Playdate with Denver
& Colorado's Front Range

Kyrie Collins

Playdate Publishing

Playdate with Denver & Colorado's Front Range by Kyrie Collins

Playdate Publishing is an imprint of Sharp End Publishing LLC

Playdate
Publishing

Published and distributed by
Sharp End Publishing, LLC
PO Box 1613
Boulder, CO 80306
t. 303.444.2698
www.playdatepublishing.com

ISBN: 978-1-892540-73-7
Library of Congress Control Number: 2010942017

Front Cover photo credits:
Butterfly girl/Kyrie Collins
Sunflower Farm/Courtesy Sunflower Farm
Denver Botanic Gardens at Chatfield/(c) Scott Dressel-Martin/Courtesy Denver Botanic Gardens
Great Plains Park/Courtesy City of Aurora

Back Cover photo credits:
Plains Conservation Center/Courtesy Plains Conservation Center
16th Street Mall/CoMedia/Larry Laszlo/Downtown Denver Partnership Inc.
Kids Crossing/Brian De Herrera-Schnering of Pinto Pictures/Courtesy FlatIron Crossing

Opening page photo credit:
Westlands Park/Patty Tucker.

If a child is to keep alive his inborn sense of wonder, he needs the companionship of at least one adult who can share it, rediscovering with him the joy, excitement and mystery of the world we live in.

~ Rachel Carlson

Acknowledgements

The Spouse of the Year Award goes to my husband, Scott, for inspiring me, encouraging me, and for filling the role of both parents many times during this process. MULU!

Atreyu, Halem, Sophie, Jackson, Conor, and Katie: you are some of the coolest kids I know! Thanks for joining us on our adventures and sharing your opinions with me, and thanks for letting your moms come too! Mary and Eva, my mommy editors, your insight was invaluable and I appreciate all the time you took with me. Thank you to Margit Crane and Amy Lang for sharing your professional experience. And, of course, my unending love and gratitude goes to my parents and to all my friends who listened, guided me, and cheered me on throughout this endeavor. I am blessed with your love!

Thank you to Matt and Amanda Kerr of Eclectic Services, Inc. for developing my website, www.PlaydateWithDenver.com.

Finally, I would like to extend my great appreciation to my publisher, Sharp End Publishing.

Author Kyrie Collins and family

3 Baby, It's Cold Outside • 65

4 Reading is FUNdamental • 83

5 Getting Wet and Staying Warm • 87

8 Fun on the Farm • 163

9 Creatures Great and Small • 173

10 Take Me Out to the Ball Game • 187

15   Appendices • 259

A Big Thank You to our Sponsors!

Page 25

Page 56

Page 91

Page 105

Page 151

Page 171

Page 193

Page 215

Page 233

Introduction

When my family and I moved to the Denver area, I had a two-year-old toddler and was six months pregnant. Immediately, I began searching for a resource of fun and interesting places to take my children. Most of the information I found was either for older children or focused on a specific area or activity. I wanted a wide array of destinations for every season of the year and for every budget. Since I couldn't find one, I decided to create one. In the process, I learned a great deal about the city we now call home, made many good friends, and discovered some true gems.

A variety of early childhood experiences is important to a child's brain development, and getting out of the house regularly is essential to most parents' sanity. *Playdate with Denver* is a travel guide for parents, grandparents, and caregivers of young children. Nearly all of the destinations in this book are appropriate for children up to age 10. However, the focus of specific activities and programs is generally on babies, toddlers, and preschoolers. Keep in mind that most places that have programs for toddlers and preschoolers also have programs for school-age children, particularly during school breaks. I have tried to include enough information about each place so that you can make an informed decision about whether or not a certain destination is right for your family.

Take your time as you visit each location. Explore with all your senses. Teach your child to observe the world. Let your child teach you to slow down and appreciate the things that have lost their wonder for you. Talk about your experiences and discover together your child's interests. I hope you enjoy using this guide as much as we enjoyed creating it.

A *few things to note:*

• Call ahead — prices and hours are subject to change.

• Check the weather. It is possible to experience all four seasons in a single day.

• Go to a local Visitor Center or visit its website (see Appendix V) for passes or coupons you may not be able to find anywhere else.

• If you find a place you love, purchase a membership. It is easier to leave a destination after a short visit if you or your child are having an off day, knowing you can return soon. Free admission is often given to very young children, so you may be able to buy an individual or couple membership, rather than one for a family.

• Most of the destinations in this book have birthday party packages.

• Many destinations have a Facebook page. Become a Fan and you'll receive special offers, discounts, and promotions.

Map of Site Locations

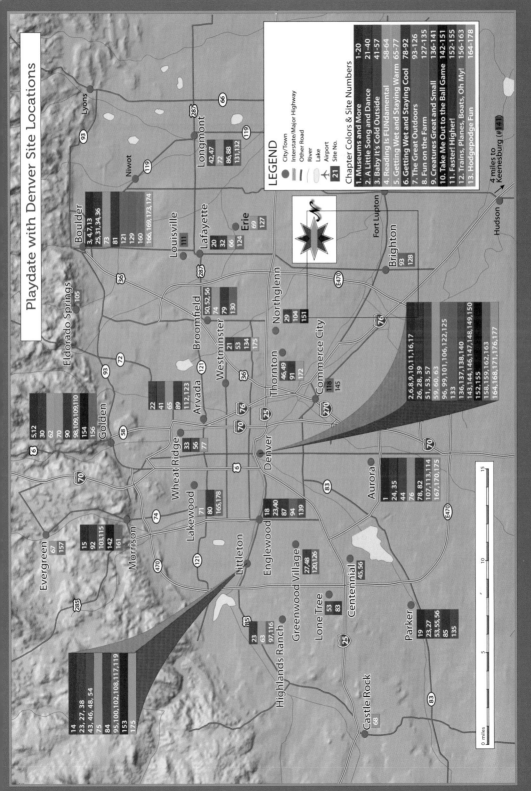

Playdate with Denver Site Locations

LEGEND
- ● City/Town
- ▬ Interstate/Major Highway
- ▬ Other Road
- River
- Lake
- ✈ Airport
- 21 Site No.

Chapter Colors & Site Numbers

Chapter	Site Numbers
1. Museums and More	1-20
2. A Little Song and Dance	21-40
3. Baby It's Cold Outside	41-57
4. Reading Is FUNdamental	58-64
5. Getting Wet and Staying Warm	65-77
6. Getting Wet and Staying Cool	78-92
7. The Great Outdoors	93-126
8. Fun on the Farm	127-135
9. Creatures Great and Small	136-141
10. Take Me Out to the Ball Game	142-151
11. Faster! Higher!	152-155
12. Trains, Planes, Boats, Oh My!	156-163
13. Hodgepodge Fun	164-178

4 miles to Keenesburg (#141)

How to Use this Guide

Each chapter is made up of a variety of places that are similar to one another. As you discover your child's interests, it will be easy to find several destinations in the metro area for exploration and discovery. Each description is similarly organized throughout the book.

THE STARS ☆☆☆☆☆

Under the name of each destination are five blank stars. In my opinion, every destination in the book rates at least three stars for my family. I did not include any place that my children didn't enjoy or that I wouldn't recommend to a friend. There are some places that we may not visit again because of distance or because they do not change, but we still had fun when we were there. Just because we had a good time doesn't mean you will. Your child may be of a different temperament or have different interests than mine do. So the stars are for YOU to rate each destination for YOUR family. One star would be a "been there, done that" kind of place while five stars would be a "buy a membership today" kind of place.

THE BASICS - Each destination's address, phone number, and website address are listed for easy reference. Following that are hours, admission, membership information, parking, food policy, and how you might be able to obtain discounts for the places that charge admission. Remember, hours and prices may change, so you should call in advance. The memberships and season passes referenced are family memberships, usually for two adults and a certain number of children. Many locations offer free admission to children under a specific age. In those instances, you could purchase an individual or couple admission for a lower rate.

WHAT TO EXPECT - A detailed description of the location will help you decide whether or not a certain destination is right for your family. Information that is pertinent to parents of young children is included, such as whether or not restrooms include diaper-changing tables.

ANNUAL EVENTS - Many locations have special celebrations each year that are particularly child-friendly. Some events may celebrate a holiday like Halloween, while others may celebrate something about the facility like its anniversary.

OTHER DESTINATIONS WITHIN 5 MILES - If you have a particularly energetic child, you may want to visit more than one destination in the same day. Maybe you just want to check out another destination on your way home from a favorite spot. Or perhaps you're considering a "staycation" this year and want a variety of activities in a specific part of town. This section will help you fulfill each of these goals.

SEE ALSO - Because many places fit into more than one section, a "See Also" section is at the end of most chapters to help you find similar places. This may be especially helpful once you've discovered some of your child's favorite types of places and things.

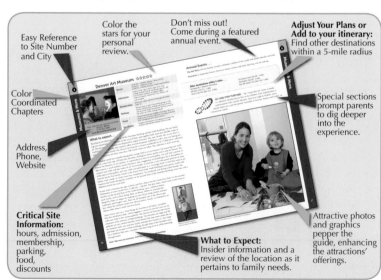

Easy Reference to Site Number and City

Color the stars for your personal review.

Don't miss out! Come during a featured annual event.

Adjust Your Plans or Add to your itinerary: Find other destinations within a 5-mile radius

Color Coordinated Chapters

Address, Phone, Website

Special sections prompt parents to dig deeper into the experience.

Critical Site Information: hours, admission, membership, parking, food, discounts

What to Expect: Insider information and a review of the location as it pertains to family needs.

Attractive photos and graphics pepper the guide, enhancing the attractions' offerings.

Keep Your Bags Packed

If you intend to visit a wide variety of places, you might consider keeping a tote box in your trunk with the essential items. Change the box when the weather changes and you'll always be prepared. (Note: If you use plastic water bottles, do not store them in the tote box, particularly in the summer. Studies are showing that the plastic can leach into the water when heated.)

Warm Weather Tote Box:

- ☐ Regular sunscreen
- ☐ Waterproof sunscreen
- ☐ Extra diapers and swim diapers
- ☐ Sun hats, swimsuits, towels, and a change of clothes for you and your child
- ☐ Beach toys like pails, shovels, rakes, sand shapers, and trucks
- ☐ Floaties, goggles, and other swimming accessories
- ☐ Baby powder (for sandbox play)
- ☐ Books, sidewalk chalk, and bubbles
- ☐ Hoodies or light jackets for you and your child
- ☐ A washable tote bag for wet or sandy clothes
- ☐ Bandages and antibiotic cream (Neo to Go sprays on and won't spill in the tote)
- ☐ Insect repellant and anti-itch cream (try Benadryl on the Go for anti-itch)
- ☐ Individually-packaged non-perishable snacks

Cold Weather Tote Box:

- ☐ Lip balm and lotion
- ☐ Sunscreen
- ☐ Extra diapers
- ☐ Extra sweatshirts, coats, hats, and gloves or mittens
- ☐ Short-sleeve shirts for you and your child, for those oddly warm days
- ☐ Swimsuits, towels, and a change of clothes for you and your child for indoor pools
- ☐ Snow boots
- ☐ Hand warmers
- ☐ An inflatable sled
- ☐ Books, coloring books, and crayons
- ☐ A washable tote bag for wet or dirty clothes
- ☐ Bandages and antibiotic cream
- ☐ Individually-packaged non-perishable snacks

Introduction

Facts about the Denver Metro Area

• The Metro Denver area is made up of seven counties — Adams, Arapahoe, Broomfield, Boulder, Denver, Douglas, and Jefferson — and covers 4,500 square miles, nearly the size of Connecticut!

• Denver lays claim to the invention of the cheeseburger, with the trademark being give to Louis Ballast in 1935. Mr. Ballast owned and operated the Humpty Dumpty Barrel Drive-In on Speer Boulevard (which, sadly, burned down a long time ago).

• Colfax Avenue in Denver is the longest continuous street in America.

• Baseline Road in Boulder marks the 40th parallel on world maps.

• The 105th meridian west of Greenwich passes through Union Station, making it the reference point for the Mountain Time Zone.

• Denver hosts the world's largest rodeo, the Western Stock Show, each year.

• The 1976 Winter Olympics were scheduled to be held in Denver. At the last minute, voters across the state chose not to host because of the cost, pollution, and population boom it would have created.

• The red marble used in the Colorado State Capitol is called "Beulah Red." All of the "Beulah Red" marble in the world went to the Capitol and, therefore, can not be replaced.

• There is an average of 30 degrees difference between the daily low and high temperatures.

• Denver International Airport is larger than Dallas-Fort Worth Airport and Chicago O'Hare Airport combined.

• At 57 stories, the tallest building in Colorado is the Republic Plaza in downtown Denver.

Have you discovered a new place? Did you find a mistake? *If you know of a great place for young children that isn't mentioned in this book, or if you want to share your experience at a specific destination, please write to me or send me an email. Your ideas could be used in future editions of this book. Contact information is located at the end of the book, page 287.*

Museums and More

The dictionary definition of a museum is a building in which objects of historical, scientific, artistic, or cultural interest are stored and exhibited. For our children, a museum can be so much more — a great place for learning, discovering, exploring, and stimulating their imaginations. This section includes children's museums, museums with discovery centers, and museums that my children loved even though they were not designed specifically with kids in mind. Children's interests grow and change as they grow and change, so many of these museums can be visited over and over again.

Morrison Natural History Museum

Aurora History Museum ☆☆☆☆☆

Courtesy Aurora History Museum

15051 East Alameda Parkway
Aurora, 80012
(303) 739-6666
www.auroramuseum.org

Hours:	9:00 AM - 4:00 PM, Tuesday - Friday 11:00 AM - 4:00 PM, Saturday and Sunday Closed major holidays.
Admission:	FREE!
Parking:	Free parking lot.
Food:	The museum asks that you not bring food or drinks, other than water, into the museum. However, there is a large grassy area outside if you want to bring a picnic lunch.

What to expect. . .

The Aurora History Museum has four galleries, two permanent and two changing. The first permanent exhibit showcases artifacts depicting the history of Aurora. The second permanent exhibit is a hands-on room for children with Lincoln Logs, building blocks, historic games, period costumes, books, a craft area with crayons and paper, and a cabinet filled with musical instruments, antlers and animal fur, tools, and other things to touch. The two rotating exhibits change every three to four months. The Collector's Corner is a display case with an Aurora resident's personal collection (of coins, sports memorabilia, stamps, etc.) that they have loaned to the museum. The Collector's Corner also changes periodically.

The museum is very small. They are working toward becoming more interactive and child-friendly. Currently, I would not make it a destination of its own, but it is next to the Aurora Public Library and it is free so I suggest adding it to a visit to the library. The men's and women's restrooms both have diaper-changing tables, and the museum is stroller-friendly.

Annual Events . . .

A **Birthday Party for the City of Aurora** is celebrated at the museum every April.

Courtesy Aurora History Museum

Other destinations within 5 miles . . .
Cinema Grill (Site 167) - less than 1 mile
Skate City - Aurora (Site 175) - 4 miles
Utah Pool (Site 76) - 4 miles

The Children's Museum of Denver Photo by Patty Tucker

Black American West Museum ☆☆☆☆☆

Hours:	10:00 AM - 2:00 PM, Tuesday - Saturday Closed major holidays.
Admission:	Under 3: Free; Age 3-12: $6; Age 13-64: $8; Age 65+: $7 American Express, Discover, MasterCard, Visa, and cash accepted.
Parking:	Free street parking.
Food:	No food or drink allowed inside the museum.
Discounts:	They will not turn away anyone who can not pay, as they want everyone to be able to experience this museum.

3091 California Street
Denver, 80205
(720) 242-7428
www.blackamericanwestmuseum.org

What to expect. . .

Miss Justina Ford was the first female African-American doctor in Colorado. She was prohibited from practicing medicine in hospitals so she worked out of her home, delivering more than 7,000 babies over the course of her 50-year career. After her death, her home was slated to be torn down, but instead was placed on the National Register of Historic Places and moved, piece by piece, to another part of town. The Black American West Museum was born.

The mission of the museum is to protect, preserve, and promote the legacy of the African-American experience. Exhibits include Dr. Ford's office, a homestead exhibit focusing on the town of Dearfield, a cowboy exhibit filled with saddles, spurs, chaps, and boots, and a military exhibit which tells the story of the Buffalo Soldiers. The halls are lined with pictures of African-American men and women who contributed to the development of the West.

The museum is very small and is not geared toward very young children, but if you call ahead, they are happy to customize your visit to be age-appropriate, including a story time and a personalized tour or presentation. They offer cards with pictures of some of the people featured in the museum, and preschool or older children can go on a "scavenger hunt" looking for the pictures. If it is a nice day, pick up a Welton Street Walking Tour pamphlet and take a self-guided tour of the "historic heart of Denver's African-American community," just one block over. A very small gift shop sells mostly books and old-fashioned candies. Since it is a historic building, there is no elevator. A unisex bathroom with a child-sized urinal is on the first floor, but it does not have a diaper-changing table.

Annual Events . . .

The Haunted History Ghost Walk, which occurs throughout the month of October, tells kid-friendly ghost stories about the people who "haunt" the museum.

Other destinations within 5 miles . . .

See Appendix I - Downtown Destinations
Tattered Cover Bookstore - Denver (Site 63) - 2 miles

Kids Kourt (Site 51) - 4 miles
Sloan's Lake Park (Site 122) - 5 miles

GO ONE STEP FURTHER - The issue of race may not be something your child understands at this point, but as they grow older, the differences between people become more apparent. Talk to your child now about similarities and differences among their group of friends. Simply asking about hair color, pets, favorite toys, and gender teaches children that there are some things that people share, and some things that make us different from others.

Boulder History Museum ☆☆☆☆☆

Courtesy Boulder History Museum

1206 Euclid Avenue
Boulder, 80302
(303) 449-3464
www.boulderhistorymuseum.org

Hours:	10:00 AM - 5:00 PM, Tuesday - Frida 12:00 PM - 4:00 PM, Saturday and S Closed major holidays.
Admission:	Under 5: Free; Age 5-17: $3; Age 18-61: $6; Age 62+: $4 American Express, MasterCard, Visa, checks, and cash accepted.
Membership:	$55 for two named adults and children under 18.
Parking:	Free parking lot on the east side of the museum. Free street parking has a two-hour limit.
Food:	The museum asks that you not bring food or drinks, other than water, into the museum. However, there is a large grassy area and a small playground behind the museum if you want to bring a picnic lunch.
Discounts:	Coupons can be found in the Entertainment Book. The museum is free on the first Sunday of the month.

What to expect...

The Boulder History Museum is located in the Harbeck-Bergheim house, itself a piece of Boulder history. It is a "two-story cube-shaped" house, a style so popular in the early 1900s that they are given the special name "American four-squares" or even "Denver Squares." Inside you'll find the Storymakers exhibit, which tells the story of the city and county of Boulder from before European settlers till the early 20th century. Artifacts, objects, documents, and photographs depicting the history

Courtesy Boulder History Museum

of Boulder are found throughout the museum. The Discovery Room is designed for children age 4 to 10 years old. The room includes an 1800s classroom, period clothing, historic games, Pansy the Cow that can be "milked," and a quilt design station. Some temporary exhibits change every few months.

The museum is a historic building, so there is no elevator to the second floor. The hallways are narrow and would make maneuvering with a stroller difficult. A unisex bathroom located on the first floor has a diaper-changing table and a stool for the sink.

Other destinations within 5 miles . . .

Colorado Music Festival Children's Concerts (Site 25) - ½ mile
CU Museum of Natural History (Site 7) - less than ½ mile
Fiske Planetarium (Site 169) - less than ½ mile
Boulder Museum of Contemporary Art (Site 4) - less than 1 mile
Tebo Train (Site 160) - 1 ½ miles
North Boulder Recreation Center Pool (Site 73) - 2 miles

Storybook Ballet (Site 36) - 2 miles
Scott Carpenter Park (Site 121) - 2 ½ miles
Rocky Mountain Theatre for Kids (Site 34) - 3 ½ miles
Kids Kabaret (Site 31) - 4 miles
NCAR (Site 173) - 4 miles

Boulder Museum of Contemporary Art ☆☆☆☆☆

Art Stop Courtesy of BMoCA

1750 13th Street
Boulder, 80302
(303) 443-2122
www.bmoca.org

Hours:	11:00 AM - 5:00 PM, Tuesday - Friday 11:00 PM - 4:00 PM, Saturday and Sunday During the Farmer's Market, the museum is open till 8:00 PM on Wednesday, and Saturday hours are 9:00 AM - 4:00 PM. Closed major holidays.
Admission:	Under 12: Free; Age 18-59: $5; Educators, Students and Seniors 60+: $4 American Express, Discover, MasterCard, Visa, and cash accepted.
Membership:	$55 for two named adults and their children under 18.
Parking:	Metered parking on 13th and 14th Streets, twelve minutes per quarter. Paid lot available at One Boulder Plaza, on 13th Street between Canyon and Walnut.
Food:	Food and drink are not allowed in the museum, but a park is across the street.
Discounts:	Museum is free on Saturday year-round and during the Boulder County Farmer's Market on Wednesday from 4:00 PM - 8:00 PM.

What to expect...

BMOCA is a historic building with at least three major exhibitions at a time. The museum is dedicated to showcasing regional, national, and international art of our time. Exhibits change three times a year, and the museum is closed between exhibits, so call in advance. Wide, open paths provide ample room to maneuver a stroller. Benches offer a chance to sit and appreciate the artwork. The museum has two unisex bathrooms on the first floor, but it does not have a diaper-changing table.

Courtesy Boulder Museum of Contemporary Art

Each Saturday at 11:00 AM, the museum offers guided tours. The tours generally last about 45 minutes, but the guides can tailor the tour if there is a large number of children in the group. If you visit on a Saturday from mid-April through early November during the Farmer's Market, your child can participate in Art Stop. Art Stop is a free activity-based program that takes place on the steps of the museum from 9:00 AM - 1:00 PM. Activities are appropriate for age three through the teen years. Assisted by local artists and educators, children have the opportunity to create their own masterpieces. If possible, the museum tries to incorporate current exhibits or the Farmer's Market into the art project to further connect the children with the artwork in the museum. Although the museum is not really geared toward young children, the artwork is impressive and it is worth a short tour, especially if you are already visiting for Art Stop.

Other destinations within 5 miles . . .

Tebo Train (Site 160) - ½ mile
Boulder History Museum (Site 3) - less than 1 mile
CU Museum of Natural History (Site 7) - less than 1 mile
Fiske Planetarium (Site 169) - less than 1 mile
Storybook Ballet (Site 36) - 1 mile

Colorado Music Festival Children's Concerts (Site 25) - 1½ miles
North Boulder Recreation Center Pool (Site 73) - 1½ miles
Rocky Mountain Theatre for Kids (Site 34) - 3 miles
Kids Kabaret (Site 31) - 3½ miles
NCAR (Site 173) - 5 miles

DID YOU KNOW? Bright colors and new shapes stimulate a baby's brain because of increased curiosity and concentration. Strap on a baby carrier and head to an art gallery as soon as your baby is big enough to face forward.

Buffalo Bill's Museum and Grave ☆☆

Courtesy of The Buffalo Bill Museum

987 ½ Lookout Mountain Road
Golden, 80401
(303) 526-0747
www.buffalobill.org

Hours:	9:00 AM - 5:00 PM daily from May 9:00 AM - 4:00 PM, Tuesday - Sunday, Closed Monday during winter ho on Christmas Day.
Admission:	Under 6: Free; Age 6-15: $1; Age 16-64: $5; Age 65+: $4 MasterCard, Visa, checks, and cash accepted.
Parking:	Free parking lot.
Food:	The museum asks that you not bring food or drinks, other than water, into the museum. However, there is a snack shop connected to the Pahaska Tepee gift shop as well as several picnic tables outside.
Discounts:	Coupons can be found in the Entertainment Book. Check the website for information on their free days, which typically occur at the end of February and mid-autumn.

What to expect. . .

At his request, William F. Cody, AKA Buffalo Bill, was buried on Lookout Mountain, overlooking the Great Plains and the Rocky Mountains. Visit on a clear day and you will see why he loved this spot. The view from the scenic overlook next to the museum is breathtaking. Telescopes are available to enhance the experience (bring quarters). Picnic tables in this area provide a great spot for you and your child to enjoy lunch.

Courtesy Buffalo Bill Museum

The museum was opened in 1921 by his foster son and its purpose is to illustrate the legend of Buffalo Bill, but it provides much more than that. A 15-minute video plays on the hour and half hour and covers the life of Buffalo Bill, as well as the controversy surrounding his funeral and burial. The museum has a wide variety of cases housing Indian artifacts, Western art, firearms, saddles, bows and arrows, and relics from Buffalo Bill's Wild West Show, which traveled the world. The Kids Cowboy Corral offers cowboy costumes, including boots and chaps, and a horse and a calf so your child can practice roping. The museum has wide walking paths and is very stroller-friendly.

The route to William Cody's actual gravesite is less than a quarter-mile long. It is paved and stroller-friendly and offers more spectacular views.

Next to the museum is the enormous Pahaska Tepee gift shop where you can purchase just about anything Western, from toys to clothing to pictures, and everything in between. The attached snack bar has a variety of standard snack bar fare, but also offers buffalo burgers and homemade fudge. Bathrooms inside the museum have diaper-changing tables. Bathrooms are located at the gift shop as well, but these do not have changing tables.

Annual Events . . .

Buffalo Bill's Birthday is celebrated at the end of February, weather permitting.

Other destinations within 5 miles . . .
Lookout Mountain Nature Center (Site 110) - 1 mile

The Children's Museum of Denver ☆☆☆☆☆

Courtesy of The Children's Museum of Denver

2121 Children's Museum Drive
Denver 80211
(303) 433-7444
www.cmdenver.org

Hours:	9:00 AM - 4:00 PM, Monday - Friday Open Wednesdays until 7:30 PM. 10:00 AM - 5:00 PM, Saturday and Sunday Closed major holidays
Admission:	Under 1: Free; Age 1: $6; Age 2-59: $8, Age 60+: $6 Discover, MasterCard, Visa, checks, and cash accepted.
Membership:	$90 for 2 named adults and their children.
Parking:	Free parking (a fee is charged for non-members on event days).
Food:	The Eat Street Café is a grab-and-go service that has a variety of healthful and kid-friendly options. You may bring in your own food and eat in the café.
Discounts:	Coupons can be found in the Entertainment Book, Chinook Book, and on ColoradoKids.com. Get a $2 discount for wearing pajamas on Wednesday evening from 4:00 - 7:30 PM. The first Tuesday of each month is free from 4:00 - 8:00 PM.

What to expect. . .

The Children's Museum of Denver offers an open-ended experience designed to grow with your child. Story time takes place daily. The educational programming is widely varied, focusing on a monthly theme. They have 11 permanent playscapes, and several temporary, mobile playscapes. Permanent exhibits include:

The Center for the Young Child is a soft and safe gated playscape designed specifically for children under four years old. No shoes are allowed in this area (cubbies are provided). There is plenty of room for little ones to practice crawling, walking, and climbing small hills. Special touches include a pond with lily pads for babies to lie on, and a glider for reading stories together.

CMD Fire Station No. 1 provides an opportunity to explore a fire truck and learn about fire safety.

Discover your creative side at **Arts a la Carte** by singing, dancing, painting, or crafting.

In **The Assembly Plant**, older children can use real tools to build a variety of projects from recycled household materials.

Bubbles lets you explore bubbles with interactive tools and one-of-a-kind machines.

Children can go grocery shopping and then prepare and serve pretend food in **My Market**.

Under My Feet and Over My Head allows your child to dress up in an insect or animal costume and climb around an anthill playscape. Be sure to stop by the window and watch the birds around the feeder.

Build a different track every time you visit **Click Clack Train Track**.

Will It Works is a place for the museum to try out ideas for future playscapes and programs, and activities are often in their early, unfinished stages.

In warmer weather, outside activities (often involving dirt or water) fill the large plaza area. There is a fabulous playground next to the parking lot, owned and maintained by the City of Denver.

The entire museum is stroller-friendly and stroller parking is available throughout the facility. The café is small with only a few tables so you may have trouble finding a seat for lunch. When the weather is warm enough, you can enjoy your meal on the patio area, in the plaza, or at the picnic tables in the playground. Lockers on the first floor provide a place to keep your diaper bag so your hands are free to play. The bathrooms are clean and spacious, with changing tables and diaper pails in all of them. The bathrooms on the first floor have child-sized toilets and sinks. The Shop, Skip, and a Jump Gift Shop, strategically located at the entrance, has a variety of educational games and toys, including many items related to the playscapes. The museum is a very popular destination and can become quite crowded, but has adopted a no-school-group policy on Monday.

Museums & More

Annual Events . . .

Bunny Trail EggVenture celebrates springtime the Saturday before Easter.

Hop, Skip, and a Jump Start is a fun-run race for the whole family that occurs in September.

Trick or Treat Street is a safe trick-or-treating experience on Halloween and the days preceding it.

Noon Year's Eve lets you ring in the New Year without keeping the children up late on December 31.

Other destinations within 5 miles . . .

See Appendix I - Downtown Destinations
The Bookery Nook (Site 59) - 3½ miles
Fish Den (Site 138) - 4 miles
Sloan's Lake Park (Site 122) - 4 miles

Tattered Cover Bookstore - Denver (Site 63) - 4 miles
Rising Curtain Theatre Academy (Site 33) - 4½ miles
Kids Kourt (Site 51) - 5 miles

GO ONE STEP FURTHER - If your child loved the Assembly Plant at the Children's Museum, check out the free kids' workshops offered by The Home Depot. Visit **www.thehomedepot.com**, click on **"Services"**, then **"Kids Workshops"**.

Photos by Patty Tucker
Photo by Eva Voss (lower right)

Museums & More

CU Museum of Natural History ☆☆☆☆☆

Courtesy CU Museum of Natural History

15th Street and Broadway Street
Boulder, 80302
(303) 492-6892
cumuseum.colorado.edu

Hours:	9:00 AM - 5:00 PM, Monday - Friday 9:00 AM - 4:00 PM, Saturday 10:00 AM - 4:00 PM, Sunday Closed most federal holidays (depending on CU's schedule).
Admission:	FREE! (Suggested donation of $1 for children over 6 and $3 for adults.) MasterCard, Visa, checks, and cash accepted.
Parking:	Paid campus lot is at Euclid and Broadway.
Food:	No food or drink allowed in the galleries. Free coffee and tea are located downstairs near Discovery Corner. There are plenty of places on campus to sit and have a picnic lunch.

What to expect...

Located on campus in the Henderson Building, the University of Colorado Museum of Natural History has three permanent exhibits and two temporary galleries. The permanent exhibits are:

Paleontology Hall has skulls, footprints, petrified wood, giant clams, and more, much of which may be touched. Check out the Discovery Cart that has touchable fossils, books, and activity backpacks.

Anthropology Hall combines biology, history, sociology, and linguistics to teach about human cultures and human history. This hall is divided into four separate focus areas.

The Bio Lounge is located in the basement and is a completely unique venue to showcase science, art, and music. Programs and exhibits change frequently. Free coffee and tea are available, and there are a number of chairs, couches, and tables.

Discovery Corner is located in a corner of the Bio Lounge, next to the coffee and tea. Filled with puppets, puzzles, books, and games, as well as fossils, antlers, and horns, your child will find plenty of items to touch, explore, and play with.

The museum offers a variety of Family Days throughout the year. Some past events have been Museum in the Dark, Navajo Weaving, and Darwin Days. Several workshops for children are available in the summer, but most of them start at kindergarten level.

The bathrooms are located on the second floor, and the women's restroom contains a diaper-changing table. If you have a child in potty-training, be sure to make a stop in the bathroom before heading down to Discovery Corner. An elevator is available and the entire museum is stroller-friendly. A very small gift shop at the entrance offers a few books and toys.

Other destinations within 5 miles . . .

Boulder History Museum (Site 3) - less than ½ mile
Fiske Planetarium (Site 169) - less than ½ mile
Boulder Museum of Contemporary Art (Site 4) - less than 1 mile
Colorado Music Festival Children's Concerts (Site 25) - 1 mile
Tebo Train (Site 160) - 1 mile
North Boulder Recreation Center Pool (Site 73) - 2 miles

Scott Carpenter Park (Site 121) - 2 miles
Storybook Ballet (Site 36) - 2 miles
Rocky Mountain Theatre for Kids (Site 34) - 3½ miles
Kids Kabaret (Site 31) - 4 miles
NCAR (Site 173) - 4 miles

DID YOU KNOW? The first Stegosaurus fossil was discovered just west of Denver in 1877. More than a century later, a fourth-grade class campaigned to make the Stegosaurus a Colorado symbol. Because of their efforts, the Stegosaurus became Colorado's official state fossil.

Denver Art Museum ☆☆☆☆☆

Photo by Christina Jackson Courtesy DAM

West 13th Avenue and Acoma Street
Denver, 80204
(720) 865-5000
www.denverartmuseum.org

Hours:	10:00 AM - 5:00 PM, Tuesday - Thurs. and Sat. 10:00 AM - 10:00 PM, Friday 12:00 PM - 5:00 PM, Sunday. Closed major holidays.
Admission:	Under 6: Free; Age 6-18: $3; Age 18-64: $10; College Students with ID and Seniors age 65+: $8. Non-Colorado residents are slightly higher. American Express, MasterCard, Visa, checks, and cash accepted.
Membership:	$70 for two adults and their children/grandchildren under 18.
Parking:	A parkng garage is located at 12th Avenue and Broadway. Rates start at $1/hour. Paid lots and parking meters are within walking distance.
Food:	Several restaurants are available in the plaza. You may bring in your own food and drink, but eating is allowed only in designated areas of the museum.
Discounts:	The museum is free the first Saturday of every month.

What to expect...

The Denver Art Museum is made up of the Hamilton Building and the North Building. The two buildings are connected via a walkway on the second floor, and together hold more than 60,000 works of art. The permanent collections are displayed by region (Oceanic Art), type (Textile Art), or era (Pre-Columbian Art). Additionally, the museum offers several temporary exhibitions with a new one being presented nearly every month. The Denver Art Museum is known worldwide for its 17,000-piece collection of Native American arts from more than 100 North American tribes. The collection is truly stunning.

Many people would not consider taking their young child to an art museum, but exposing your child to art at a very early age will help him develop a feeling for artistic quality and a taste for beauty. The Denver Art Museum, in my opinion, is a great place to start. In each gallery, you will find a picture of their mascot, a small monkey named Seymour, and a suggestion of something to do in that gallery to connect your child with the works of art. For example, it could be a card with partial pictures of some of the items in that gallery and your child can participate in a "scavenger hunt" to find that work of art. Visit the Just for Fun Family Center in the lower level of the North Building to play games, build with blocks, read a book, or create your own masterpiece. On weekends and during school breaks, the museum has Family Backpacks available on the second floor of the Hamilton Building, each one with a different activity for your child.

If your child is between the ages of three and five, drop in on the Create Play Dates on the second Wednesday of every month from 11:00 AM - 1:00 PM. The play dates, which meet in the Duncan Pavilion on the second floor of the North Building, have a different theme each month, such as Roar, Bang, Blob, or Stomp. When we attended the Bang Play Date, we began by making our own drum using Quaker oatmeal containers and Pringles cans. Then we all tromped over to the African gallery, where the children could view African drums. Finally, we listened to an African fable about a turtle and two drums.

Upon arrival, pick up a "Free Things for Families to do Today" pamphlet from the admittance desk, which suggests a variety of activities you can do with your child in the various galleries. The Denver Art Museum has family restrooms at the entrance of both buildings. The elevators are large and the galleries are very stroller-friendly. Small details like step stools under the water fountains show you just how family-oriented this museum is. Very large gift shops are located in both buildings; the gift shop in the Hamilton area has a fabulous kids area, complete with bean bags to sit in while browsing through books.

Photo by Christina Jackson
Courtesy Denver Art Museum

Note: Like most art museums, DAM has nude statues and paintings.

Annual Events . . .

Dia del Nino, the last Sunday of April, celebrates children of the world with family-friendly activities.

Powwow in September honors American Indian culture with food, dancing, and art making.

Other destinations within 5 miles . . .

See Appendix I - Downtown Destinations
Kids Kourt (Site 51) - 3 miles
Sloan's Lake Park (Site 122) - 4 miles

The Bookery Nook (Site 59) - 5 miles
The Bookies (Site 60) - 5 miles
Four Mile Historic Park (Site 106) - 5 miles

GO ONE STEP FURTHER - The "Touch the Art" series of books is a fabulous introduction to fine art for children. Each reproduction is super-imposed with a tactile element. From Van Gogh to Warhol, every volume draws on a specific period. Available online at **www.touchtheheart.com** or at your local bookstore.

Photo by Christina Jackson Courtesy Denver Art Museum

Denver Firefighters Museum ☆☆☆☆☆

Hours:	10:00 AM - 4:00 PM, Monday - Saturday Closed major holidays.
Admission:	Under 1: Free; Age 1-12: $4; Age 18-64: $6; Students and Seniors 65+: $5 Discover, MasterCard, Visa, checks, and cash accepted.
Membership:	$60 for two adults at the same address, a nanny, and all children under 18
Parking:	Metered street parking and paid lots are available.
Food:	Food and drink are not allowed in the museum except for baby bottles.
Discounts:	Coupons can be found in the Entertainment Book, Chinook Book, and on ColoradoKids.com. There are several free days each year; check the website calendar for the current year's dates.

1326 Tremont Place
Denver, 80204
(303) 892-1436
www.denverfirefightersmuseum.org

What to expect...

The building that houses the Denver Firefighters Museum was Fire Station One, one of Denver's oldest, and served as a working fire station until 1975. It was then placed on the National Register of Historic Places and opened to the public. Its mission is to preserve and share the history of the Denver Fire Department and to teach fire safety and prevention.

The main floor is mainly dedicated to the history of firefighting. You'll find historical fire gear, clothing, and the history of 9-1-1 and this station house. Children will love climbing up the step stool and sliding down the fire pole, dressing up in real firefighter gear and climbing into the driver's seat of an actual fire engine.

The second floor has more history, showcasing living quarters and officers' quarters. Lockers display gear, supplies, and toiletries that may have been used by firefighters as far back as the 1800s. The Kids Gallery has a Stop, Drop, and Roll practice mat, books and DVDs on fire safety and prevention, and six computer stations with games. A miniature house lets families practice getting out safely. Senior citizens and children under seven are the most at risk of dying in a fire, so early fire safety is essential. On the first Wednesday of every month at 11:00 AM, Tales for Tots takes place in the Kids Gallery with fire-themed books, rhymes, puppetry, and more.

Because it is a historical building, there is no elevator to get to the second floor. Bathrooms are located on both floors, and diaper-changing tables are in both the men's and women's. A small gift shop has t-shirts, toys, games, glasses, mugs, and much more, all firefighter-themed.

Annual Events...

Wee Wednesday is a six-week fire safety program designed for children 2 to 5. It occurs once in the spring and once in the fall.

Father's Day Spaghetti Dinner begins with a social hour and photos on the fire truck.

Fun at the Firehouse, an annual safety fair, takes place the first weekend in August. Try your hand with a fire hose and maneuver through a safety obstacle course.

Fire Safety Week marks the anniversary of the 1871 Great Chicago Fire in early October. Learn more about fire safety with hands-on activities and special presentations.

Firehouse Ghosts for Families is an overnight adventure in October that includes a spaghetti dinner, ghost stories, and Halloween crafts. It is appropriate for ages 4 and up.

Other destinations within 5 miles . . .

See Appendix I - Downtown Destinations
Kids Kourt (Site 51) - 2½ miles
The Bookies (Site 60) - 4½ miles

Four Mile Historic Park (Site 106) - 4½ miles
Family Arts at DAVA (Site 44) - 5 miles

Denver Museum of Miniatures, Dolls, and Toys ☆☆☆☆☆

Courtesy of Denver Museum of Miniatures, Dolls, & Toys

1880 Gaylord Street
Denver, 80206
(303) 322-1053
www.dmmdt.org

Hours:	10:00 AM - 4:00 PM, Wednesday - Saturday 1:00 PM - 4:00 PM, Sunday Closed major holidays.
Admission:	Under 5: Free; Age 5-16: $4; Age 17-61: $6; Age 62+: $5 MasterCard, Visa, checks, and cash accepted.
Membership:	$45 for two adults and their children under 18.
Parking:	Free street parking, but you may have some difficulty finding a space.
Food:	No food or drink is allowed in the museum, but you may use the picnic table in the backyard.
Discounts:	Coupons can be found in the Entertainment Book and the Chinook Book. The museum is free on the first Sunday of every month and includes a free hands-on workshop.

What to expect. . .

The purpose of the museum is to "provide educational and cultural services to the greater Rocky Mountain Region through the preservation, exhibition, collection, and interpretation of visual art using miniatures, dolls, and toys." Inside this gorgeous Victorian home, you will find 10 different themed rooms, such as the Pink Room and the ABC Room. Each room is filled with hundreds of toys: antique dolls from around the world, dollhouses, giant teddy bears, miniature trains and planes, and more. Three of the galleries have hands-on activities for your child, such as Legos-brand building blocks. Many of the rooms have books for children and adults. The basement area is for crafts, workshops, and birthday parties. Free Sundays always have crafts for the children. Temporary exhibits in the museum change every quarter.

Because it is a historic building, no elevator is available. A unisex bathroom with a diaper-changing table is located on the first floor. You'll find a stool under the sink to make hand-washing easier for little ones. A small gift shop sells a variety of collectibles, dollhouse furnishings and accessories, magazines about miniatures, books, coloring books, and more.

Annual Events . . .

Not-So-Haunted Halloween takes place on the first Sunday of the month after Halloween.

Courtesy of Denver Museum of Miniatures, Dolls, & Toys

Gingerbread House Workshops are weekends in December.

The museum sponsors **various workshops** throughout the year during school breaks.

Other destinations within 5 miles . . .

See Appendix I - Downtown Destinations
Kids Kourt (Site 51) - 3½ miles
Sloan's Lake Park (Site 122) - 3½ miles

The Bookery Nook (Site 59) - 4½ miles
Fish Den (Site 138) - 5 miles

Denver Museum of Nature and Science ☆☆☆☆☆

Museums & More

2001 Colorado Boulevard
Denver, 80205
(303) 370-6000
www.dmns.org

Hours:	9:00 AM - 5:00 PM daily Closed Christmas Day.
Admission:	Under 3: Free; Age 3-18: $6; Age 18-64: $11; Students and Seniors 65+: $6. Additional fee for Phipps IMAX Theater or Gates Planetarium. All major credit cards accepted.
Membership:	$80 for two named adults in the same household and their children under 18.
Parking:	Free parking lot and underground garage.
Food:	The T-Rex Café provides lunch from 11:00 AM - 2:00 PM and snacks all day long. No food or drink other than water are allowed in the museum, but you may bring your own lunch in to the area near the café.
Discounts:	The museum has many Free Days each year. The free days are for Colorado residents only, and do not include Phipps IMAX Theater or Gates Planetarium. Visit the website for the current year's free days.

What to expect. . .

We have visited this museum more than half a dozen times and still have not seen all of it. This is partly because my children are enamored with specific areas, and partly because it is so massive. The exhibits are very interactive and provide a great deal of information about the subjects inside. Permanent exhibits include:

Discovery Zone, an educational center that incorporates all of the other exhibits into its hands-on activities. Both my children spend hours here.

Egyptian Mummies showcases tomb artifacts, human mummies, animal mummies, and a model of an Egyptian temple.

Expedition Health uses interactive, personalized activities to teach you about "the amazing, incredible you." This is a must-see for us each time we go and we spend at least an hour in here.

Gems and Minerals is a re-created mine that allows you to view scores of crystals, gems, and minerals.

North American Indian Cultures is one we haven't seen but I think is pretty self-explanatory.

Prehistoric Journey is another must-see for us because my children are dinosaur fanatics. This exhibit takes you through the evolution of life, ending with a Paleontology Lab where you can watch them working on fossils.

Space Odyssey is an interactive and informational exhibit about the universe. This is another must-see and usually takes us at least an hour. The entrance to Gates Planetarium is through this exhibit.

We have seen very little of the **Wildlife Exhibits**, or the "zoo where the animals stand still," but the dioramas that we saw were incredible and surprisingly interactive.

Temporary exhibits change every few months and usually require an additional fee. The IMAX theater has shows starting at 10:30 AM. They cover topics ranging from prehistoric animals to the ocean to space, and usually two different films show alternately in the same day. Films last 45 minutes to an hour. You can purchase a ticket to just the IMAX theater, but you save money by buying a combination ticket. Gates Planetarium has three to four different shows alternating over the course of the day, and also last about 45 minutes. You can purchase tickets just to the planetarium, but only after 3:00 PM.

Family bathrooms are located on the first floor near Gems and Minerals. The family bathroom has a large open area with a sink, diaper-changing tables, and some comfortable chairs. Three unisex bathrooms in here have private toilets and sinks. Other bathrooms in the museum have diaper-changing tables. The gift shop is enormous and has exhibit-related souvenirs and gifts, including a large variety of items for children.

Other destinations within 5 miles . . .

Foothills Art Center ☆☆☆☆☆

Courtesy Foothills Arts Center

809 15th Street
Golden, 80401
(303) 279-3922
www.foothillsartcenter.org

Hours:	10:00 AM - 5:00 PM, Monday - Saturday 1:00 PM - 5:00 PM, Sunday Closed all major holidays.
Admission:	Under 18: Free; Age 18-64: $5; Age 65+: $3 American Express, Discover, MasterCard, Visa, checks, and cash accepted.
Membership:	$45 for two named adults and their children under 18.
Parking:	Free small parking lot and free street parking.
Food:	Food and drink are not allowed in the museum, but you may eat at the picnic tables behind the building or the granite table in the small sculpture garden.
Discounts:	Six or more Family Free Days each year; check the website calendar.

What to expect. . .

The motto of the Foothills Art Center is "Engaging the mind and inspiring the spirit — offering the world of art through exhibition and education." With six different exhibitions each year, the range of artwork displayed is large and varied. The Main Building has the largest collections. All the pieces are out in the open, and many are down low, so you may want to use a stroller if you're taking an energetic toddler. The aisles are wide and the building is stroller-friendly. The Community Gallery is next door to the main center. Smaller exhibitions, usually featuring Colorado artists, are held here. The Carriage House is a large room where art classes are held for children as young as three. Sidewalk sales occur several times a year.

Family Free Days occur whenever the Art Center changes exhibits. These days are very family-oriented with snacks, crafts, and art activities for children. Sometimes cookie decorating is the art activity and the snack. Check the website calendar to find the next Family Free Day.

Men's and women's restrooms are available in the Main Building and a unisex bathroom is in the Community Gallery, but none of them have diaper-changing tables.

Annual Events . . .

The Watercolor Media Show is their most popular exhibition and shows from August through October.

The Holiday Art Market features works by over 100 Colorado artists and includes everything from ceramic to jewelry to holiday decorations. It runs from mid-November through December.

Other destinations within 5 miles . . .

Clear Creek Books (Site 62) - 3 blocks
Clear Creek History Park (Site 98) - ½ mile
Golden Community Center (Site 70) less than 1 mile
Lions Park (Site 109) - less than 1 mile

Colorado Railroad Museum (Site 156) - 2½ miles
Splash at Fossil Trace (Site 90) - 2½ miles
Heritage Square Amusement Park (Site 154) - 3 miles
Heritage Square Music Hall (Site 30) - 3 miles

Leanin' Tree Museum of Western Art ☆☆☆☆☆

Courtesy of Leanin' Tree Museum

6055 Longbow Drive
Boulder, 80301
(303) 729-3440
www.leanintreemuseum.com

Hours:	8:00 AM - 5:00 PM, Monday - Friday 10:00 AM - 5:00 PM, Saturday and Sunday Closed all major holidays.
Admission:	FREE!
Parking:	Free parking lot.
Food:	No food or drink allowed in the museum, but there is a picnic table next to the parking lot and several benches and grassy spots in the Sculpture Garden.

What to expect. . .

The Leanin' Tree Museum of Western Art is a private collection consisting of more than 250 paintings and 150 bronze sculptures. The owner of the collection, Ed Trumble, has a close friendship with nearly every artist represented in the museum. His collection is the result of his pursuit of fine artwork to reproduce on Leanin' Tree greeting cards. Depicting cowboys, trains, Native Americans, pioneers, mountains, and Colorado wildlife, all of the pieces in the museum are truly stunning. Many pieces have information cards next to them, providing information about the artist, the artwork, or both.

The Sculpture Garden contains 25 brilliant, life-size bronze statues, mainly of wildlife. Two of the sculptures, a burro and a saddle, may be climbed on and are great photo opportunities.

The museum has a very large elevator and wide, stroller-friendly aisles. The bathrooms are clean but do not have diaper-changing tables. Take the time to stroll through the gift shop. In addition to the usual hats, books, t-shirts, and knickknacks, you'll also find a special collection of greeting cards and calendars featuring some of the very artwork you just enjoyed. The gift shop accepts American Express, MasterCard, Visa, checks, and cash.

Other destinations within 5 miles . . .
Celestial Seasonings (Site 166) - less than 1 mile
Boulder Reservoir (Site 81) - 4½ miles

Courtesy Leanin' Tree Museum

Museums & More

Littleton Museum ☆☆☆☆☆

Photo by Nicole Hager Printed with permission

6028 South Gallup Street
Littleton, 80120
(303) 795-3950
www.littletongov.org/museum

Hours:	8:00 AM - 5:00 PM, Tuesday - Friday 10:00 AM - 5:00 PM, Saturday 1:00 PM - 5:00 PM, Sunday Closed major holidays.
Admission:	FREE!
Parking:	Free parking lot.
Food:	Other than water, food and drink are not allowed in the museum area, including the outdoor areas of the farm, but Gallup Park is across the street.

What to expect. . .

The Littleton Museum offers a link between Littleton's past and present. Inside you'll find a permanent exhibit with photographs, artifacts, and information about the history of Littleton. Attached to the permanent gallery is a fine arts gallery with original photography and art collections; the collections change every two to three months. The temporary exhibit displays traveling exhibits from other museums, including the Smithsonian Institution (the Littleton Museum is the only museum in Colorado to be recognized as an affiliate of the Smithsonian). This exhibit changes a few times per year. The last area before heading outside is Kids Connection, which provides interactive and hands-on activities. You'll find a room with pillows and books, computers that let your child design and launch a satellite, a wheat mill, and an old-fashioned kitchen. The exhibits are roomy and make it easy to maneuver a stroller.

Outside the building are two farm sites, one from the 1860s and one from the 1890s. Ketring Lake sits between them. Along the path, you'll come across a real homestead cabin, schoolhouse, barn, and animal pens. Museum staff and volunteers are dressed in period clothing and can be seen working on the farm or tending to the homestead. Live animals occupy the pens but are for looking only — it is not a petting zoo. The path is crushed gravel, so wear closed-toe shoes. A sturdy stroller should be manageable. At Ketring Lake, take a break in the gazebo and watch the waterfowl that lives there. Continue on the path into the 1890s farm site and see what a difference a few decades can make in the buildings, which include a home, a barn, a tool shed, and a blacksmith shop.

Bathrooms are located in the front and rear of the museum and offer diaper-changing tables in both the men's and women's. A small gift shop near the entrance of the building offers t-shirts, toys, beeswax candles, knickknacks and more. The museum can not accommodate large groups without notice, so if your group has 10 or more people, they ask that you make a reservation and contribute $1 per person.

Other destinations within 5 miles . . .

The Town Hall Arts Center (Site 38) - 1 mile
Cornerstone Park (Site 100) - 1½ miles
Pirates Cove Family Aquatic Center (Site 87) - 1½ miles
Hudson Gardens (Site 108) - 2 miles
Belleview Park (Site 94) - 2½ miles
Skate City - Littleton (Site 175) - 2½ miles
Carson Nature Center and South Platte Park (Site 95) - 4 miles

Scales 'n' Tails - Englewood (Site 139) - 4 miles
CYT Denver - Aspen Academy (Site 27) - 4½ miles
Younger Generation Players (Site 40) - 4½ miles
The Hop - Littleton (Site 46) - 5 miles
Museum of Outdoor Arts (Site 18) - 5 miles
Robert F. Clement Park (Site 117) - 5 miles

Morrison Natural History Museum ☆☆☆☆☆

501 Colorado Highway 8
Morrison, 80465
(303) 697-1873
www.mnhm.org

Hours:	10:00 AM - 5:00 PM daily May through mid-August 10:00 AM - 4:00 PM Tuesday - Saturday mid-August through April 12:00 PM - 4:00 PM, Sunday Closed major holidays.
Admission:	Under 4: Free; Age 4-12: $4; Age 13-64: $5; Age 65+:$4. All major credit cards accepted.
Membership:	$36 for all persons in a single household.
Parking:	Free parking lot.
Food:	No food or drink are allowed inside the museum. You may bring your own food and picnic at one of the tables outside or inside the Discovery Outpost if they are not hosting a birthday party.
Discounts:	Coupons can be found in the Entertainment Book, on ColoradoKids.com, and on their website.

What to expect. . .

The Morrison Natural History Museum is dedicated to focusing on the local discoveries of dinosaur fossils. They are engaged in long-term research projects and participate on active digs. Additionally, this museum is home to both the first Stegosaurus fossil and the first Apatosaurus fossil ever discovered. Upon entering the museum, the first major exhibit is the skull of a Tyrannosaurus. The first floor is filled with fossils, skulls, and tracks from a variety of Jurassic dinosaurs, positioned low enough for children to reach, and nearly everything is available for touching. Little ones will love the collection of infant and juvenile Stegosaurus and Apatosaurus tracks.

The second floor has Cretaceous and late Ice Age fossils, as well as living reptiles, such as snakes and turtles. Come on a Friday afternoon between 12:00 and 4:00 PM and you can get a closer look at the snakes, touch them, and possibly even participate in feeding them. The working paleontology lab is located in this area. On most days you will find Matthew Mossbruker, the director of the museum, working on a fossil. Children can don goggles and use a real paleo tool to break down some of the rock. The process gives them a greater sense of appreciation for the work being done here.

In front of the museum is a boulder "garden" with a covered area containing fossils too large to take inside. When there are enough volunteers and non-threatening rain, people work out here to uncover the fossils and children can help in this process too. If there isn't anyone working on a real fossil, a large sandbox is located beyond this area where your child can dig for petrified wood and shells.

The Morrison Natural History Museum was featured in *Smithsonian Magazine* in 2008. Although it is much smaller than many museums, it can actually offer more. Without making a reservation, you can get a guided tour by a knowledgeable, highly-trained guide. The museum receives new items all the time; Memorial Day weekend is usually when they showcase their new items to the public. Check the calendar on the website for upcoming events and special announcements throughout the year, and also to make sure you are not going when a large group is scheduled.

A unisex bathroom is available on the first floor, but does not contain a diaper-changing table. There is no elevator, but a wheelchair- and stroller-friendly ramp has been installed on the outside of the building that will lead you to the second floor.

Other destinations within 5 miles . . .

Bandimere Speedway (Site 142) - 1½ miles
Bear Creek Lake Park Swim Beach (Site 80) - 1½ miles

Red Rocks (Site 115) - 2½ miles
Dinosaur Ridge (Site 103) - 4 miles

Museo de las Americas ☆☆☆☆☆

Courtesy of Museo de las Americas

861 Santa Fe Drive
Denver, 80204
(303) 571-4401
www.museo.org

Hours:	10:00 AM - 5:00 PM, Tuesday - Friday 12:00 PM - 5:00 PM, Saturday - Sunday Closed major holidays.
Admission:	Under 13: Free; Age 18-64: $4; Students and Seniors age 65+: $3 American Express, Discover, MasterCard, Visa, checks, and cash accepted.
Membership:	$70 for two adults and their children under age 18.
Parking:	Free street parking is available, but you may have difficulty finding a space and it is limited to two hours Monday through Saturday. Some paid lots are in the area.
Food:	No food or drink are allowed in the museum. Several restaurants are within walking distance.
Discounts:	Free on the first Friday of each month from 5:00 PM - 9:00 PM. Other free events may take place throughout the year; visit the website for details.

What to expect. . .

Museo de las Americas was the first gallery in this area, and what is now called The Art District sprouted up around it. Its mission is to educate our community about the diversity of Latino American art and culture. The Museo's permanent collection contains more than 4,000 objects, much of it thanks to the generosity of the Tragen and Bloodworth families. The temporary art exhibits change every few months. All the art is labeled in both English and Spanish.

Family Free Day takes place on the second Saturday of the month, and this is probably your best opportunity to teach your children about Latino American culture. Admission is free for the entire family and the Museo hosts workshops for children in their basement, usually centered around whatever cultural holiday has just past or is upcoming. These workshops involve arts and crafts, and often include a PowerPoint presentation to provide some historical context. While your child is participating in the workshop, you can stay upstairs to admire the artwork.

The gallery is closed between exhibits. This information is not always on the website, so it is best to call ahead. There are restrooms in the Museo, but they do not have diaper-changing tables.

Other destinations within 5 miles . . .

See Appendix I - Downtown Destinations
Kids Kourt (Site 51) - 3 miles

Sloan's Lake Park (Site 122) - 4½ miles
Four Mile Historic Park (Site 106) - 5 miles

GO ONE STEP FURTHER - Check out the Global Wonders DVD series, which can help introduce your child to a variety of cultures. **www.globalwonders.com**.

Museums & More

Museum of Contemporary Art ☆☆☆☆☆

Photo by Dean Kaufman Courtesy MCA Denver

1485 Delgany Street
Denver, 80202
(303) 298-7554
www.mcadenver.org

Hours:	10:00 AM - 6:00 PM, Tuesday - Sunday Open Friday till 10:00 PM. Closed major holidays.
Admission:	Under 6: Free; Age 6-17: $5; Age 18-64: $10; Age 65+: $5 All major credit cards accepted.
Membership:	$75 for two adults and their children under age 18. An adult member may bring two additional guests at no charge each time they visit the museum.
Parking:	Very limited free street parking and a paid lot across the street.
Food:	No food or drink is allowed in the galleries. A café with a variety of soups, salads, and sandwiches is located on the third level. You may bring your own lunch and eat in the outdoor garden, also located on the third level.
Discounts:	Coupons can be found in the Entertainment Book. The museum has quarterly free days. Visit the website for current information.

What to expect...

MCA Denver is an innovative forum for contemporary art that is designed to inspire and challenge audiences of all ages. The best way to visit with children, in my opinion, is from the top down. The third floor has an outdoor area with a Skylight Promenade and a very small garden. Inside is The Idea Box, a creative space designed by the artists to encourage investigation into contemporary art. Children can create their own art, including postcards that can be sent to family, using the tissue paper, construction paper, glue, markers, crayons, and scissors provided. Art left behind by others is displayed on the walls. From the Idea Box, a ramp leads a little further up to a room with more children's creations on display. The projects rotate to complement the art on display. The far wall is a large window looking out to downtown Denver with bean bags on the floor. We sat here for a bit, admiring the view, enjoying the sunshine warming us, and discussing the art we had just created.

The second floor has several large galleries with vaulted ceilings, creating a very open feel. One room had giant raindrops, each painted with a different colorful design, from ceiling to floor. Another room had self-inflating whoopee cushions in separate boxes, pushed at different times to create a sort of song. The exhibits change every four to six months, so these will no longer be available when you visit; these are just examples of the type of art we saw. The exhibits are changed one at a time, so you'll always find something new, and the museum doesn't have to close between exhibits.

The first floor contains two exhibitions, a gift shop, and a hands-on library where kids can touch objects from the exhibiting artists. The basement has an area with couches and a video showing on the wall. The video can be anything related to the exhibits in the museum, including film of the artists creating their works.

The entire museum is very stroller-friendly with an enormous elevator and plenty of room to maneuver. Bathrooms can be found on the different floors; none of them have diaper-changing tables but the museum is planning to install some soon.

Other destinations within 5 miles...

See Appendix I - Downtown Destinations
The Bookery Nook (Site 59) - 3½ miles
Fish Den (Site 138) - 4 miles

Sloan's Lake Park (Site 122) - 4 miles
Kids Kourt (Site 51) - 4½ miles
Rising Curtain Theatre Academy (Site 33) - 4½ miles

DID YOU KNOW? Denver International Airport has the largest public art program in the nation. Pieces are located in the landscape, the terminal, the concourses, and in the train tunnels. DIA also has several venues with changing exhibits. For more information, visit www.flydenver.com/guide/art.

Museum of Outdoor Arts ☆☆☆☆☆

Courtesy Museum of Outdoor Arts

1000 Englewood Parkway, 2nd Floor
Englewood, 80110
(303) 806-0444
www.moaonline.org

Hours:	9:00 AM - 5:00 PM, Monday - Thursday 9:00 AM - 4:00 PM, Friday 11:00 AM - 4PM, Saturday Closed major holidays.
Admission:	FREE!
Parking:	Free parking in the piazza in front of the building and also a free parking garage to the west of the museum.
Food:	Food and drink are not allowed in the museum, but there is a small area in the building with vending machines and a table and chairs. A large grassy area in front of the building is a great place to enjoy a picnic lunch.

What to expect...

In spite of the name, the Museum of Outdoor Arts has a small gallery located inside the Englewood Civic Center. The exhibits change three to four times a year, and the museum is closed in between exhibits for two to four weeks, so check the website or call ahead. More interactive and family-friendly exhibits are generally showing in the fall. When we went, we experienced the Color of Sound, which was an exhibit that combined light and music components. A special exhibit for the blind offered pieces that can be touched. The exhibits may be different when you go; these are simply examples of what we experienced.

MOA's outdoor art collection is on display in public locations throughout Denver, including Samson Park (Site 120). Several pieces are located in front of the building and in the corridor between the parking garage and the Civic Center. Grab a map from inside the gallery, then get on the free shuttle for a self-guided art tour of a dozen pieces. The shuttle runs every 10 minutes from 6:30 AM - 6:30 PM.

Courtesy Museum of Outdoor Arts

Bathrooms are located next to the entrance to the indoor gallery. The women's restroom has a diaper-changing table. The piazza in front of the building has a large grassy area and a fountain with geysers that run in the summertime. The Englewood Library is located on the first floor of the Civic Center.

Other destinations within 5 miles . . .

Museums & More

The Wildlife Experience ☆☆☆☆☆

Photo by Eva Voss

10035 South Peoria Avenue
Parker, 80134
(720) 488-3300
www.thewildlifeexperience.org

Hours:	9:00 AM - 5:00 PM, Tuesday - Sunday Closed Monday, Thanksgiving, and Christmas. Usually open on a holiday Monday (e.g., Memorial Day or Labor Day).
Admission:	Under 3: Free; Age 3-12: $6; Age 13-64: $10; Age 65+: $9 American Express, MasterCard, Visa, checks, and cash accepted.
Membership:	$80 (for six individuals, children or adult)
Parking:	Free parking lot.
Food:	The Toucan Café offers a variety of healthful, affordable options. Outside food and drink are not allowed inside the museum or café, but there are plenty of tables and chairs outside where you can enjoy your own picnic lunch.
Discounts:	Coupons can be found in the Entertainment Book, Chinook Book, and on ColoradoKids.com.

What to expect. . .

The Wildlife Experience is a museum that combines fine art and natural history in a way that connects visitors with wildlife and the surrounding environment. Its purpose it to educate about conservation, environment, wildlife, and habitat in a fun and entertaining atmosphere, and since September 2002, they have been doing just that. The museum offers a nice mix of permanent and changing exhibits. Exhibits include:

Extreme Screen Theater shows films hourly from 10:00 AM - 4:00 PM. The films last approximately 45 minutes, covering anything from coral reefs to safaris. There is an additional fee for the movie, but you can save money by buying a combination ticket.

Cubs Corner is a toddler-focused area with costumes, Tuesday Tales (story time), Theater Thursdays (puppet shows), and a safe place to crawl around or climb. Tuesday Tales and Theater Thursdays take place before noon.

The Exhibit Gallery on the first floor features fine art, sculptures, and photography, all based on wildlife. This exhibit changes every few months.

Discovery Den provides interactive games, costumes, arts and crafts, and a variety of educational programming for school-age children (although my toddler always enjoys playing in here too). Comfy chairs outside this room give parents a place to sit and relax while the children play.

The Exhibit Gallery on the second floor is a 5,000 square foot exhibit that changes every four to six months, and is designed with children of all ages in mind. Past exhibits have included Grossology and Amazing Butterflies.

Globeology is a quarter-mile walking path that takes you through seven different biomes, including a rainforest, highlands, desert, under the sea, and Wild Colorado.

The Nature Trail takes visitors around the museum to view native plants and sculptures. This is where Winter Wonderlights takes place.

Globeology and Wild Colorado are immersive exhibits featuring animatronics and computer-based learning that allow you to step into the environment. A cell phone audio tour is available through most of the museum.

We usually start in the Exhibit Gallery on the second floor and then go through Globeology, which brings us back down to the first floor. I bring a magazine or a book whenever we go to The Wildlife Experience. Seriously. I enjoy the museum, and I love participating and playing with my children, but there are a couple of areas where they like to spend way more time than I do. In the Coral Reef section of Globeology, there is a bit of the ocean projected onto the floor and the fish will swim away when the children run toward them. My boys will spend 30 minutes or more chasing the fish, and thankfully, there is a bench to sit on. They are happy to spend an hour or more in Discovery Den or Cubs Corner, as well.

The bathrooms throughout the museum have changing tables in both the men's and women's restrooms. The computer displays throughout the museum are too advanced for most little ones, but will provide more learning opportunities as they grow. The large gift shop offers a variety of environmentally-friendly products, including soy candles, handbags made from recycled tires, and shirts made from bamboo.

Annual Events . . .

Kids Bowl is a one-day event the Saturday before the Super Bowl that features sports-themed activities and events throughout the museum

Spring Eggstravaganza is a one-day event the Saturday before Easter that celebrates the beginning of spring.

Trick or Treat Off the Street is a Halloween party that occurs for two days at the end of October.

Winter Wonderlights includes an outdoor trail of lights, a Christmas village, Santa, and live reindeer.

Santa Breakfast happens every Saturday morning in December.

Other destinations within 5 miles . . .

Cook Creek Pool (Site 83) - 3½ miles

Little Monkey Bizness (Lone Tree or Parker) Site 53 - 5 miles

Party On (Site 55) - 5 miles

Pump It Up - Parker (Site 56) - 5 miles

Photo by Patty Tucker

# of Wonder Children's Museum

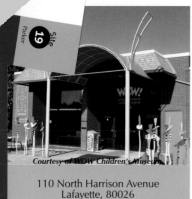

Parker · Site 19

Courtesy of WOW Children's Museum

110 North Harrison Avenue
Lafayette, 80026
(303) 604-2424
www.wowmuseum.com

Hours:	9:00 AM - 5:00 PM, Tuesday and Wednesday 10:00 AM - 6:00 PM, Thursday - Saturday 12:00 PM - 4:00 PM, Sunday Closed Sundays in the summer, all major holidays plus Mother's Day and Father's Day.
Admission:	Under 15 months: Free; Age 15 months - 11 years: $7; Age 12+: Free Discover, MasterCard, Visa, checks, and cash ac- cepted.
Membership:	$65 for one child; $10 for each additional child.
Parking:	Free parking lot and free street parking.
Food:	You are welcome to bring in your own food. There is a designated eating area inside, and picnic tables outside. You may also leave to eat and return the same day without having to purchase another admission.
Discounts:	Coupons can be found in the Entertainment Book, Chinook Book, and in the EcoMetro Guide. Discount of $1 per child for active military families. A 10-pass punch card is $60. Coupons are also distributed at Boulder County festivals and town fairs.

What to expect. . .

World of Wonder (or WOW! as they are known) is an interactive and educational facility that focuses on science, art, and imaginative play in which children and parents can explore, discover, and learn together. The building was Lafayette's original firehouse, and the city donated the building to World of Wonder when the firehouse relocated. The museum is made up of two very large rooms, with each room containing half a dozen or more exhibits. They include:

Photo by Angel McCall

A **Pirate Ship and Lighthouse** where kids can run, climb, and dress up like a pirate or a fish.

A **Science Lab** with a magnetic table, gravity walls, books, and more.

An **Art Studio** with plenty of room for a dozen children and art supplies such as scissors, glue, paper, paint, and colored pencils. Tiny art aprons are provided, and there are clips to hang the artwork till it dries.

A **Light and Shadow Room** where music, lights, and shadows are coordinated together.

A **Credit Union** that allows children to play teller or customer, complete with a vault and a drive-up window. The car ride in this area runs on tokens, which the museum will provide for free.

The **Whole Foods Market** has play food and a mini kitchen, and teaches where the ingredients from a pizza come from (from farm to table).

A **Dance Studio** with costumes, tap and ballet shoes, and mirrors.

A **Theatre in the Round** which includes a puppet stage.

Blowing in the Wind teaches about air and wind using paper cups, scarves, and more.

Inside the Bubble where a child can stand on a platform and pull a bubble wand up over their head so they are literally inside the bubble.

Courtesy of World of Wonder Children's Museum

A Train Station with costumes and trains.

A Toddler Area is somewhat separated from all the activity. Blocks, legos, books, and more are available for play.

Pipes is an exhibit that explores hydraulics and pulley systems by letting children build large structures with PVC pipes and make pulley chairs.

A Changing Exhibit that is usually on loan from a children's museum in another state. This exhibit changes every three to five months.

Toddler hour is on Tuesday and Wednesday mornings from 9:00 AM - 11:00 AM. This is generally a quieter time, with few older children. Most areas in the museum have books related to the exhibit. World of Wonder is much smaller than many other children's museums I've visited, but offers a tremendous amount of activities. The *Boulder Daily Camera* listed WOW! in "The Best of Boulder" as a great place for families with children, and *Child Magazine* ranked it as one of the top 50 children's museums in the country.

The bathrooms are located next to the bubble exhibit and diaper-changing tables are in both the men's and women's. A stool for children to reach the sink is also provided in each bathroom. A very small gift shop is located near the admissions desk, and has toys from Crawdaddy Toys, books, t-shirts, and hats.

Annual Events . . .

Irish Dancers entertain for St. Patrick's Day.

A Birthday Party for the museum happens every November.

A New Year's Eve Celebration takes place at noon on December 31.

Other destinations within 5 miles . . .

Bob L. Burger Recreation Center Indoor Pool (Site 66) - 3 blocks
Peanut Butter Players (Site 32) - less than 1 mile
Waneka Lake Park (Site 124) - 3 miles

Erie Community Center Leisure Pool (Site 69) - 4½ miles
Rock Creek Farm Pumpkin Patch (Site 130) - 4½ miles

See Also

The Arvada Center (Site 22)

Clear Creek History Park (Site 98)

Colorado Railroad Museum (Site 156)

Dinosaur Ridge (Site 103)

Family Arts at DAVA (Site 44)

Fiske Planetarium (Site 169)

Forney Museum of Transportation (Site 158)

Four Mile Historic Park (Site 106)

Ghost Town and Wild West Museum (Site 186)

May Natural History Museum of the Tropics (Site 188)

Pro Rodeo Hall of Fame (Site 189)

Rock Ledge Ranch (Site 190)

Rocky Mountain Dinosaur Resource Center (Site 191)

Western Museum of Mining and Industry (Site 194)

Wings Over the Rockies Air and Space Museum (Site 163)

DID YOU KNOW? The History Colorado Center, formerly called Colorado History Museum is closed for relocation. It is scheduled to reopen in March 2012, just a block south from its previous location. Visit **www.coloradohistory.org** for details.

Morrison Natural History Museum

DID YOU KNOW? The Mizel Museum, a place "where adults and children of every race and culture are welcome to learn about one another and celebrate life," is undergoing renovations to become more child-friendly. They are scheduled to re-open Fall 2010. Visit **www.mizelmuseum.org**.

A Little Song and Dance

Like a good book, music, dance and live theater can carry its audience to faraway lands and exciting adventures. Children seem to have a natural ability to engage in a "willing suspension of disbelief" and just get lost in the story being told. The Denver metro area provides tremendous opportunities to expose your child to age-appropriate musical and theatrical performances. Sign up on the various mailing lists so you are always aware of upcoming productions, and discover the magic of live theater with your child.

Arts on the Move Courtesy Town Hall Arts Center

A Little Song & Dance

The 73rd Avenue Theatre Company ☆☆☆☆☆

Fauna Rock Courtesy 73rd Avenue Theatre Company

7287 Lowell Boulevard
Westminster, 80030
(720) 276-6936
www.the73rdavenuetheatrecompany.com

Season:	Season runs year-round with four or five children's productions each year. The productions generally run for four to eight weeks.
Shows:	Performances are at 1:30 PM on Saturday and 11:00 AM on Sunday.
Tickets:	Age 1-12: $6; Age 13+: $8 Reservations can be made over the phone. Tickets may be purchased at the door using American Express, Discover, MasterCard, Visa, checks, or cash.
Parking:	Free parking lot and free street parking.
Food:	Food and drink are permitted inside the theatre. A few concessions are offered by the theatre company on a donation basis.
Discounts:	Group discounts are available

What to expect. . .

The 73rd Avenue Theatre Company is a relatively new company that was created with the idea of giving back to the community that hosts it and the understanding that the performing arts enriches the lives of those who get involved, including audience, artists, and performers. Shows are performed by professional adult actors, last about one hour, and are usually familiar literature-based stories based. At least one children's performance each year is bilingual. After each performance, children have the opportunity to meet the cast who will autograph the cast photo included with the purchase of every ticket.

The theatre is a black box, which means it is a simple, unadorned performance space. It can seat up to 50 patrons. Unisex bathrooms are located on the outside of the building and do not have diaper-changing tables.

The 73rd Avenue Theatre Company

Other destinations within 5 miles . . .

The Arvada Center (Site 22) - 3 miles
Squiggles Playground (Site 123) - 3 miles
Secrest Pool (Site 89) - 3½ miles
Lakeside Amusement Park (Site 155) - 4½ miles

Majestic View Nature Center (Site 112) - 4½ miles
Denver Puppet Theater (Site 28) - 5 miles
Fish Den (Site 138) - 5 miles

"Children's theatre . . . no other study can paint a lesson in colors that will stay and stay and never fade." ~ Mark Twain

The Arvada Center ☆☆☆☆☆

Courtesy The Arvada Center

6901 Wadsworth Boulevard
Arvada, 80003
(720) 898-7200 (Box Office)
www.arvadacenter.org

Season:	At least two different children's shows are pr[...] each year, one in the fall and one in the sprin[...] production has dozens of performances on the [...] Stage over a six-week period, then in the Black Box theater for a three-week period.
Shows:	Weekday performances for children's programming are at 10:00 AM and 12:00 PM. Saturday shows are at 11:00 AM and 1:00 PM.
Tickets:	$8 for weekday performances; $10 for Saturday performances (children's programming). Tickets can be purchased online or over the phone using Discover, MasterCard, and Visa. The box office also accepts checks and cash.
Parking:	Free parking.
Food:	Drinks are allowed in the theater. A coffee cart may be set up just inside the entrance.

What to expect. . .

Over 90,000 children are served each year by the Arvada Center children's theater program. *Kids' Pages Family Magazine* awarded the Arvada Center as its readers' choice for "Best Place for Families in 2008." The Arvada Center has also been the recipient of three *Denver Post* Ovation awards and four Colorado Theatre Guild Henry awards. Children's shows are performed by professional adult actors and generally last 90 minutes or less. In addition to the children's theater, the regular season may include family-friendly performances, although these productions are likely to last two hours or longer. Musical performances are held in the amphitheater during the summer. Whichever performance you choose to attend, plan to arrive early or stay late so you and your child have the opportunity to explore Squiggles Playground (Site 123).

In addition to theater, the Arvada Center is home to the Arvada History Museum, a 3,000 square foot permanent exhibit depicting the historical and cultural heritage of Arvada. Additionally, two floors of gallery space showcase 12 to 15 art exhibitions each year, emphasizing contemporary art. The museum and gallery are open weekdays from 9:00 AM - 6:00 PM, Saturday from 9:00 AM - 5:00 PM, and Sunday from 1:00 PM to 5:00 PM. Food and drink are not permitted in the gallery or the museum, and both are free to the public.

The Main Stage seats 500 and the Black Box Theater seats about 260. Both theaters are designed so that every seat is a good one. The Center is fully accessible and offers shadowed performances for the deaf and audio-described shows for the blind. Diaper-changing counters are available in most of the bathrooms.

Annual Events . . .

Several **Family Arts Days** each year provide families the opportunity to explore theater together. Visit www.arvadacenter.org/education for current information. Children must be 5 years or older and accompanied by an adult.

Other destinations within 5 miles . . .

Squiggles Playground (Site 123) - same location
Secrest Pool (Site 89) - 1 mile
Majestic View Nature Center (Site 112) - 1½ miles
The 73rd Avenue Theatre Company (Site 21) - 3 miles
Apex Center Indoor Pool (Site 65) - 4 miles
Clubhouse Adventure Playground (Site 41) - 4 miles

Lakeside Amusement Park (Site 155) - 4 miles
Fish Den (Site 138) - 4½ miles
Rising Curtain Theatre Academy (Site 33) - 4½ miles
The Bookery Nook (Site 59) - 5 miles
Wheat Ridge Recreation Center Pool (Site 77) - 5 miles

Audience of One ☆☆☆☆☆

Courtesy Audience of One Theatre Company

(720) 979-5765
www.audienceofonetheater.org

Season:	Three full-scale productions and an improv comedy show are produced each spring and fall. Each production has several performances over a one- to two-week period, including four weekday shows for home-schoolers, preschoolers, and classroom field trips.
Shows:	Day and evening performances vary.
Tickets:	$10 for weekend theatrical productions; $5 for weekday; $5 for improv. Tickets can be purchased online using MasterCard or Visa.
Parking:	Free parking available at both venues.
Food:	Water bottles are permitted in the theatre. Concessions are sold by the acting company before the show and during intermission.

Multiple Locations. . .

The Burgundy Theatre & Events Center
9136 West Bowles Avenue
Littleton, 80123

Parker Mainstreet Center
19650 East Main Street
Parker, 80134

What to expect. . .

Audience of One is a non-profit organization that offers after-school theatrical training for children 5-18. Each training session culminates in a full-scale professionally-directed production at an affordable price. Shows are performed by youth actors and generally last under 90 minutes. One production features children age 5-7, while the others feature children 8-18. Teens age 12-18 make up the improv team. Productions may be based on children's literature or children's

Courtesy Audience of One Theatre Company

Broadway musicals. The actors are very talented, and the costumes and props are well-designed. The older troupes serve as mentors for the younger ones.

Other destinations within 5 miles . . .

See My Art Workshop (Site 54) for destinations near The Burgundy Theatre & Events Center.
See H2O'Brien Pool (Site 85) for destinations near Parker Mainstreet Center.

Aurora Fox Theatre ☆☆☆☆☆

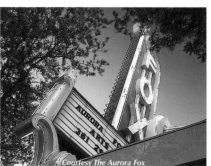
Courtesy The Aurora Fox

9900 East Colfax Avenue
Aurora, 80010
(303) 739-1970
www.aurorafox.org

Season:	Season runs from June to July, with a different production each month. Each production will have 18 performances over a three-week period.
Shows:	Performances are typically at 10:00 AM on Tuesday through Friday, and 1:00 PM on Monday, Wednesday, and Saturday.
Tickets:	$7 for Little Foxes Summer Children's Theatre. Tickets can be purchased online using American Express, Discover, MasterCard, and Visa. The box office also accepts checks or cash.
Parking:	Free parking.
Food:	Food and drink are discouraged, except for water bottles.
Discounts:	Season and group discounts are available.

A Little Song & Dance

What to expect. . .

The Aurora Fox building was originally constructed as a family movie theater for military families in the area. A fire in 1985 nearly destroyed the building, but the City of Aurora rescued The Fox and restored it for use as a year-round live theater. The Aurora Fox's Little Foxes Summer Children's Theatre program casts children and youth in a majority of the roles, with one or two adult professional actors who serve as mentors of professional behavior for the rest of the cast. The Fox provides an excellent theatrical experience for youth participants and audiences alike by hiring a professional production team consisting of lighting, set, costume, and properties designers, as well as directors and stage managers.

The Little Foxes perform in the main auditorium, a proscenium theater which holds approximately 245 patrons. Performances generally last about an hour. Bathrooms are located in the lobby near the box office. Most productions are based on children's books. Past shows include *The Hobbit, A Little Princess,* and *Charlie and the Chocolate Factory.*

Other destinations within 5 miles . . .
Family Arts at DAVA (Site 44) - ½ mile
Wings Over the Rockies Museum (Site 163) - 2½ miles
Cinema Grill (Site 167) - 4½ miles
Little Monkey Bizness - Denver (Site 53) - 4½ miles

Tattered Cover - Denver (Site 63) - 4½ miles
Urban Farm (Site 133) - 4½ miles
Morrison Nature Center (Site 113) - 5 miles

The Cultural Services Division is the largest single provider of arts & culture in the City of Aurora offering programs in performing arts, fine arts, history, public art, special events and festivals, and community volunteerism.

Colorado Music Festival Children's Concerts ☆☆☆☆☆

Courtesy Colorado Music Festival

900 Baseline Road
Boulder, 80302
449-1397
(303) 440-7666 (Tickets)
www.COmusic.org

Season:	The Festival Season runs for six weeks from the end of June till the beginning of August.
Shows:	Young People Concerts are at 10:00 AM on both Saturday and Monday as the festival opens in late June. Family Fun Concerts are typically at 2:00 on select Friday afternoons.
Tickets:	$8 for Young People Concerts and $5 for Family Fun Concerts. Tickets may be purchased online and over the phone using MasterCard and Visa. The box office also accepts checks and cash.
Parking:	Free parking, but very limited within Chautauqua Park. Additional parking is available in the neighborhoods around Baseline Road.
Food:	Food and drink are not permitted in the auditorium. The Chautauqua Dining Hall is located down the hill from the auditorium. You may bring your own food and picnic in Chautauqua Park.
Discounts:	Group discounts are available.

What to expect...

The mission of the Colorado Music Festival and Rocky Mountain Center for Musical Arts is to inspire and connect community members of all ages by providing access to the best of the world's music through education and performance. Summer performances take place in Chautauqua Auditorium, which seats 1,200 guests. The season opens on a Saturday with the Young People's Concert. The program is repeated the following Monday. With the purpose of getting young children excited about classical music, each concert is followed by a music fair in Chautauqua Park, complete with an instrument "petting zoo," performances by Boulder Suzuki Strings, face painting, and other fun activities. Family Fun Concerts are geared toward children age 4 to 8 and take

Courtesy Colorado Music Festival

place three times each season. These 45-minute performances introduce children to the various instruments by featuring different sections of the orchestra such as percussion, brass, strings, or woodwinds. Family Fun Concerts are held on select Friday afternoons throughout the Festival season.

The Colorado Music Festival has merged with the Rocky Mountain Center for Musical Arts, so the children's programming will be expanding.

Other destinations within 5 miles . . .

Boulder History Museum (Site 3) - ½ mile
CU Museum of Natural History (Site 7) - 1 mile
Fiske Planetarium (Site 169) - 1 mile
Boulder Museum of Contemporary Art (Site 4) - 1½ miles
North Boulder Recreation Center Pool (Site 73) - 1½ miles
Tebo Train (Site 160) - 1½ miles

Scott Carpenter Park (Site 121) - 2½ miles
Storybook Ballet (Site 36) - 2½ miles
NCAR (Site 173) - 4 miles
Rocky Mountain Theatre for Kids (Site 34) - 4½ miles
Kids Kabaret (Site 31) - 5 miles

The Colorado Symphony Family Series ☆☆☆☆☆

Courtesy The Colorado Symphony

Boettcher Concert Hall
1000 14th Street
Denver, 80202
(303) 623-7876
www.coloradosymphony.org

Season:	Season runs from October through May with five performances in the series.
Shows:	Performances are on Sunday afternoon at 2:30 PM, except for the Halloween performance, which may be on a weekday in the evening.
Tickets:	Under 18: $13; Age 18+: $25. Tickets can be purchased online using American Express, Discover, MasterCard, and Visa. The box office also accepts checks or cash.
Parking:	Metered parking, paid lots, and a parking garage at the Performing Arts Complex available.
Food:	Food and drink are not permitted, except for water bottles.
Discounts:	Season discounts are available.

A Little Song & Dance

What to expect. . .

Established in 1989, The Colorado Symphony has a 21-week Masterworks series of classical programs, as well as Pops, Holiday, and Summer Parks concerts. Additionally, CSO has created a series specifically for children. The Family Series concerts are shorter than other concerts, lasting about an hour. Concerts may have special features to entertain children, such as narration, storytelling, or costumes. The doors to the Concert Hall open 90 minutes before each concert for pre-performance activities like craft projects, storytelling, an instrument petting zoo, or their popular Halloween costume contest before October's concert. Drums of the World is the most popular concert in the series and is always the Sunday after Thanksgiving.

Petite Musique is a program designed for toddlers and young school-age children. The 45-minute interactive program introduces children to instruments through a favorite story. Petite Musique is offered at 10:00 AM and 11:30 AM on two Mondays and two Tuesdays each spring and fall at different venues around the metro area. Tickets are $5 for children and $7 for adults. Information about the upcoming Petite Musique series is on the website under the **Learn** link.

The Concert Hall is stroller-friendly. Diaper-changing tables are available in both the men's and women's bathrooms.

Note: On the website click on Current Season, then Family, then scroll down and click on CSO Family Series.

Other destinations within 5 miles . . .

See Appendix I - Downtown Destinations
The Bookery Nook (Site 59) - 4 miles
Kids Kourt (Site 51) - 4 miles

Sloan's Lake Park (Site 122) - 4 miles
Fish Den (Site 138) - 5 miles
Rising Curtain Theatre Academy (Site 33) - 5 miles

CYT Denver ☆☆☆☆☆

Courtesy CYT Denver

(303) 653-4716
www.cytdenver.org

Season:	Season runs year-round. At least two productions take place each fall, winter, and spring. Each production has three performances per weekend for one or two weekends.
Shows:	Performances are typically at 7:00 PM on Friday, and 2:00 PM and 7:00 PM on Saturday.
Tickets:	$15 for advance purchase; $17.50 at the door. Tickets can be purchased online using Discover, MasterCard, or Visa. Tickets can also be purchased at the door using credit cards, checks, or cash.
Parking:	Free parking at both locations.
Food:	Food and drink are discouraged inside the theater. Concessions are sold before the performances.
Discounts:	Group discounts are available.

Multiple Locations. . .

Aspen Academy Theater 5859 South University Boulevard Greenwood Village, 80121	Parker Mainstreet Center 19650 East Mainstreet Parker, 80134

What to expect. . .

Founded in 1981, CYT is a nationwide theater arts program dedicated to developing character in children and adults through training in the arts and by producing wholesome family entertainment. CYT Denver offers a variety of full-scale musical productions each year, most of which will already be familiar to you and your family. The shows are acted by children who participate in the after-school education program, ranging in age from 8-18. Many of the actors have been a part of this company for several years and excel in both singing and acting abilities.

Courtesy CYT Denver

Generally, different shows are offered at each venue, so you may be able to see more than one production each season. The Parker Mainstreet Center seats a little more than 200 people, while the Aspen Academy can hold 500. Both theaters are set up so that every seat in the house is a good one.

Other destinations within 5 miles . . .

See H2O'Brien Pool (Site 85) for destinations near Aspen Academy Theatre.
See H2O'Brien Pool (Site 85) for destinations near Parker Mainstreet Center.

Denver Puppet Theater ☆☆☆☆☆

3156 West 38th Avenue
Denver, 80211
(303) 458-6446
www.denverpuppettheater.com

Season:	Season runs year-round except for Septe[...] six different productions each year. Eac[...] runs for six to eight weeks, except for th[...] show which only runs in December.
Shows:	Performances are typically at 10:00 AM and 1:00 PM on Thursday and Friday, and 1:00 PM on Saturday and Sunday
Tickets:	$7. Tickets are purchased at the door using MasterCard, Visa, checks, or cash.
Parking:	Free parking lot and free street parking.
Food:	Food and drink are not allowed in the theater. A coffee shop and ice cream parlor is attached to the puppet theater. When the weather is warm, bring your own lunch and eat in the courtyard.
Discounts:	Purchase a 10-pack of tickets for $60. The 10-pack can be used throughout the season. Coupons can be found in the Entertainment Book and the Chinook Book.

Little Song & Dance

What to expect. . .

For 13 years, Annie Zook has been entertaining children throughout Denver with her hand-made, one-of-a-kind marionettes. The entire theater, including the bathrooms, is decorated with hundreds of puppets. Marionettes, hand puppets, stick puppets, feather boas, and theater masks cover virtually every spare inch of space and create a fun atmosphere. Doors open for 30 minutes before each show. Children are invited to decorate their tickets, which are paper puppets, in the art room next to the lobby. The shows last 45-50 minutes and are appropriate for children 3 and older. Stories may be familiar, like Little Red Riding Hood, or original tales. The theater stays open for 30 minutes after the show to give the children the opportunity to play with some of the puppets. Small stages are set up in a few corners of the theater so the kids truly have the chance to practice the craft.

Courtesy of The Denver Puppet Theatre

The Denver Puppet Theater is in a beautiful home built in the 1930s. Reservations are encouraged for groups of 10 or more; payment is made when you arrive at the theater. Both adult-sized chairs and kid-sized chairs are arranged in front of the stage. Bathrooms are available in the lobby but do not have diaper-changing tables.

Other destinations within 5 miles . . .

The Bookery Nook (Site 59) - 1 mile
Fish Den (Site 138) - 2 miles
Lakeside Amusement Park (Site 155) - 2 miles
Rising Curtain Theatre Academy (Site 33) - 2 miles
Sloan's Lake Park (Site 122) - 3 miles

Casa Bonita (Site 165) - 4½ miles
The 73rd Avenue Theatre Company (Site 21) - 5 miles
Scales 'n' Tails - Lakewood (Site 139) - 5 miles
Tattered Cover Bookstore - Denver (Site 63) - 5 miles

D.L. Parsons Theatre ☆☆☆☆☆

Courtesy D.L. Parsons Theatre

Northglenn Recreation Center
11801 Community Center Drive
Northglenn, 80233
(303) 450-8800
www.northglenn.org/p153.html

Season:	Season runs year-round with three productions by Northglenn Youth Theatre. The Northland Chorale performs twice each year. Magical Mornings, which are productions by outside artists, occur about a dozen times per year.
Shows:	Performances are typically at 7:00 or 7:30 PM on Friday and Saturday, and 2:00 or 2:30 PM on Sunday. Weekday performances are held at 10:00 AM.
Tickets:	Tickets for Northland Chorale are generally $15 or less. Tickets for Northglenn Youth Theatre are generally $8 or less. Tickets for Magical Mornings are generally $5 or less. Tickets may be purchased over the phone using MasterCard and Visa. The box office also accepts checks or cash, and is open during Recreation Center hours.
Parking:	Free parking.
Food:	Food and drink are not permitted in the theater.
Discounts:	Group discounts are available.

What to expect. . .

D.L. Parsons Theatre offers a variety of family-friendly and child-oriented shows year-round. The Northglenn Youth Theatre (NYT), which has won more national youth theater awards than any other children's theater in Colorado, encourages children to expand their talents and cultivate a life-long love for the arts. NYT provides three family-friendly theatrical productions at D.L. Parsons Theatre each year. The actors are youths ranging in age from 8-18. These shows are full-scale productions that can last approximately two hours. Past productions include *Aida, Beauty and the Beast,* and *Into the*

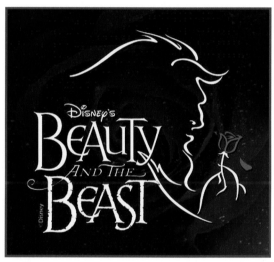

Woods. Outside artists also perform at various times throughout the year as part of the Magical Mornings program. These productions are shorter, generally one hour or less, and are geared toward toddlers and preschoolers. From puppet shows to musical theater, these productions are a great opportunity to introduce younger children to live performances. The Northland Chorale also performs at D.L. Parsons Theatre twice each year. The Northland Chorale is an adult choir that combines music, dancing, and comedy, and has been entertaining audiences for 40 years.

The D.L. Parsons theater seats 300, but still maintains an intimate feeling and every seat is a good one. Bathrooms are located near the entrance, but do not have diaper-changing tables.

Other destinations within 5 miles . . .

E.B. Rains Jr. Memorial Park (Site 104) - across the street
Boondocks Fun Center (Site 151) - less than ½ mile
Krispy Kreme (Site 172) - 1 mile
Skate City - Westminster (Site 175) - 1 mile

The Hop - Thornton (Site 46) - 1½ miles
Scales 'n' Tails - Northglenn (Site 139) - 2½ miles
Jungle Quest (Site 49) - 4 miles
Little Monkey Bizness - Westminster (Site 53) - 4½ miles

Heritage Square Music Hall ☆☆☆☆☆

Courtesy Heritage Square Music Hall

18301 West Colfax Avenue
Golden, 80401
(303) 279-7800
www.hsmusichall.com

Season:	Season runs year-round, with three or four different productions each year.
Shows:	Performances are at 1:30 PM on Saturday. Select Saturdays may also have a 3:00 PM performance.
Tickets:	Under 62: $6; Age 62+: $5. Tickets can be purchased over the phone or in person at the Music Hall Box Office. American Express, MasterCard, Visa, checks, and cash are accepted.
Parking:	Free parking.
Food:	No outside food and drink are permitted in the theater for the children's productions. Dinner theater productions provide a buffet.

What to expect. . .

Heritage Square Music Hall has been entertaining audiences for over 20 years. Children's productions are geared toward kids as young as 2 years old. The shows are performed by professional adult actors and generally last about an hour. Each production is highly interactive with lots of audience participation, and children may even be invited on stage to play certain roles. The theater holds 300 patrons, and seats are reserved so call early to get your choice of seats. Bathrooms are located in the lobby but do not have diaper-changing tables.

Sleeping Beauty

Heritage Square Music Hall also offers year-round dinner theater featuring an extensive buffet and a family-friendly comedy followed by a musical and comedy revue. Dinner and a show can last four hours or more, so this is probably a better option for older children.

Other destinations within 5 miles . . .
Heritage Square Amusement Park (Site 154) - same location
Splash at Fossil Trace (Site 90) - 1½ miles
Clear Creek History Park (Site 98) - 3 miles
Foothills Art Center (Site 12) - 3 miles

Clear Creek Books (Site 62) - 3½ miles
Red Rocks (Site 115) - 4 miles
Lions Park (Site 109) - 4½ miles
Dinosaur Ridge (Site 103) - 5 miles

HELPFUL TIP - The theater department of most high schools will have at least two productions each school year, many of which are child-friendly. Contact the school nearest you for more information. Many local colleges also have family shows.

Kids Kabaret ☆☆☆☆☆

A Little Song & Dance

Kids Kabaret Courtesy Boulder's Dinner Theatre

Boulder's Dinner Theatre
5501 Arapahoe Avenue
Boulder, 80303
(303) 449-6000
www.theatreinboulder.com

Season:	Two productions each year, one in the spring and one in the fall, generally run for six to eight weeks.
Shows:	Performances are typically at 10:00 AM on Wednesday through Friday, and 11:00 AM on Saturday.
Tickets:	$8. Tickets can be purchased online using Discover, MasterCard, and Visa. The box office also accepts checks and cash.
Parking:	Free parking.
Food:	Food and drink are discouraged, except for water bottles.
Discounts:	Group discounts are available. Coupons can be found in both the Entertainment Book and the Chinook Book.

What to expect. . .

Throughout the year, Boulder's Dinner Theatre offers live entertainment combined with a fine-dining experience. Many of the productions are family-friendly, such as "Singin' in the Rain" and "Peter Pan," but the entire evening can last up to four hours. Most young children can't last that long. Fortunately, Boulder's Dinner Theatre also offers Kids Kabaret, a great introduction to live theater. Always based on children's literature and performed by professional adult actors, the productions usually invite audience participation from the children, much of it on stage. Performances last about an hour and are followed by a question-and-answer period with the actors. Lights and sounds not used in the performance may be demonstrated, or the backdrop moved so everyone can see backstage.

The stage is a three-quarter thrust, with tables and chairs surrounding three sides. Every seat offers a great view of the stage. Because the performances are short and usually take place on days when there is an evening show, no food is served or allowed inside the theater. Bathrooms are located in the lobby but they do not have diaper-changing tables. When your child is ready for the full dinner theater experience, tickets start at $35 (meal included) and coupons can be found in the Entertainment Book and the Chinook Book.

Other destinations within 5 miles . . .

Rocky Mountain Theatre for Kids (Site 34) - ½ mile
Scott Carpenter Park (Site 121) - 2 miles
Cottonwood Farm Pumpkin Patch (Site 129) - 2½ miles
Storybook Ballet (Site 36) - 2½ miles
Boulder Museum of Contemporary Art (Site 4) - 3½ miles
Tebo Train (Site 160) - 3½ miles

Boulder History Museum (Site 3) - 4 miles
CU Museum of Natural History (Site 7) - 4 miles
Fiske Planetarium (Site 169) - 4 miles
Celestial Seasonings (Site 166) - 5 miles
Colorado Music Festival (Site 25) - 5 miles
North Boulder Recreation Center Pool (Site 73) - 5 miles

Peanut Butter Players ☆☆☆☆☆

Courtesy Peanut Butter Players

Harlequin Center for the Performing Arts
990 Public Road
Lafayette, 80026
(303) 786-8727
www.peanutbutterplayers.com

Season:	Productions run year-round, with five or six different shows each year. Each show runs for approximately six weeks, except for the holiday show which is only for the month of December.
Shows:	Performances are typically on Saturday at 11:00 AM with a noon lunch, or a 1:00 PM lunch with a 1:45 performance.
Tickets:	$12.00 for lunch and a show. Reservations can be made by calling the box office. Tickets are purchased at the theatre on the day of the show. American Express, Discover, MasterCard, Visa, checks, and cash accepted.
Parking:	Free parking.
Food:	Lunch is included in your admission. Water bottles are allowed.
Discounts:	Group discounts are available.

A Little Song & Dance

What to expect. . .

You may have experienced dinner theater before, but you probably haven't experienced Children's Luncheon Theater. These performances are designed especially for kids and their families. When you arrive, you will be greeted, seated, and served by the Lunch Bunch. The Lunch Bunch are professional actors, ranging in age from 7-17, who perform at least once a week for six months out of the year. Since they are acting *and* waiting tables, they are truly learning everything they need to know for a career in acting!

Courtesy Peanut Butter Players

Choices for lunch may vary; ours were hot dogs, peanut butter and jelly sandwiches, or salad in a pita pocket. Sandwiches are served on whole-wheat bread and came with 100% juice, potato chips, Oreo cookies, and orange slices. To raise money, the Lunch Bunch also sold candy before the show. Bathrooms are located in the lobby but do not have diaper-changing tables.

Shows generally last about 45 minutes and may invite audience participation. The actors are children who have received training in singing, dancing, and acting. Props and costumes are very limited, encouraging the audience and the actors to call on their imaginations. Productions may be familiar to you already, such as *Peter Pan* or *The Wizard of Oz*, or they may be less well-known. Either way, we found the performance engaging and enjoyable for everyone in the audience. The Peanut Butter Players were ranked as the "Best of Boulder" in kids' entertainment 10 times, and were runner-up to the Pearl Street Mall twice. They were also voted Best Day Camp in Boulder County for the past two years.

Other destinations within 5 miles . . .

World of Wonder Children's Museum (Site 20) - less than 1 mile
Bob L. Burger Recreation Center Indoor Pool (Site 66) - 1 mile

Waneka Lake Park (Site 124) - 2 miles
Louisville Community Park (Site 111) - 4½ miles

"I believe that in a great city, or even a small city or village, a great theater is the outward and visible sign of an inward and visible culture."
~ *Laurence Olivier*

Rising Curtain Theatre Academy ☆☆☆☆☆

Photo by Eric Franklin Courtesy RCT Academy

The Curtain Playhouse
6690 West 38th Avenue
Wheat Ridge, 80033
(720) 887-0122
www.curtainproductions.org

Season:	The season runs year-round with ten to fourteen family-friendly performances, and three to five geared toward children.
Shows:	Most performances are held at 7:30 PM on Friday, Saturday, or Sunday.
Tickets:	Prices vary depending on the show. Curtains Up Theatre tickets are $18 - $24; Theatre for Young Audiences tickets are $8; Junior Company Theatre tickets are $10 - $12. Tickets may be purchased online or over the phone using Discover, Master-Card, or Visa. Tickets may also be purchased at the door but are slightly more expensive, and you run the risk of a sold-out show.
Parking:	Free parking lot.
Food:	Food and drink other than water are not permitted in the theater, but a free dessert service is offered in the lobby at intermission.

What to expect. . .

The Rising Curtain Theatre Company is the junior company made up of children age 3-18, while the Curtains Up Theatre Company is the professional division. Both companies are housed in the same theater and each offers a variety of family-friendly productions throughout the year. The junior company is theater for children performed by children, while the other shows for children are performed by professional adult actors. Tickets for both companies are available through the website. Performances may last anywhere from 45 minutes to 2.5 hours, depending on the show. Contact the theater to ask questions and determine the production most appropriate for your family.

The theater is a very small venue, seating approximately 50 patrons. A unisex bathroom with a diaper-changing table is available in the lobby.

Other destinations within 5 miles . . .

See Appendix I - Downtown Destinations
Fish Den (Site 138) - 1½ miles
The Bookery Nook (Site 59) - 2 miles
Denver Puppet Theater (Site 28) - 2 miles
Lakeside Amusement Park (Site 155) - 2 miles
Scales 'n' Tails - Lakewood (Site 139) - 2½ miles

Sloan's Lake Park (Site 122) - 2½ miles
Wheat Ridge Recreation Center Pool (Site 77) - 2½ miles
Casa Bonita (Site 165) - 3 miles
The Arvada Center (Site 22) - 3 miles
Squiggles Playground (Site 123) - 3 miles
Secrest Pool (Site 89) - 4½ miles

Photo by Eric Franklin Courtesy Rising Curtain Theatre Academy

Rocky Mountain Theatre for Kids ☆☆☆☆☆

Courtesy Rocky Mountain Theatre for Kids

The Magic Playhouse
5311 Western Avenue
Boulder, 80301
(303) 245-8150
www.theaterforkids.net

Season:	Several productions are offered each spring, summer, and fall or winter. The major production will generally run for two successive weekends. Minor productions generally run for one weekend.
Shows:	Times may vary but most shows have matinee and evening performances.
Tickets:	Prices vary depending on the show, but are usually less than $12. Tickets may be purchased online using Discover, MasterCard, Visa, or e-check.
Parking:	Free parking at all theaters.
Food:	Food and drink other than water are not permitted in the theater. Children's tickets for matinees of the major production include a snack and a drink.

What to expect. . .

Since 1996, the award-winning Rocky Mountain Theatre for Kids has given students a professional theater experience and the opportunity to study in a true workshop environment. RMTK has junior and senior acting groups in both Denver and Boulder, so they are able to offer several productions after each session. Shows are performed by talented youth actors as young as 8 years old. Upcoming shows are listed on the website with performance dates, ticket prices, and a brief description of each show including the running time. Costumes and props look very professional and are well-designed. A video of excerpts from various productions is available on the home page.

The Boulder Youth Repertory performs at the Magic Playhouse in Boulder; the Denver Youth Repertory performs at various theaters in the Denver area.

Courtesy Rocky Mountain Theatre for Kids

Other destinations within 5 miles . . .

Kids Kabaret (Site 31) - ½ mile
Scott Carpenter Park (Site 121) - 1½ miles
Storybook Ballet (Site 36) - 2½ miles
Boulder Museum of Contemporary Art (Site 4) - 3 miles
Cottonwood Farm Pumpkin Patch (Site 129) - 3 miles
Boulder History Museum (Site 3) - 3½ miles

CU Museum of Natural History (Site 7) - 3½ miles
Fiske Planetarium (Site 169) - 3½ miles
Tebo Train (Site 160) - 3½ miles
Colorado Music Festival (Site 25) - 4½ miles
North Boulder Recreation Center Pool (Site 73) - 4½ miles

Shoestring Children's Theater Company ☆☆☆☆

Courtesy Shoestring Children's Theater Company

PO Box 461295
Aurora, 80046
(720) 984-8278
www.shoestringchildrenstheatercompany.com

Season:	Season runs from September through June, with three mainstage productions. Each production has four performances, including matinee and evening shows.
Shows:	Performances are typically on the weekend, with matinees at 2:00 PM and evening performances at 7:00 PM.
Tickets:	$8. MasterCard and Visa are accepted for online purchases. Reservations can be made over the phone and the tickets paid for at the door with checks or cash.
Parking:	Free parking at all venues.
Food:	Varies from venue to venue; generally only water is allowed in the theater. Refreshments are available for purchase before and after the show.
Discounts:	A free children's event takes places with the Aurora Symphony Orchestra in the spring, usually March.

What to expect. . .

Shoestring Children's Theater Company is a very unique program that uses live theatrical performances to promote literacy in our community by bringing children's books from local authors to the stage. The productions are cast with children from 7-16 years old, and encompass all levels of abilities. Supplemental activities such as a craft project or educational curriculum accompany each production to further the adventure into the book. Following the performance, stay and talk with the author and meet some of the cast.

The company sets seasonal goals to donate books to children within Colorado. You can help them meet these goals by bringing a new or gently used book to the performance. Shoestring Children's Theater company received the "Best Theatre Educational Program Award for 2009" from Alliance for Colorado Theatre.

Storybook Ballet ☆☆☆☆☆

Aurora

Site 35

Storybook Ballet Courtesy Boulder Ballet

Dairy Center for the Arts
2590 Walnut Street, Boulder, 80302
443-0028
(303) 444-7328 (Tickets)
www.boulderballet.org/sperfs.html

Season:	A Storybook Ballet is produced each spring and performed for one weekend.
Shows:	Performances are at 7:00 PM on Friday and Saturday, and 2:00 PM on Saturday and Sunday.
Tickets:	Under 12: $10; Age 12 and up: $15. Tickets may be purchased over the phone or online at **www.thedairy.org** using American Express, Discover, MasterCard, and Visa. The box office also accepts checks and cash.
Parking:	Free parking.
Food:	Food and drink are not permitted inside the theater.

What to expect. . .

Storybook Ballet is an original ballet performed by students of the Boulder Ballet School. Familiar children's stories are brought to life through dance and music. Past productions have included *The Wizard of Oz* and *Alice in Wonderland*. Each performance only lasts about an hour. Storybook Ballet is the perfect way to introduce your child to the beautiful art of ballet.

Order your tickets early, as performances usually sell out. The Storybook Ballet takes place in the Performance Space at the Dairy Center for the Arts, a small 250-seat theater. Bathrooms are located just outside the Performance Space but do not have diaper-changing tables.

Storybook Ballet Courtesy Boulder Ballet

Other destinations within 5 miles . . .

Boulder Museum of Contemporary Art (Site 4) - 1 mile
Tebo Train (Site 160) - 1½ miles
Boulder History Museum (Site 3) - 2 miles
CU Museum of Natural History (Site 7) - 2 miles
Fiske Planetarium (Site 169) - 2 miles
Colorado Music Festival (Site 25) - 2½ miles

Kids Kabaret (Site 31) - 2½ miles
North Boulder Recreation Center Pool (Site 73) - 2½ miles
Rocky Mountain Theatre for Kids (Site 34) - 2½ miles
Celestial Seasonings (Site 166) - 4½ miles
Boulder Reservoir Swim Beach (Site 81) - 5 miles
NCAR (Site 173) - 5 miles

Tiny Tots "Inside the Orchestra" ☆☆☆

Photo by Jack Eberhard   Courtesy Junior S...

(303) 355-7855
www.jrsg.org

Season:	Season runs from the end of Janua... Februray, with a total of eighteen p...
Shows:	Performances are typically at 9:30... 10:30 AM, and may take place on Monday, Tuesday, Wednesday, or Thursday.
Tickets:	$5. Tickets can be purchased by downloading a ticket order form from the website and mailing cash or a check.
Parking:	Varies by location.
Food:	Food and drink are discouraged, except for water bottles.
Discounts:	They've never turned anyone away who could not pay.

What to expect. . .

For more than 22 years, the Junior Symphony Guild has provided a unique experience for audiences of all ages by allowing them to experience classical music from "inside the orchestra." Parents and children sit on the floor surrounded by the 30-member orchestra. The conductor engages the children by connecting the music with their everyday lives: music that sounds like a timeout versus music that sounds like playtime, or music that seems like an inside voice compared to music that is more like an outside voice. Special guests of these concerts may include ballerinas, opera singers, and soloists as young as eight years old. After the concert, children are encouraged to take a closer look at the instruments and speak with the musicians.

In 1997, the American Symphony Orchestra League in Washington DC honored the JSG's "Inside the Orchestra" programs with "best in the nation" for educational outreach. This recognition compared the

Photo by Jack Eberhard Courtesy Junior Symphony Guild

Junior Symphony Guild's work with major symphonies' efforts from coast to coast. To reach the most children, performances are held at a variety of locations across the Denver metro area, so you're sure to find one near you. Locations may vary from year to year, but are typically at Temple Emanuel, Temple Sinai, Wildlife Experience, Mile Hi Church, Boettcher Concert Hall, and El Jebel. Concerts sell out, so send your form in as early as possible to ensure that you can attend with your child.

DID YOU KNOW? Babies as young as 3 months old can pick out the complex structure of classical music and recognize classical selections they have heard before.

The Town Hall Arts Center ☆☆☆☆☆

Courtesy Town Hall Arts Center

2450 West Main Street
Littleton, 80120
(303) 794-2787
www.townhallartscenter.com

Season:	Family theater runs year round; children's productions occur once in the fall and once in late winter. Each children's show runs for a two- to three-week period.
Shows:	Performances are typically at 10:00 AM on Monday through Thursday, and 10:00 AM and 1:00 PM on Saturday.
Tickets:	$7. American Express, Discover, MasterCard, and Visa accepted for online purchases. The box office also accepts checks and cash.
Parking:	Free street parking and a paid public lot are available.
Food:	You may bring your own snacks and drinks into the theater. Concessions are sold during regular season performances.

What to expect. . .

The Town Hall Arts Center has been producing professional children's theater since 1997 with the goal of helping children develop a life-long appreciation of the performing arts. Children's shows are performed by professional adult actors and last approximately one hour. Most shows are original stories. Many of the shows during the regular season are also family-friendly. These shows may last two hours or more and tickets are slightly more expensive.

Aesop-a-Rebop Courtesy Town Hall Arts Center

Located on the second floor of the building, the theatre is a three-quarter thrust that holds about 260 patrons, and every seat in the house is a good one. Behind the lobby on the first floor is a small art gallery featuring Littleton artists. The art changes with every major show through the regular season. An elevator is in this area for those unable to use the stairs to the theater. Men's, women's, and a unisex bathroom are located between the lobby and the art gallery, but they do not have diaper-changing tables.

Other destinations within 5 miles . . .

Hudson Gardens (Site 108) - less than 1 mile
Littleton Museum (Site 14) - 1 mile
Cornerstone Park (Site 100) - 1½ miles
Pirates Cove Family Aquatic Center (Site 87) - 1½ miles
Skate City - Littleton (Site 175) - 1½ miles
Belleview Park (Site 94) - 2 miles
Carson Nature Center and South Platte Park (Site 95) - 3 miles
Younger Generation Players (Site 40) - 3 miles

Audience of One - Burgundy Theater (Site 23) - 5 miles
Museum of Outdoor Arts (Site 18) - 3½ miles
Robert F. Clement Park (Site 117) - 3½ miles
The Hop - Littleton (Site 46) - 4 miles
Scales 'n' Tails - Englewood (Site 139) - 4½ miles
Bumble Bounce's House of Bounce (Site 43) - 5 miles
CYT Denver - Aspen Academy (Site 27) - 5 miles
My Art Workshop (Site 54) - 5 miles

A Little Song & Dance

Trunks ☆☆☆☆☆

Trunks Courtesy Buntport Theatre

Buntport Theater
717 Lipan Street, Denver, 80204
(720) 946-1388
www.buntport.com/trunks

Season:	Season runs from October through April. See the website for dates.
Shows:	Performances are every other Saturday at 1:00 PM and 3:00 PM.
Tickets:	$5 - $7, depending on the dice you roll at the door. Reservations are suggested but not required, and can be made online or over the phone. You can pay online using PayPal or at the door with checks or cash.
Parking:	Free street parking.
Food:	Food and drink other than water are not permitted in the theater.
Discounts:	$1 discount if you wear a superhero costume.

What to expect. . .

Trunks is an award-winning live comic book series. The season begins with an original episode, and every two weeks there is an all-new episode based on audience suggestion. Before the show, children are asked to write the name of one of their favorite books on a slip of paper. After the show, one of the superheroes in the cast will randomly select one of the slips of paper, and the next show will be loosely based on that book while continuing to tell the story of the superheroes. Each episode can stand alone so you don't have to attend the whole series (but you'll want to). You can visit the **Episodes** page on the website for the full story of each episode. The theater is very small so seats are not reserved, but you will have a great seat regardless of where you sit. A bathroom is available in the waiting area but does not have a diaper-changing table.

Other destinations within 5 miles . . .

See Appendix I - Downtown Destinations
Kids Kourt (Site 51) - 3 miles

Sloan's Lake Park (Site 122) - 4½ miles
Four Mile Historic Park (Site 106) - 5 miles

GO ONE STEP FURTHER: Sales of graphic novels climbed from $43 million in 2001 to almost $400 million in 2009. Much of that success is due to the fact that librarians endorsed graphic novels as a tool to encourage reading among children and teens. Ask your librarian for recommendations for your child's age group.

Younger Generation Players ☆☆☆☆☆

Courtesy Younger Generation Players

2701 West Oxford Avenue #3
Englewood, 80110
(303) 789-4444
www.ygplayers.org

Season:	The season runs year-round with different productions in spring, summer, fall, and winter. Generally, each production will run for one or two weeks.
Shows:	Performances are typically in the evening from Thursday through Saturday. Sunday matinees may also be available.
Tickets:	$13. Tickets may be purchased online or over the phone using MasterCard or Visa. The box office also accepts checks and cash.
Parking:	Free parking lot.
Food:	Food and drink are not permitted in the theater. Concessions are sold in the lobby during intermission.

What to expect. . .

The Younger Generation Players have been entertaining audiences with their song and dance for more than 30 years. These actors, age 6-18, present a variety of Broadway hits and adapted stories. Past shows include *Hansel and Gretel, Guys and Dolls, Oklahoma!, Snow White and the Seven Dwarfs,* and more than 150 other productions. Most shows are full-length productions and the Christmas performance includes a musical revue afterward; performances are generally at least two hours. The theater can accommodate approximately 120 guests. Every

"Sleeping Beauty" Courtesy Younger Generation Players

seat affords a good view of the stage. Cushions are available as boosters for smaller children.

The theater is located in a set of industrial complex warehouses so it may be difficult to spot. Shows start on time so give yourself plenty of travel time. Bathrooms are located in the small lobby of the theater but do not have diaper-changing tables.

Other destinations within 5 miles . . .

Museum of Outdoor Arts (Site 18) - 2 miles
Cornerstone Park (Site 100) - 2½ miles
Belleview Park (Site 94) - 3 miles
Pirates Cove Family Aquatic Center (Site 87) - 3 miles
Scales 'n' Tails - Englewood (Site 139) - 3 miles

Skate City - Littleton (Site 175) - 3 miles
The Town Hall Arts Center (Site 38) - 3 miles
Hudson Gardens (Site 108) - 3½ miles
Littleton Museum (Site 14) - 4½ miles
White Fence Farm (Site 178) - 5 miles

See Also

Casa Bonita (Site 165)

Elitch Gardens (Site 152)

Flying W Ranch (Site 184)

Baby, It's Cold Outside

Denver has a pretty ideal climate. Averaging 300 days of sunshine each year — that's more than some beach cities on either coast! And with less than sixteen inches of precipitation each year, we're pretty dry too. Still, there are some days when it is just too cold, too rainy, too snowy, or too muddy to play outside. There are only so many hours I can stay in my house before I start to go stir-crazy, so I am thankful that Denver also has plenty of clean, safe places where we can go, from indoor playgrounds to bounce houses to arts and crafts.

Courtesy Jumpstreet

Apex Center Clubhouse Adventure Playground ☆☆☆☆☆

Baby It's Cold Outside

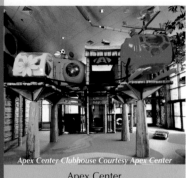

Apex Center Clubhouse Courtesy Apex Center

Apex Center
13150 West 72nd Avenue
Arvada, 80005
(303) 424-2739
www.apexprd.org/facilities/apex-center

Hours:	**Fall/Winter/Spring Hours** 7:30 AM - 9:00 PM, Monday - Friday 7:30 AM - 6:30 PM, Saturday 10:00 AM - 7:00 PM, Sunday **Summer Hours (Memorial Day - Labor Day)** 7:30 AM - 8:30 PM, Monday - Friday 7:30 AM - 7:30 PM, Saturday 10:00 AM - 6:30 PM Sunday
Admission:	FREE!
Parking:	Free parking lot.
Food:	No food or drink allowed inside the Clubhouse. You may bring in your own lunch and eat at the tables in the lobby. A snack bar is available with hot dogs, burritos, chicken strips, burgers, and the like.

What to expect. . .

The Apex Center is immense, and admission is required for general use of the facility. The Clubhouse, however, is totally free and is a great indoor playground for children under 10 (children 8 and under must be accompanied by an adult). With trees, grass, and sky painted on the walls and a giant treehouse structure, the Clubhouse is designed to look like a treehouse in someone's backyard. The treehouse is actually two separate structures that are connected at the top; one of the structures is perfect for toddlers. With tubes, slides, and ladders, your child will have fun exploring this multi-level play area. Parents are encouraged to join in the fun, but padded benches are available when you run out of energy (which will, no doubt, be long before your child does). A number of different-sized balls are available for kicking and rolling.

The Clubhouse is in its own room with only one door, so it would be difficult for your little one to escape without you seeing her. The floor is soft and cushioned. Cubbies are provided for jackets and shoes. A unisex child's bathroom with a diaper-changing table is connected to the Clubhouse.

Other destinations within 5 miles . . .

Apex Center Indoor Pool (Site 65) - same location
Majestic View Nature Center (Site 112) - 3½ miles
The Arvada Center (Site 22) - 4 miles

Squiggles Playground (Site 123) - 4 miles
Secrest Pool (Site 89) - 4½ miles

B&C BounceTown ☆☆☆☆☆

Courtesy B&C BounceTown

Hours:	10:00 AM - 2:00 PM, Monday, Wednesday, and Friday 10:00 AM - 7:00 PM, Tuesday and Thursday All other times are reserved for parties.
Admission:	Under 2: Free with a paying child or $4 without; Children 2 and up: $8 MasterCard, Visa, checks, and cash accepted.
Parking:	Free parking lot.
Food:	You may bring in your own food or order Blackjack Pizza to be delivered. Eating is only in the party room.
Discounts:	Coupons can usually be found on ColoradoKids. com, BestofLongmont.com, and on their Facebook fan page. Admission is only $5 on Mad Monday (excluding holidays and no-school days) and Grand- parents Day, which is the last Tuesday of the month. Multi-visit and summer Bounce Passes are available at a discounted rate.

1821 Lefthand Circle, Unit C
Longmont, 80501
(303) 774-9550
www.bncbouncetown.com

Baby It's Cold Outside

What to expect. . .

Unlike most bounce houses, B&C
BounceTown does not have a lobby that
is separate from the bouncing room. As
soon as you enter, you are at the front
counter. Anyone who wants to cross
the threshold, including "adults, non-
participants, and boring people," must
remove their shoes and enter wearing
only their socks (which they have for
sale if you forget yours). B&C is a 5,000
square foot facility with five different
inflatables. They own more than five, so
inflatables may vary, but you can generally expect at least one slide, a bounce
house for older kids, a bounce house for
younger kids, and an obstacle course.

Courtesy B&C BounceTown

A few Little Tykes rocking horses and kid-sized benches can also be found in here. Among all the
inflatables, parents can relax on one of two very comfortable leather couches or an easy chair. Several
magazines are available, and you can also access their free wireless internet.

Bounce sessions are parent-supervised. Your admission is good for the entire day, but there is no re-
entry. The party room has four large picnic tables where you can eat your lunch. Both the men's and
women's bathrooms provide diaper-changing tables and step stools for the sink. Although the bounce
area is not separated from the entrance, a staff member is always at the front desk and children are not
permitted to leave unless accompanied by an adult. The entire facility, including the inside and outside
of every inflatable, is cleaned each night.

Other destinations within 5 miles . . .

Kanemoto Park and Pool (Site 86) - 1½ miles
Longmont Recreation Center Leisure Pool (Site 72) - 2 miles
Sunflower Farm (Site 132) - 2½ miles

Itty Bitty City (Site 47) - 3 miles
Roosevelt Activity Pool (Site 88) - 3 miles

Bumble Bounce's House of Bounce ☆☆☆☆☆

Hours:	10:00 AM - 4:00 PM, Tuesday - Thursday 10:00 AM - 8:00 PM, Friday 10:00 AM - 1:00 PM, Sunday All day Saturday and Sunday afternoons are reserved for parties.
Admission:	Under 13 months: Free; 13 months - 23 months: $2; Age 2-10: $5; Adults 18 and over: $2.50 (one free adult admission with each paid child admission) American Express, Discover, MasterCard, Visa, and cash accepted.
Parking:	Free parking lot.
Food:	You are welcome to bring your own food and drink and eat in the party room or lobby. Food and drink are not allowed in the bouncers.
Discounts:	Purchase an 8-visit punch card for $25. Buy a Bumble Bounce t-shirt for $10 and your child's admission is $3 every time they wear it to Bumble Bounce.

(720) 283-2899
www.houseofbounce.net

What to expect. . .

Bumble Bounce's House of Bounce is a family-owned business, opened by parents who have a son with a January birthday. They simply wanted a bouncer for his birthday, and the business expanded into a place to bounce when the weather was too cold and snowy outside. The first room you enter is the lobby, a large room with a few tables and chairs, and some coin-operated rides (one of which is a 50-year old race car). The bounce room is 6,000 square feet and has some themed inflatables, including a dinosaur bouncer, an obstacle course, and a pirate ship. A small bouncer is reserved for children two and under and a large bounce castle is available for older children. A gym mat is on the floor at the entrance of each inflatable so children have a soft landing when they exit. Benches are placed near every bouncer and comfortable couches are in the center of the room so you can keep an eye on your child if you're not bouncing with her. A loft gives you a birds-eye view of the entire room. It only has a few barstools for sitting, but it's a great spot to video your child, especially in the obstacle course.

Bounce sessions are parent-supervised. Shoes are not allowed and socks are required (they sell them if you forget yours). Cubbies for shoes and hangers for jackets are provided. Water fountains and bathrooms are available inside the bounce room and in the lobby as well; all the bathrooms have diaper-changing tables. The entrances to the bouncers are cleaned several times a day, and all the bouncers are sanitized inside and out each week.

Note: Bumble Bounce's House of Bounce is relocating. Please visit the website for the new address.

Other destinations within 5 miles . . .

Pump It Up - Littleton (Site 56) - 2 miles
Tattered Cover Bookstore - Highlands Ranch (Site 63) - 2 miles
Civic Green Park (Site 97) - 2½ miles
Carson Nature Center and South Platte Park (Site 95) - 3 miles
The Hop - Littleton (Site 46) - 3 miles
Hudson Gardens (Site 108) - 4 miles

Littleton Museum (Site 14) - 4 miles
Belleview Park (Site 94) - 4½ miles
Pirates Cove Family Aquatic Center (Site 87) - 4½ miles
Redstone Park (Site 116) - 5 miles
The Town Hall Arts Center (Site 38) - 5 miles

Family Arts at DAVA ☆☆☆☆☆

	Family Arts
	10:00 AM - 12:00 PM, Tuesday and Friday
Hours:	**Gallery Hours**
	9:00 AM - 5:00 PM, Monday - Friday
	Closed weekends and major holidays.
Admission:	FREE!
Parking:	Free parking lot and free street parking.
	Food and drink are not allowed inside the gallery.
Food:	You may bring snacks and a drink to Family Arts.
	They provide a snack toward the end of the class.

1419 Florence Street
Aurora, 80205
(303) 367-5886
www.davarts.org

Baby It's Cold Outside

What to expect. . .

"Crafts are for school!" I was so relieved when I heard another parent say this, since I have worked hard to keep crafts (other than coloring books or play-dough) out of my house. The set up, the clean up, the cost, and trying to figure out where to store it all is just too much for me. So imagine my excitement when I discovered a few places in the Denver area where my children could participate in arts and crafts from a very young age.

Since 1994, Downtown Aurora Visual Arts (DAVA) has supported thousands of young people by providing free on-site art programs, creative opportunities, and art-based job training. Through Family Arts, DAVA offers a semi-weekly opportunity for you and your child to make art together using ceramics, paints, and other projects. Our visit began with 20 minutes of unstructured crafting (since families with young children can't always arrive on time), followed by a structured art activity, a story, a snack, and then another craft. Family Arts is for children age 3 to 6, and parents are expected to participate with their children. DAVA tries to connect the craft with the current exhibit in the gallery. For example, during the Health/Wellness/Prevention exhibit, children could create clay superhero foods, like Powerful Peppers or Terrific Tomatoes. The gallery is very small; exhibits generally feature local artists and change every two to three months.

Pre-registration is not required to participate. The unisex bathroom is located in the gallery and a diaper-changing table is provided.

Other destinations within 5 miles . . .

See Appendix I - Downtown Destinations
Aurora Fox Theatre (Site 24) - ½ mile
Wings Over the Rockies Museum (Site 163) - 2½ miles

Cinema Grill (Site 167) - 4 miles
Urban Farm (Site 133) - 4½ miles
Morrison Nature Center at Star K Ranch (Site 113) - 5 miles

DID YOU KNOW? Many craft stores offer classes just for children. Some are free and some charge a nominal fee to cover the cost of supplies. Visit **www.michaels.com**, **www.lakeshorelearning.com**, or **www.hobbylobby.com** to find a class near you.

Family Sports Center ☆☆☆☆☆

Courtesy South Suburban Parks and Recreation

6901 South Peoria Street
Centennial, 80112
(303) 708-9500
www.ssprd.org

Hours:	10:00 AM - 8:00 PM, Monday - Thursday and Saturday 10:00 AM - 10:00 PM, Friday 10:00 AM - 7:00 PM, Sunday
Admission:	Cost is based on the activities you choose. Discover, MasterCard, Visa, checks, and cash accepted.
Parking:	Free parking lot.
Food:	No outside food or drink are allowed. A concession stand and vending machines are available on the first level. The Avalanche Grill, a sports bar, is located on the second floor.
Discounts:	See below for a full description of all available discounts.

What to expect...

Family Sports Center, part of the South Suburban Parks and Recreation District, offers miniature golf, laser tag, a climbing wall, arcade games, rides, ice skating, and a variety of inflatable games. The arcade games and some of the smaller rides operate on one or two tokens. Some of the games dispense tickets, which can be cashed out for prizes. Larger rides such as bumper cars, the Sizzler, and a motion simulator require from two to five tickets each. Kidopolis is a two-story climbing structure with a slide, and it is free (no shoes allowed and socks are required). A new interactive gaming area is scheduled to open shortly after the release of this book.

Courtesy South Suburban Parks and Recreation

The ice facility, which houses two NHL-size rinks, is home to the Arapahoe Warriors Hockey Program. Additionally, the Colorado Avalanche (Site 143) practices here and the public may watch. Bathrooms are available on both levels of the Sports Center and diaper-changing tables are provided in all of them. We experienced some issues with games being out of order but not being labeled as such, or games not giving tickets when they were supposed to, but the staff was very cooperative about replacing tokens for the ones we lost.

Monday through Thursday (excluding holidays), an Individual Fun Pass can be purchased for $13.95. It includes unlimited rides, one attraction, and $5 in tokens. For $15.95, you'll get two attractions. Rock 'n' Skate is available for $10 on the second Friday of every month. $2 Tuesdays is offered the second Tuesday of each month and Blades for a Buck is on the first Friday of each month; both have special prices for skating admission, skate rentals, and concessions. Sunday is Family Day and there are two discounted packages available. Additionally, coupons can be found on the website, in the the District Catalog, and on ColoradoKids.com.

Note: On the website click on Facilities/Parks, then Family Sports Center under Recreation Centers

Other destinations within 5 miles . . .
Samson Park (Site 120) - 3½ miles
Westlands Park (Site 126) - 4½ miles

The Hop ☆☆☆☆☆

www.denverhop.com

Hours:	9:00 AM - 12:00 PM and 1:00 PM - 4:00 PM, Monday - Friday. Weekends are reserved for parties.
Admission:	Under 2: Free with a paying child or $2 without; Children 2 and up: $6. American Express, Discover, MasterCard, Visa, checks, and cash accepted.
Parking:	Free parking.
Food:	You may bring in your own food and drink and eat in the lobby. No food or drink allowed inside the bouncing arena.
Discounts:	Coupons can sometimes be found on their website or on ColoradoKids.com. Purchase a 6-visit punchcard for $25 or a 13-visit punchcard for $50. Bring a non-perishable food item in the months of November and December and receive $1 off admission.

Multiple Locations. . .

8257 Southpark Circle Littleton, 80120 (303) 655-7399	12301 North Grant, Ste 260 Thornton, 80241 (303) 902-5775

What to expect. . .

Although my children seemed to love all the bounce places equally, The Hop is my personal favorite because I feel it offers the best value. The family-owned and family-operated 5,000 square foot facility holds a variety of inflatables: a big inflatable slide, sports-themed inflatables, a pirate-themed bouncer, and a jungle-themed bouncer just for toddlers. In addition to playing on the inflatables, children can also enjoy a game of air hockey or foosball, which are both free. Parents and children alike will have a blast playing old school games like Frogger, Donkey Kong, Galaga, Dig Dug, and more than 60 others on the complimentary video arcade games. The bounce arena also includes a parent lounge with comfortable couches, a flat screen TV, and a karaoke machine. In the middle of all the bouncers is another table where you can keep an eye on your child if you're not bouncing too. Not a bad deal for six bucks, and your admission is good for the full three hours of open play time.

The owners are grandparents who have been involved with youth and youth sports for well over 25 years, so they really understand kids and how to keep them entertained. They wanted to provide a clean, comfortable, safe place for children of all ages to be active. Before entering the play room, everyone is asked to use antibacterial hand sanitizer. The inflatables are cleaned four times a day and after every party on the weekends. Hooks and cubbies are available for jackets and shoes. Socks are required (they sell them if you forget yours). The lobby has benches that convert to half a picnic table. The bathroom has a diaper-changing table. Like the other bounce houses, bounce sessions are parent-supervised.

Other destinations within 5 miles . . .

See Carson Nature Center and South Platte Park (Site 95) for destinations near Littleton location.
See Boondocks Fun Center (Site 151) for destinations near Thornton location.

Itty Bitty City ☆☆☆☆☆

Courtesy Longmont Recreation Services

Hours:	9:00 AM - 11:00 AM, Friday, mid-August through mid-May
Admission:	Children: $2.00; Adults: Free MasterCard, Visa, checks, and cash accepted.
Parking:	Free parking lot and free street parking.
Food:	You may bring in your own food. Vending machines offer soda, water, chips, cookies, candy, and frozen treats.
Discounts:	Itty Bitty Punch Pass gives you 10 visits for $17.00.

700 Longs Peak Ave
Longmont, 80501
(303) 651-8405
www.ci.longmont.co.us/rec/childrens/
ittybitty.htm

What to expect. . .

Itty Bitty City is a drop-in playtime located in the gym of the St. Vrain Memorial Building. Created especially for preschool-aged children, you will find plenty of activities to entertain your child. Tricycles, scooters, and roller skates, a mini-trampoline, and more balls than you can count will keep him active. Giant building blocks and tables for coloring encourage creative play. A Baby Zone sits in the back of the gym on an extra thick mat, providing a safe place for very little ones to play.

Itty Bitty City Courtesy Longmont Recreation Services

Itty Bitty City is available nearly every Friday during the school year. Occasionally, it is cancelled due to a special event, so call or check the website before you go. The bathrooms are just outside the gym and the women's bathroom has a diaper-changing table. Parents can get a key from the front desk to the family bathroom, which also has a diaper-changing table. Eating is allowed provided you sit on the bleachers. You may also use the tables and chairs located near the entrance to the gym.

Other destinations within 5 miles . . .

Roosevelt Activity Pool (Site 88) - 3 blocks
Kanemoto Park and Pool (Site 86) - 1½ miles
Longmont Recreation Center Leisure Pool (Site 72) - 2 miles

B&C BounceTown (Site 42) - 3 miles
Sunflower Farm (Site 132) - 3½ miles
Rocky Mountain Pumpkin Ranch (Site 131) - 4½ miles

Jump Street ☆☆☆☆☆

Courtesy Jumpstreet

10081 West Bowles Avenue
Littleton, 80127
(303) 339-3030
www.gotjump.com

Hours:	1:00 AM - 9:00 PM, Sunday and Monday 10:00 AM - 10:00 PM, Tuesday - Thursday 10:00 AM - midnight, Friday and Saturday
Admission:	The pricing structure varies by age and day. To participate in the toddler area only, expect to pay $4 - $8 for weekday admission. American Express, Discover, MasterCard, Visa, and cash accepted.
Parking:	Free parking lot.
Food:	No outside food or drink are allowed, except baby food. Earthquake Coffee offers a variety of gourmet coffees and teas, pastries, muffins, as well as snack-bar type foods like burgers, hot dogs, and nachos.
Discounts:	Coupons can sometimes be found on ColoradoKids.com or DenverKids.com. However, you can not use your coupon in conjunction with any other offer, including specially-priced days or times.

Other Locations. . .

7969 E. Arapahoe Rd.
Greenwood Village, 80112
(303) 586-5530

What to expect. . .

With "streets" of trampolines, arcade games, a laser maze, a batting cage, a bubble ball field, and foosball, JumpStreet really caters to older children, but the Littleton and Greenwood Village locations are striving to offer something for everyone. The area for children 7 and under is called Earthquake and features its own miniature street of trampolines (level with the ground), inflatables, coin-operated rides (each ride is 50 cents), a play house, and a climbing area with Little Tykes equipment. At the Littleton location, Earthquake is connected to Earthquake Coffee, where you can relax with a cup of joe, take advantage of free wireless access, or tune in to one of the televisions mounted in the corners. Earthquake is not gated off from the rest of the 40,000 square foot facility so you still have to watch your child pretty closely (it's more fun to play anyway). Admission is for the whole day, but there is no re-entry.

Earthquake is deep-cleaned weekly and thoroughly wiped down daily. Shoes are not allowed on the trampoline and socks are optional. Adults can jump on the street in Earthquake without having to pay admission as long as they are jumping with their children. Bathrooms are in the back of the building and diaper-changing tables are available in both men's and women's.

Note: Jump Street also has a Thornton location, but it does not include an Earthquake area.

Other destinations within 5 miles . . .

Audience of One - Burgundy Theater (Site 23) - ½ mile
My Art Workshop (Site 54) - ½ mile
Fun City (Site 153) - 1½ miles
Robert F. Clement Park (Site 117) - 2 miles

Ridge Recreation Center Activity Pool (Site 75) - 2½ miles
Deer Creek Pool (Site 84) - 4 miles
Weaver Hollow Park and Pool (Site 92) - 4 miles
Skate City - Littleton (Site 175) - 4½ miles

Courtesy Jumpstreet

Jungle Quest ☆☆☆☆☆

Courtesy Jungle Quest

9499 Washington Street
Thornton, 80229
(303) 920-9404
www.junglequest.net

Hours:	10:00 AM - 6:00 PM daily Open till 8:00 PM on Friday.
Admission:	Full facility access: $15 for 1 ½ hours; Toddler area only: $5 for 1 ½ hours American Express, Discover, MasterCard, Visa, and cash accepted.
Parking:	Free parking lot.
Food:	Tables and chairs are available in the observation areas. Jungle Quest offers a few snacks and drinks.
Discounts:	Coupons can be found in the Chinook Book and on ColoradoKids.com. Get a Frequent Flyer Pass and your 11th visit is free. Adults play free on Friday from 4:00 - 8:00 PM when accompanied by a paying child. Join the VIP program by texting JUNGLE to 74700 to receive the most current offers.

What to expect. . .

More than any other indoor play area, Jungle Quest is the place my children kept begging to visit again. The 12,000 square foot "jungle" offers something unique to keep children active: the longest indoor zip line in the country, jungle swings, a rock wall, and a multi-level toddler area with rope bridges and tube slides. Anyone participating on the zip lines, jungle swings, and rock wall is fitted with a harness and watches a safety video. Friendly, helpful staff members are available at each launch platform to ensure that the participant is attached properly. The

Courtesy Jungle Quest

platforms are seven, nine, and eleven feet high, and each one has a safari swing and two zip-lines. Their safety record is excellent. For children who are not quite ready to fly on a zip line or jungle swing, the Mayan temple toddler area offers plenty of fun. Consider yourself warned: the curly blue slide from the top level in the toddler area is curlier than it looks — I had a difficult time sliding down.

If you aren't going to participate in the swinging (but seriously, it is so much fun), there are two observation areas with tables, chairs, free wireless access, and room to park a stroller. Diaper-changing tables are available in both the men's and women's bathrooms. I recommend a trip to the bathroom prior to putting on the harness. Bring drinks and snacks, as you and your child will both be hungry and thirsty after playing so hard. Also, closed-toe, rubber-soled shoes are required.

Note: Jungle Quest also has a Littleton (8000 S Lincoln St. #10, (303) 738-9844)) location, but it does not have a toddler area.

Other destinations within 5 miles . . .

Thornton City Pool (Site 91) - 1 mile
Scales 'n' Tails - Northglenn (Site 139) - 2½ miles
Boondocks Fun Center (Site 151) - 3 miles
Krispy Kreme (Site 172) - 3½ miles

D.L. Parsons Theatre (Site 29) - 4 miles
E.B. Rains Jr. Memorial Park (Site 104) - 4 miles
The Hop - Thornton (Site 46) - 4½ miles
Skate City - Westminster (Site 175) - 4½ miles

Kids Crossing Play Area ☆☆☆☆☆

Hours:	10:00 AM - 9:00 PM, Monday - Saturday 11:00 AM - 6:00 PM, Sunday Department stores, restaurants, theater, and holiday hours may vary.
Admission:	FREE!
Parking:	Free parking lot. For the easiest access, park near Old Navy and The Village or Crate and Barrel, or by Dick's Sporting Goods on the North side of the mall. Look for the New Parent and Family parking.
Food:	No food is allowed in the play area. The indoor playground is located in The Food Court. The Food Court and the patio area outside have plenty of tables, chairs, and benches.

Flatiron Crossing Mall
1 Flatiron Crossing Drive and Interlocken Blvd
Broomfield, 80021
(720) 887-7467
www.flatironcrossing.com

Baby It's Cold Outside

What to expect...

This indoor playground provides a variety of activities for your child. The triangular-shaped play area features soft foam-molded dinosaurs, dino eggs, a mammoth, flowers, ladybugs, and more. The floor is extra padded, and soft benches are installed around the perimeter. Interactive games, puzzles, and mirrors are mounted into the walls. Just outside the entrance to the play area are a couple of kid-sized picnic tables with chalkboard tops (you might want to bring your own chalk,

Photo by Brian De Herrera-Schnering of Pinto Pictures Courtesy Flatiron Crossing

as it isn't always well-stocked). If the weather is nice, step outside and enjoy the giant sandbox, filled with trucks, buckets, shovels, and other beach toys, or check out the small playground in The Village near Bloom.

The vaulted ceiling and windows give the play area a bright, open feel, especially in the daylight. The play area has only one way in and out, so it is easy to keep an eye on your child. Other details include cubbies for shoes, hooks for jackets, a hand sanitizer dispenser, and space for stroller parking. The nearest restrooms are behind the Dairy Queen. Diaper-changing tables are provided in both the men's and women's bathrooms, and a family restroom is available too.

Other destinations within 5 miles ...

Kids Kourt ☆☆☆☆☆

Courtesy CCSC /Photo by Steve Crecelius

Cherry Creek Mall Shopping Center
3000 East 1st Avenue
Denver, 80206
(303) 388-3900
www.shopcherrycreek.com

Hours:	10:00 AM - 9:00 PM, Monday - Saturday 11:00 AM - 6:00 PM, Sunday Kids Kourt is closed for cleaning 2:00 - 2:30 PM, and 6:00 - 6:30 PM daily.
Admission:	FREE!
Parking:	Free parking garage. Use the East entrance, by Macy's.
Food:	No food or drink are allowed in the play area. Plenty of restaurants are available in the mall, and you may bring in your own food to eat in one of the dining areas.

What to expect. . .

Kids Kourt at the Cherry Creek Mall Shopping Center has a brand new soft foam-molded indoor playground with a Looney Tunes theme. Believe me when I say that your child will get a kick out of climbing over, under, and around Bugs Bunny, Taz, Pepe, and other Looney Tunes favorites! Sponsored by Rocky Mountain Hospital for children, it's focused on active, healthy lifestyles. The play area is L-shaped, and if you sit on the

Kids Kourt photo by Steve Crecelius Courtesy Cherry Creek Shopping Center

bench in the corner, you can have a view of both sides. The floor is extra cushioned, and padded benches are installed around the edges. Stroller parking is available near the entrance to the play area, as are antibacterial wipes at "kid height." Because this mall is so popular, Kids Kourt can get crowded.

The bathrooms are located just a few stores down from the play area. Both the men's and women's have nice changing areas with sinks and changing pads. The women's bathroom also has a couple of comfortable chairs for breastfeeding. Next to the men's and women's bathrooms is what I consider to be the best family restroom in the city. The door is automatic and just needs to be nudged with an elbow or a stroller to open. Inside you'll find an adult-sized toilet and sink next to a child-sized toilet and sink, as well as a diaper dispenser, a changing pad, and antibacterial wipes.

Other destinations within 5 miles . . .

See Appendix I - Downtown Destinations
The Bookies (Site 60) - 2 miles

Four Mile Historic Park (Site 106) - 2 miles
Wings Over the Rockies Air and Space Museum (Site 163) - 4 miles

Kids Zone ☆☆☆☆☆

Courtesy of Paul Derda Recreation Center

Paul Derda Recreation Center
13201 Lowell Boulevard
Broomfield, 80020
(303) 460-6900
www.ci.broomfield.co.us/recreation

Hours:	5:00 AM - 10:00 PM, Monday - Thursday 5:00 AM - 6:30 PM, Friday 7:00 AM - 8:00 PM, Saturday 8:00 AM - 6:00 PM, Sunday The Rec Center closes for one week, usually in late August, for maintenance.
Admission:	Under 4: Free; Age 4-7: $4 American Express, MasterCard, Visa, checks, and cash accepted.
Parking:	Free parking lot.
Food:	Only water is allowed inside Kids Zone. You may bring in your own food and drink to consume in the Columbine Room. Vending machines are available throughout the facility.
Discounts:	Discounted pricing is available for residents of Broomfield.

What to expect...

One of the amenities you'll find inside the Paul Derda Recreation Center is a large indoor play area with a multi-level treehouse structure. Rope bridges, tunnels, obstacle courses, climbing structures, and some very odd stairs will keep your child moving up to the top of the treehouse. All routes ultimately lead to the slides. In front of the treehouse is a small area with soft foam-molded flower, rock, log, and animal structures.

Kids Zone is in its own room with only one door, so it would be hard for your little one to escape. The floor is soft and cushioned. Cubbies are provided for jackets and shoes. Stroller parking and bathrooms are just outside the play area; diaper-changing tables are available in both the men's and women's restrooms.

Other destinations within 5 miles . . .

Paul Derda Recreation Center Indoor Pool (Site 74) - same location
The Bay Aquatic Park (Site 79) - 2½ miles
Scales 'n' Tails - Northglenn (Site 139) - 2½ miles
Little Monkey Bizness - Westminster (Site 53) - 4 miles

Skate City - Westminster (Site 175) - 4 miles
Boondocks Fun Center (Site 151) - 4½ miles
The Butterfly Pavilion (Site 134) - 5 miles
Krispy Kreme (Site 172) - 5 miles

DID YOU KNOW? The percentage of overweight and obese children and teens has more than doubled over the past 30 years. Although many factors contribute to this epidemic, children are becoming more sedentary. The National Association for Sport and Physical Education (NASPE) offers expanded guidelines for daily activity for children:

- **Toddlers** - 30 minutes planned physical activity AND 60 minutes unstructured physical activity (free play)

- **Preschoolers** - 60 minutes planned physical activity AND 60 minutes unstructured physical activity (free play)

- **School-age children** - 60 minutes or more, broken up into bouts of 15 minutes or more

Baby It's Cold Outside

Little Monkey Bizness ☆☆☆☆☆

Baby It's Cold Outside

Hours:	Hours vary by location, but most generally open between 8:00 and 9:00 AM, and close between 5:00 and 6:00 PM. All locations offer a Family Night, when they are open till 8:00 PM.
Admission:	Infants and adults: Free; Crawlers under 1: $5; Children over 1: $7.50 Forms of payment accepted vary by location.
Parking:	All locations have free parking.
Food:	No outside food or drink allowed, other than baby food, sippy cups or bottles, or in the case of food allergies. The on-site café offers a variety of healthful options.
Discounts:	All locations have a Family Night with discounted admission. All locations have an electronic punchcard system. After your 8th visit, you receive a free open play. You will also receive occasional coupons via email when you are a part of the punchcard system.

730 Colorado Boulevard, 2nd Floor
Denver, 80206
(303) 623-2218
www.monkeybizness.com

Multiple Locations. . .

7600 East Park Meadows Drive Lone Tree, 80124 (720) 880-5800	14693 Orchard Parkway Westminster, 80023 (303) 252-9999	10430 South Progress Way, Ste 101 Parker, 80134 (303) 841-5888

What to expect. . .

The whole concept of Little Monkey Bizness is that it is a place for parents and a place for children under 6. The play area is about 3,000 square feet and is filled with a variety of activities designed to keep your child active and engaged. A crawl area for children under 2 is separate from the rest of the play area. The floor is extra padded in this area, and babies and toddlers can play with age-appropriate toys, soft climbing structures, and activity centers. The rest of the play area has a multi-level playground, clubhouses, a bounce house, plastic slides of varying size, and more. Surrounded by a low wall with a locking gate, a person must be tall enough to reach over to the other side to open the gate and leave the play area. This allows parents the choice of playing with their children or relaxing in the lounge without having to worry about their little ones escaping. You can see the entire play area from virtually any seat in the lounge. The coffee shop area has plenty of room to sit, including a few comfy armchairs, free wireless access, and features Seattle's Best Coffee. During open play hours, the Party Room doubles as an arts and crafts room.

Employees clean throughout the day and the entire play area is sanitized every night. The staff is enthusiastic and helpful. At least one member of the staff can be found in the play area to help keep watch on the children (but keep in mind that this is a parent-supervised facility), while others can be found in the arts and crafts room, or making coffee. Both the men's and women's bathrooms have diaper-changing tables and step stools under the sink. The women's bathroom also has a chair for breastfeeding. Your admission does not have a time limit; you may stay as long as you like and can re-enter throughout the day as long as you have your receipt.

Note: On the website click on Little Monkey Bizness, *then click on* Find A Location

Other destinations within 5 miles . . .

See Appendix I - Downtown Destinations for destinations near the Denver location.
See Cook Creek Pool (Site 83) for destinations near Lone Tree location.
See Party On (Site 55) for destinations near the Parker location.
See Paul Derda Recreation Center (Site 74) for destinations near Westminster location.

My Art Workshop ☆☆☆☆☆

Courtesy My Art Workshop

The Shoppes at Columbine Valley
5950 S. Platte Canyon
Littleton, CO 80123
(303) 948-3598
www.myartworkshop.com

Hours:	10:00 AM - 6:00 PM, Monday - Friday 10:00 AM - 4:00 PM, Saturday Closed Memorial Day, Independence Day, Labor Day, Thanksgiving, and Christmas through December 28.
Admission:	Cost is based on the craft you choose. American Express, Discover, MasterCard, Visa, checks, and cash accepted.
Parking:	Free parking lot.
Food:	You are welcome to bring in your own food.
Discounts:	Coupons can be found on their website, and occasionally on GoCityKids.com, ColoradoKids.com, or ColoradoParent.com.

What to expect. . .

My Art Workshop is a drop-in arts and crafts center for children that provides set up, clean up, materials, and instruction. Activities include tie dye,
wood projects, pottery painting, clay sculpting, mosaics, fashion design,
sand art, and more. You pay for the type of craft you choose, not for the
amount of time you are there, so your child will never feel rushed. My boys
had a blast decorating wooden swords with paint, plastic gemstones, fuzzy
balls, and googly eyes. They are one-of-a-kind masterpieces that cost us
about $12 each, about the same as a plastic sword would have been at a

Courtesy My Art Workshop

toy store. The staff was very helpful and worked with my kids at their individual levels. My Art Workshop has
won multiple awards, including *Kids' Pages Magazine* Best Places for Families 2007 and 2008, Comcast on
Demand Best of the City 2008, and *Colorado Parent Magazine* Family Favorite 2009.

The women's restroom has a diaper-changing table, and men can have a staff member let them into the wom-
en's bathroom if the need arises. Both bathrooms have step stools for the sink. A lounge chair sits near the
bathrooms, for breastfeeding or simply relaxing. In addition to their annual events, My Art Workshop offers
special events throughout the year, particularly around holidays and during Jefferson County school breaks.

Annual Events . . .

Mother's Day Crafting Night and Pizza Party generally takes place in the week before Mother's
Day. Dads and kids can come in and create a present for mom.

Father's Day Crafting Night and Pizza Party takes place right before Father's Day.

Halloween Fun and Pizza Party occurs shortly before Halloween.

*Note: My Art Workshop was in the process of moving 3 miles east of their original location as this
book was going to press. The above address is their new location. However, not all of the nearby
destinations will still be within a 5-mile radius of the new location.*

Other destinations within 5 miles . . .

Audience of One - Burgundy Theater (Site 23) - same location
Jump Street (Site 48) - ½ mile
Robert F. Clement Park (Site 117) - 1½ miles
Fun City (Site 153) - 2½ miles
Ridge Recreation Center Activity Pool (Site 75) - 3 miles
Deer Creek Pool (Site 84) - 4 miles

Skate City - Littleton (Site 175) - 4 miles
Weaver Hollow Park and Pool (Site 92) - 4½ miles
Denver Botanic Gardens at Chatfield (Site 102) - 5 miles
Hudson Gardens (Site 108) - 5 miles
The Town Hall Arts Center (Site 38) - 5 miles

Baby It's Cold Outside

Party On ☆☆☆☆☆

Courtesy Party On

10505 South Progress Way
Parker, 80134
(303) 840-4849
www.partyonparker.com

Hours:	10:00 AM - 3:00 PM, Monday and Tuesday 10:00 AM - 8:00 PM, Wednesday Closed Thursday and Friday. Weekends and weekday evenings, other than Wednesdays, are reserved for private parties.
Admission:	Under 2: Free with a paying child; Children 2 and up: $7.50 Discover, MasterCard, Visa, checks, and cash accepted.
Parking:	Free parking lot.
Food:	You may bring in your own snacks and drinks to consume in the lobby.
Discounts:	Coupons can be found on their website and sometimes in *Search Parker* magazine. Purchase a 10-visit punchcard for $55. Discounted admission on Wednesday from 3:00 - 8:00 PM.

What to expect. . .

Party On is a bright, colorful, and spacious bounce house that is locally owned and operated. Like most bounce houses, it is designed for children up to age 10, but Party On offers a few extras that are ideal for the younger set. Inflatables include side-by-side slides, a pirate ship, a fire truck, and a maze, as well as a large, circus-themed bouncer reserved for children two and under. In front of the "Toddler Big-Top" is a small learning center with cardboard blocks, wooden puzzles, and books. A coin-operated carousel sits off to the side. More than a dozen chairs provide seating for parents, and magazines are provided for parents' reading pleasure. The admission gives you an hour and a half of bouncy fun.

Bounce sessions are parent-supervised. A gym mat is at the entrance of each bouncer so children will always have a soft landing. The inflatables are disinfected daily. Diaper-changing tables are available in both the men's and women's bathrooms. Shoes are not allowed and socks are required (they sell socks if you forget yours). Cubbies and hooks provided for shoes and jackets are located in the lobby.

Other destinations within 5 miles . . .

Little Monkey Bizness - Parker (Site 53) - 1 block
Pump It Up - Parker (Site 56) - ½ mile
Audience of One - Parker (Site 23) - 1 mile

CYT Denver - Parker (Site 27) - 1 mile
H2O'Brien Pool (Site 85) - 1 mile
The Wildlife Experience (Site 19) - 5 miles

Courtesy Party On

Pump It Up ☆☆☆☆☆

Hours:	Pop-In Playtimes vary by location. Weekends are usually reserved for parties.
Admission:	Prices and forms of payment accepted vary by location.
Parking:	Free parking at all locations.
Food:	No food or drink are allowed inside the bouncing arena.
Discounts:	Coupons can be found in the Entertainment Book. Punch card programs are available at each location; terms and prices may vary.

Pump It Up Photo by Susan Clark

www.pumpitupparty.com

Baby It's Cold Outside

Multiple Locations. . .

8150 South University Boulevard, Ste 100 Littleton 80122 (303) 770-7867	18850 Clarke Road Parker, 80134 (720) 842-0200

What to expect. . .

Although each Pump It Up facility is independently owned and operated, you can expect certain things from every location. The bouncing arenas are spacious, clean, and brightly colored. Generally about 5,000 square feet, each arena has a variety of bouncers: inflatable slides, obstacle courses, boxing arenas, and/or standard bounce houses. Each inflatable is designed and installed with safety in mind. Some facilities may have quarter-operated games like basketball or air hockey. Some may have Cozy Coupes and plastic slides available as well.

Pop-In Playtime is a parent-supervised activity, and parents are encouraged to join in the jumping, bouncing, and sliding. A few benches are provided for when you get tired — and believe me, you will get tired! Each session has a time limit, usually about an hour and a half, but that's all my children can handle. Shoes are not allowed in the inflatables but socks are required (they sell them if you forget yours). Cubbies and hooks are available for shoes and jackets. Both men's and women's bathrooms provide diaper-changing tables. Pump It Up prides itself in great customer service, a strong safety record, and extreme cleanliness. The inflatables are cleaned and disinfected daily.

Note: After you select your location, Pop-In Playtime is listed under Party Packages.

Other destinations within 5 miles . . .

See Civic Green Park (Site 97) for destinations near the Littleton location.
See Party On (Site 55) for destinations near the Parker location.

Baby It's Cold Outside

REI ☆☆☆☆☆

Hours:	10:00 AM - 9:00 PM, Monday - Friday 10:00 AM - 7:00 PM, Saturday 10:00 AM - 6:00 PM, Sunday
Admission:	FREE!
Parking:	Free underground parking.
Food:	Eating is discouraged in the play area. A few tables and chairs are available outside for picnicking. A Starbucks with inside seating and an outside patio is located on the first floor.

1416 Platte Street
Denver, 80202
(303) 756-3100
www.rei.com/stores/18

What to expect...

If you happen to be downtown or need to shop for outdoor gear or apparel, the Denver Flagship REI store has an indoor playground on the third floor that is open to the public during store hours. Naturally, it has an outdoor theme. There are two small slides, one shaped like a canoe and one built into a smiling tree, as well as a dark tunnel with a plastic bear hibernating inside. A fake water feature completes the look. The water feature is made of clear plastic and your child will enjoy looking at the crawdad, turtle, frog, and other water creatures "under" the water. The play area is quite small, well suited for babies and toddlers.

This store is also home to the Pinnacle, one of the tallest, freestanding indoor climbing walls in the Denver area. For $10, children four feet and taller can attempt to climb the 47-foot rock on weekends from 10:00 AM - 4:00 PM. Chalk, bags, shoes, and harnesses are provided by REI. The Pinnacle is closed during sales and certain special events. Contact the store in advance if you intend to climb.

Bathrooms are located on the Mezzanine level (second floor) and are clean and spacious. Diaper decks are in both the men's and women's, and there is also a hand sanitizer dispenser mounted on the wall.

Other destinations within 5 miles . . .
See Appendix I - Downtown Destinations
The Bookery Nook (Site 59) - 3 miles
Sloan's Lake Park (Site 122) - 3½ miles

Fish Den (Site 138) - 4 miles
Kids Kourt (Site 51) - 5 miles

See Also

Boondocks Fun Center (Site 151)

The Butterfly Pavilion (Site 134)

The Children's Museum of Denver (Site 6)

Denver Art Museum (Site 8)

Denver Museum of Nature and Science (Site 11)

Downtown Aquarium (Site 137)

Fun City (Site 153)

The Wildlife Experience (Site 19)

World of Wonder Children's Museum (Site 20)

Reading is FUNdamental

Reading aloud to your child daily is one of the best things you can do to help ensure later academic success. According to Jim Trelease's **The Read Aloud Handbook**, this single activity can increase a child's vocabulary, improve grammar and writing skills, improve problem-solving and critical-thinking skills, and improve attention span. In addition to all its academic benefits, reading aloud nurtures emotional development, offers entertainment, and stimulates the imagination. Few things offer a better bonding activity than snuggling with your child and sharing a story. Continue your read-aloud adventures (and enjoy their benefits) at one of the Denver area's many libraries or bookstores.

Boulder Public Library Photo by Sonia Knapp

Site **58**
Various

Barnes and Noble
☆☆☆☆☆
www.bn.com
(Click on **Stores and Events**)

Many locations in the Denver metro area.

Virtually every store offers a regular story time, but days and times vary. Check the website.

Site **59**
Denver

The Bookery Nook
☆☆☆☆☆
4280 Tennyson Street
Denver, 80212
(303) 433-3439
www.thebookerynook.com

Story time at 10:00 AM on Tuesday.

Other destinations within 5 miles . . .
See Appendix I - Downtown Destinations
Fish Den (Site 138) - ½ mile
Denver Puppet Theater (Site 28) - 1 mile
Lakeside Amusement Park (Site 155) - 1 mile
Rising Curtain Theatre Academy (Site 33) - 2 miles
Sloan's Lake Park (Site 122) - 2½ miles
Casa Bonita (Site 165) - 4 miles
Pump It Up - Wheat Ridge (Site 56) - 4½ miles
Secrest Pool (Site 89) - 4½ miles
Scales 'n' Tails (Northglenn) Site 139 - 4½ miles
The Arvada Center (Site 22) - 5 miles
Squiggles Playground (Site 123) - 5 miles
Wheat Ridge Recreation Center Pool (Site 77) - 5 miles

Site **60**
Denver

The Bookies
☆☆☆☆☆
4315 East Mississippi Avenue
Denver, 80246
(303) 759-1117
www.thebookies.com

Story time at 10:30 AM on Tuesday.

Other destinations within 5 miles . . .
See Appendix I - Downtown Destinations
Four Mile Historic Park (Site 106) - 1 mile
Kids Kourt (Site 51) - 2 miles
Wings Over the Rockies Air and Space Museum (Site 163) - 4½ miles

Site **61**
Various

Borders
☆☆☆☆☆
www.borders.com
(Click on **Store Locator**.)

Several locations in the Denver metro area.
Virtually every store offers a regular story time, but days and times vary. Check the website.

GO ONE STEP FURTHER - Gather new or gently used books with your child to donate to Basic Reads (**www.basicreads.org**), a local non-profit organization whose purpose is to get books into the hands of low-income children in the Denver area.

Clear Creek Books

Site 62
Golden

☆☆☆☆☆
1200 Washington Avenue
Golden, 80401
(303) 278-4593
www.clearcreekbooks.com

Story time at 10:30 AM on Friday.

Other destinations within 5 miles . . .
Foothills Art Center (Site 12) - 3 blocks
Clear Creek History Park (Site 98) - 4 blocks
Lions Park (Site 109) - ½ mile
Colorado Railroad Museum (Site 156) - 2 miles
Splash at Fossil Trace (Site 90) - 2½ miles
Heritage Square Amusement Park (Site 154) - 3½ miles
Heritage Square Music Hall (Site 30) - 3½ miles

Tattered Cover Bookstore

Site 63
Various

☆☆☆☆☆
2526 East Colfax Avenue
Denver, 80206
(303) 322-7727

9315 Dorchester Street
Highlands Ranch, 80129
(303) 470-7050
www.tatteredcover.com

Story time at 10:30 on Tuesday at the Colfax location.
Story time at 10:30 on Tuesday and Saturday at the Highlands Ranch location.

Note: Tattered Cover also has a LoDo location but it does not have a story time.

Other destinations within 5 miles . . .
See Appendix I - Downtown Destinations for destinations near the Denver location.
See Civic Green Park (Site 97) for destinations near the Highlands Ranch location.

HELPFUL TIP - Talk to the librarian in the children's section for book recommendations for your child. Most bookstores also keep lists of suggested books, divided by age. The following internet resources offer lists of great children's books as well:

Carnegie Library of Pittsburgh - www.carnegielibrary.org/kids/books/

Reading is Fundamental, Inc. -www.rif.org/us/about-rif.htm

Caldecott Medal Winners and Honor Books - www.ala.org/alsc/caldecott.cfm

Newbery Medal Books - www.ala.org/alsc/newbery.cfm

Denver Public Library - www.kids.denverlibrary.org

Boulder Public Library Photo by Sonia Knapp

Site 64 Public Libraries

☆☆☆☆☆

We are fortunate to have so many public libraries in our area — too many to list them all! Libraries generally offer story time from several times a week to several times a day, depending on the location. Many have an evening or a Saturday story time, so parents who work outside the home can still share this special time with their children. Additionally, the children's section of the library, like the children's section of most bookstores, is designed just for them. Bright colors, comfortable chairs, puzzles, puppet shows and games are just some of the activities your child might discover, making a trip to the library even more fun and exciting.

Arapahoe County Libraries: **www.arapahoelibraries.org**

Aurora Libraries: **www.auroralibrary.org**

Boulder Libraries: **www.boulderlibrary.org**

Broomfield Library: **www.ci.broomfield.co.us/library/**

Denver Libraries: **www.denverlibrary.org**

Douglas County Libraries: **www.douglascountylibraries.org**

Elbert County Library: **www.elbertcountylibrary.org**

Englewood Library: **www.englewoodgov.org**

Erie Library: **www.mylibrary.us**

Jefferson County Libraries: **www.jefferson.lib.co.us**

Lafayette Library: **www.cityoflafayette.com/library/**

Littleton Library:
www.littletonlibrary.org or **www.littletongov.org/bemis/**

Longmont Library: **www.ci.longmont.co.us/library/**

Louisville Library: **http://www.louisville-library.org/**

Westminster Library: **www.westminsterlibrary.org**

See Also

Children's Museum of Denver (Site 6)

Denver Art Museum (Site 8)

Denver Botanic Gardens (Site 101)

Denver Firefighters Museum (Site 9)

Family Arts at DAVA (Site 44)

Four Mile Historic Park (Site 106)

Rocky Mountain Dinosaur Resource Center (Site 191)

The Wildlife Experience (Site 19)

A Little Song and Dance Chapter. Children's theater is often based on children's literature.

Getting Wet and Staying Warm

If your baby likes baths, an indoor activity or leisure pool is a great next step. Many of the pools are designed to entertain children as soon as they are able to sit up on their own. We love visiting indoor pools in the middle of winter for a change of pace, but they are great to visit in the summertime too, especially if your child has fair skin and burns easily. They are usually less crowded in the summer as well. All of the facilities in this chapter permit you to bring in your own food and drink, but glass and alcohol are prohibited at all locations.

A special note: the term "safety breaks" is used throughout this chapter. It refers to a time when everyone must get out of the pool for a specific period of time (adults are sometimes permitted to continue swimming). Plan your visit carefully, as it is no fun to start playing in the water, only to be told a few minutes later to exit the pool!

Courtesy Wheat Ridge Parks & Recreation

Apex Center Indoor Pool ☆☆☆☆☆

Courtesy Apex Center

Hours:	Hours for the pool vary daily and change seasonally. Visit the website.
Admission:	Under 4: Free; Age 4-5: $4; Age 6-18: $5.75, Age 19-61: $6.75; 62+: $5.75Admission includes full access to the recreation center, except for ice skating. American Express, Discover, MasterCard, Visa, checks, and cash accepted.
Parking:	Free parking lot.
Food:	You may bring your own food and drink into the pool area (no glass or alcohol), or use the eating area overlooking the pool. Blue View Café sells hot dogs, burgers, burritos, and sandwiches. Vending machines on the lower level sell snacks and drinks.
Discounts:	Residents of the Apex Parks and Rec District receive discounted pricing. Discounted 20 punch passes are available. Join the e-mail list to receive coupons and discount offers. Special rates are offered on select holidays.

13150 West 72nd Avenue,
Arvada, 80005
(303) 424-2739
www.apexprd.org/facilities/apex-center

What to expect...

The Apex Center is an enormous recreational complex. The pool area alone is 23,000 square feet and is the largest indoor aquatic facility in the Denver metro area. In addition to an indoor pool, the Apex Center has a climbing wall, a wellness studio that offers Pilates and massage, indoor cycling, a group fitness room, an indoor running track, two NHL-size ice skating rinks, and the Apex Center Clubhouse Adventure Playground (Site 41). This indoor playground is completely free; you don't even have to pay the daily admission. Daily admission to the Apex Center does not include ice skating. The Apex Center was selected "Best Place to Get Wet and Wild Indoors" by *Westword Magazine*.

All the pools are maintained between 85 and 88 degrees. The lap pool has a wheelchair ramp into the water. Next to the lap pool is the toddler play area, which is completely separate from the other pools. It has zero-depth entry and is only 18 inches at its deepest point. The play structure is huge, with two slides, a tunnel, fountains, water curtains, and more. Past the toddler zone is a pool with plastic floating log sections on which you can try to balance to cross, a small current pool, a swimming area, and a splashdown area for two 150-foot water slides. This pool ranges from three to four feet deep. Children must be 6 or older to ride the water slides alone, but lap riding is permitted. The Apex Center also has two spas in here, a family spa kept at 94 degrees and an adult-only spa kept at 104 degrees.

Safety breaks are only held when the pool is very busy and last a maximum of 15 minutes. The pool is on the lower level of the Apex Center and is stroller- and wheelchair-accessible. Diaper-changing tables are provided in both the men's and women's locker rooms. In addition, the family locker room has five private cabanas, each with a toilet, sink, shower, dressing area, and diaper-changing table. Lockers in the locker rooms are available at no charge but you must bring your own lock, or you can use the lockers by the admission desk, which are a quarter each time you open them.

Annual Events...

Fourth of July Ice Cream Social has a bounce house, ice cream, and a special admission rate.

Halloween Carnival, usually the Friday before Halloween, is especially for children age 4 to 7.

Other destinations within 5 miles...

Clubhouse Adventure Playground (Site 41) - same location
Majestic View Nature Center (Site 112) - 3½ miles
The Arvada Center (Site 22) - 4 miles

Squiggles Playground (Site 123) - 4 miles
Secrest Pool (Site 89) - 4½ miles

Bob L. Burger Recreation Center Indoor Pool ☆☆☆☆☆

Courtesy of City of Lafayette Recreation Department

111 West Baseline Road
Lafayette, 80026
(303) 665-0469
www.cityoflafayette.com/recreation

Hours:	The pool is open when the recreation center is, but hours vary by season. Check the website.
Admission:	Under 2: Free; Age 2-5: $2.50; Age 6-17: $3; Age 18-54: $4.50; Age 55+: $2.75. Admission includes full access to the recreation center. American Express, Discover, MasterCard, Visa, checks, and cash accepted.
Parking:	Free parking lot.
Food:	Food and drink, other than water, are not allowed in the pool area. You may bring in food to eat in the lobby area of the recreation center and on the outdoor patios. Tables and chairs are provided. Vending machines offer candy, drinks, and ice cream.
Discounts:	20-visit punch cards may be purchased; prices vary depending on age. The Family "Bail-Out" is admission for two adults and two children for $10. A group discount is available to groups of 20 or more. Parents and grandparents get in free on Mother's Day and Father's Day with a paid child admission.

What to expect. . .

The Bob L. Burger Recreation Center offers an indoor walking track, a basketball court, a lap pool, a fitness area, a preschool, and scores of classes to enjoy, including swimming classes for children as young as six months old. A playground and an inline skating rink are located outside. The Rec Center is the starting point for a two-mile stroller-friendly walking path.

The indoor pool has some great features for families with young children. The Toddler Play Pool is maintained at a very warm 88 degrees. It has zero-depth (beach) entry on one side and gets as deep as 3.5 feet. One side has a large rock wall with a waterfall. Children can stand inside the cave area and watch as the water comes down. Other features include a small waterslide, a vortex, and mushroom raindrops spraying water. The Lazy River is separate from the Play Pool and has inner tubes for floating. The water temperature is kept around 86 degrees, slightly cooler than the Play Pool but still quite comfortable. The island in the center of the Lazy River is the splashdown area for the 150-foot Water Slide. The slide does not have any height restrictions. Riders must be able to swim, and lap riding is permitted for parents with very young children. Strong swimmers and older children will have fun in the large Activity Pool with basketball nets, diving boards, and a rope swing.

Three to six lifeguards are on duty, depending on the season and the time of day. There are no mandatory safety breaks. Children under 6 must be within arm's reach of an adult. The men's and women's locker rooms have diaper-changing tables, showers, dressing areas, and a special machine that will wring out your suit before you pack it up. The family locker room has two private cabanas, each with a toilet, sink, shower, and diaper-changing table. Children 4 and older must use the gender-appropriate locker room or the family locker room. Complimentary locks for the lockers and water toys are available for you to check out from the front desk with ID.

Annual Events . . .

TV Turn Off Week is every April. Turn off the TV and youth receive a free week's pass to the recreation center.

Other destinations within 5 miles . . .

World of Wonder Children's Museum (Site 20) - 3 blocks
Peanut Butter Players (Site 32) - 1 mile

Waneka Lake Park (Site 124) - 2 miles
Erie Community Center Leisure Pool (Site 69) - 4½ miles

Getting Wet and Staying Warm

Site 66 Lafayette

Buchanan Park Recreation Center Indoor Pool ☆☆☆☆☆

Getting Wet and Staying Warm

Courtesy Evergreen Park and Recreation District

32003 Ellingwood Trail
Evergreen, 80439
(720) 880-1100
www.evergreenrecreation.com

Hours:	6:00 AM - 8:00 PM, Monday - Friday, 11:00 AM - 6:00 PM, Saturday, 9:00 AM - 6:00 PM, Sunday Water features (e.g., water slide) are turned on at approximately 11:00 AM.
Admission:	Under 4: Free; Age 4-18: $6; Age 19-59: $7.75; Age 60+: $5.75. Admission includes full access to the recreation center. American Express, Discover, MasterCard, Visa, checks, and cash accepted.
Parking:	Free parking lot.
Food:	Only water is allowed in the pool area. You may bring in your own food and drink and eat in the lounge area that looks into the pool, or on the patio overlooking Buchanan Pond. Vending machines.
Discounts:	Residents receive discounted pricing. Punch cards for 5, 15, or 20 visits are available at a discounted rate. Family of Four pass is $18.75 ($13.75 for residents). $3 admission from 3:00-6:00 PM on Wednesday, Friday, and Saturday.

What to expect. . .

Located on the lower level of the Buchanan Park Recreation Center, the indoor pool has a very small vortex, a water slide, a toddler area with a play structure, and two lap lanes separated from the toddler area by a dividing wall. The water temperature is maintained at 86 degrees. Generally, two lifeguards are on duty during the week and three are on duty on the weekends. In addition to the pool, the Recreation Center has a fitness area, a preschool, and plenty of classes to try, including swimming lessons for children as young as eight months old. There is a climbing wall downstairs; children must be at least four years old and 35 pounds. When the weather is nice, take a walk on the paved path around Buchanan Pond or burn off some energy at the playground.

The vortex is very small and usually has people walking against the current. The water slide does not have height restrictions but the rider must know how to swim. Lap riding is permitted. The splashdown area for the slide is 3.5 feet deep. The toddler area has zero-depth (beach) entry with a few geysers and is only two feet at its deepest point. The play structure has a curly slide and some water spraying down, but it is easy to avoid for children who don't like to be sprayed. A hot tub is located in one corner of the room. The water is maintained at 102 degrees, and children are allowed in it when accompanied by an adult.

Mandatory safety breaks occur at the top of the hour for five minutes if there are more than 25 people in the pool. Men's and women's locker rooms have showers, dressing areas, and lockers (bring your own lock) but do not have diaper-changing tables. The Recreation Center has a family locker room with six private cabanas with showers and dressing areas. Diaper-changing tables are only in a few of the cabanas. Children 5 and older must use same-gender locker rooms or the family locker room. The door to the family locker room is blue and has a sign on it, but it is before the "Locker Rooms" sign so it is easy to miss. This indoor pool is smaller than most in the Denver area but provides a fun place to play and swim for young children if you live in or are visiting Evergreen.

Note: On the website click on Facilities, then choose Buchanan Park Recreation Center.

Other destinations within 5 miles . . .

Evergreen Towne Trolley (Site 157) - 4½ miles

Castle Rock Recreation Center Leisure Pool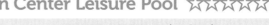

Getting Wet and Staying Warm

Courtesy of Castle Rock Recreation Center

2301 North Woodlands Boulevard
Castle Rock, 80104
(303) 660-1036
www.crgov.com

Hours:	10:00 AM - 7:00 PM, Monday - Saturday 10:00 AM - 5:00 PM, Sunday Visit the website for holiday closures.
Admission:	Under 3: Free; Age 3-17: $5.25; Age 18-61: $6.50, Age 62+: $5.75 Admission includes full access to the recreation center. MasterCard, Visa, checks, and cash accepted.
Parking:	Free parking lot.
Food:	Vending machines offer soda, water, candy, and chips. You are welcome to bring your own food to eat in the pool area; you can even have pizza delivered. Several tables with chairs are around the perimeter of the pool.
Discounts:	Discounted pricing is available for individuals with a Castle Rock Recreation ID. Sunday is Family Day, when you can purchase a full-day pass to the Recreation Center for a family of four for $17 ($14 for residents).

What to expect. . .

Located on the lower floor of the Castle Rock Recreation Center, the leisure pool is wheelchair and stroller accessible. The water temperature is maintained at a comfortable 87 degrees. At least two lifeguards are on duty at all times, and there can be as many as five when the pool gets crowded. In addition to the leisure pool, the Recreation Center has a basketball court, a lap pool, a fitness area, a preschool, and scores of classes to enjoy, including swimming classes for children as young as six months old. There's a decent-sized playground outside and a stroller-friendly walking path.

The leisure pool is divided into four main sections. The Interactive Play Structure has a zero-depth (beach) entry and is only three feet at its deepest point. Water geysers at the beach entry and stream geysers on the side provide unlimited fascination for babies. The structure has a small slide, wheels that control the flow of water when turned, dumping buckets, and various spouts and shower sprays. The Lazy River has a water curtain, for those who love the feel of water pouring down on them (it can easily be avoided for those who don't). Two water slides are fully enclosed. You must be at least 48 inches tall to ride the slides. The slides are mounted on the outside of the building. Since they are somewhat "in-visible" from the pool area, you don't have to try to explain to your toddler why she can not go on the slides yet. A rectangular pool gets as deep as five feet. Swim lessons for babies take place in this area. Older children play water basketball or swim in this area.

Mandatory 15-minute safety breaks where everyone is required to get out of the pool take place every two hours, with the first one at 11:45 AM. In addition to men's and women's locker rooms, the Recreation Center has a family locker room. Children under 18 must be accompanied by an adult inside the locker room. In the family locker room, there are two private changing areas, and three private shower areas with toilets and changing tables inside. Lockers are provided in the family locker room at no charge, but you must provide your own lock. This pool is smaller than most indoor pools in the Denver area, but is a great choice if you live in Castle Rock or Parker.

Note: When visiting the website click on Recreation.

DID YOU KNOW? Swimming is a low-impact, full-body activity that builds cardio-respiratory fitness and promotes endurance, coordination, and flexibility. Swimming and other water activities are something the entire family can enjoy together. What other physical activity do you know that can give you face-to-face and skin-to-skin contact with your child? And because there's almost no impact with swimming, it's a form of exercise that can be continued for a lifetime.

Erie Community Center Leisure Pool ☆☆☆☆☆

Courtesy Erie Parks

450 Powers Street
Erie, 80516
(303) 926-2550
www.eriecommunitycenter.com

Hours:	Hours for the Leisure Pool vary daily and change seasonally. Visit the website.
Admission:	Under 4: Free; Age 4-17: $2.75; Age 18-59: $5.50; Age 60+: $3.40, Admission includes full access to the recreation center. American Express, MasterCard, Visa, checks, and cash accepted.
Parking:	Free parking lot.
Food:	Only water is allowed in the pool area. Vending machines in the lobby sell snacks and drinks. You may bring your own food and drink. Tables and chairs are available in the lobby.
Discounts:	Discounted pricing is available for Erie residents. Daily admission for a family of two adults and two children (age 4-17) is $12.50 ($10 for residents). Punchcards for 10 or 20 visits are available at a discounted rate.

What to expect. . .

The Erie Community Center is only a few years old, so everything is bright and new. The water temperature of the leisure pool is maintained at about 84 degrees. They keep a ratio of one lifeguard for every 10 children. In addition to the leisure pool, the Recreation Center has two climbing walls, a lap pool, a fitness area, racquetball courts, a kids' game room, and plenty of classes to enjoy, including swimming classes for children as young as six months. Before or after your swim, take time to play a game on the NEOS, an interactive game for the whole family (think "Dance Dance Revolution" meets "Simon"). Small playgrounds are available both inside and outside the Recreation Center. The Erie Community Library and Erie Community Park are also located on this property.

The leisure pool has zero-depth (beach) entry with a large play structure. The play structure has two long slides, pipes with water flowing out, and wheels controlling the flow of water. This area of the pool has geysers in the beach section, and only gets as deep as one foot. A swimming area on the other side gets as deep as 3.5 feet. The current river has a small vortex in it and is also 3.5 feet deep. The 144-foot water slide lands in 3.5 feet of water. You must be 46 inches tall to ride the slide, or you can pass a swim test. Lap riding is not allowed. Strong swimmers can swing on a rope and drop into 10 feet of water in the lap pool.

The Erie Community Center does not do mandatory safety breaks. In addition to men's and women's locker rooms, the Recreation Center has a family locker room with four private cabanas. Each cabana has a toilet, sink, shower, bench, and a diaper-changing table. Lockers are provided at no charge, but you must provide your own lock. In addition to swim diapers, children who are not potty-trained are required to wear plastic pants over the diaper (available for purchase at Guest Service).

Other destinations within 5 miles . . .
Bob L. Burger Recreation Center Indoor Pool (Site 66) - 4½ miles
World of Wonder Children's Museum (Site 20) - 4½ miles

Golden Community Center Leisure Pool ☆☆☆☆☆

Courtesy City of Golden

1470 10th Street
Golden, 80401
(303) 384-8100
www.cityofgolden.net

Hours:	Hours vary daily and change seasonally. A current schedule is available at the front desk.
Admission:	Under 5: $2; Age 6-18: $3.75; Age 19-59: $5.50; Age 60+: $4 Admission includes full access to the recreation center. American Express, Discover, MasterCard, Visa, checks, and cash accepted.
Parking:	Free parking lot.
Food:	Food and drink other than water are not permitted in the pool area. Eating is permitted in the lobby. One vending machine sells snack items and another sells lunch items like frozen burritos. A microwave is provided. You may also bring in your own food.
Discounts:	A 20-visit punchcard can be purchased at a discount.

What to expect. . .

The Golden Community Center is a very large recreational facility adjacent to Lions Park (Site 109). The water temperature of the leisure pool is maintained at about 90 degrees. Two or more lifeguards are on duty. In addition to the leisure pool, the Recreation Center has a climbing wall, a lap pool, a fitness area, an indoor jogging track, and more than 100 classes to enjoy, including swimming classes for children as young as six months old. A very small indoor playground with a miniature climbing wall are located in the lobby. Lions Park has a large outdoor playground.

The leisure pool has zero-depth (beach) entry and gets as deep as three feet. The play area includes a small slide that lands in one foot of water, pipes that spray down, and a water curtain. Next to the toddler zone are plastic floating log sections on which you can try to balance to cross. A 150-foot water slide has a splashdown area next to the logs. The water for the logs and water slide is 3.5 feet deep. Children must be able to swim to participate alone on either, although lap riding is permitted on the slide.

Safety breaks are the last 10 minutes of every hour; adults may continue to swim during this time. The men's and women's locker rooms both have diaper-changing tables. Additionally, a family locker room has three private dressing areas and a separate bathroom with a diaper-changing table. Lockers are provided at no charge, but you must provide your own lock.

*Note: **Click on** Golden Community Center **under the** Residents & Visitors **tab***

Other destinations within 5 miles . . .

Lions Park (Site 109) - next door
Clear Creek Books (Site 62) - ½ mile
Clear Creek History Park (Site 98) - ½ mile
Foothills Art Center (Site 12) - ½ mile

Colorado Railroad Museum (Site 156) - 2½ miles
Splash at Fossil Trace (Site 90) - 4 miles
Heritage Square Amusement Park (Site 154) - 4½ miles
Heritage Square Music Hall (Site 30) - 4½ miles

Courtesy City of Golden

Getting Wet and Staying Warm

Lakewood Link Recreation Center Pool ☆☆☆☆☆

Courtesy Lakewood Link Recreation Center

1295 South Reed Street
Lakewood, 80232
(303) 987-5400
www.Lakewood.org/Recreation

Hours:	Varies daily and changes seasonally; visit the website for the current schedule.
Admission:	Under 3: Free; Age 3-17: $4, Age 18-61: $5; Age 62+: $4 Admission includes full access to the recreation center. MasterCard, Visa, checks, and cash accepted.
Parking:	Free parking lot.
Food:	Vending machines offer soda, water, candy, chips, and ice cream. An eating area is next to the pool with a few small tables and chairs. During warm weather, enjoy the fenced-in patio connected to the pool area. Guests are welcome to bring in their own food and drink.
Discounts:	Military discounts are available with active ID. Multi-visit punchcards can be purchased at a discounted rate.

Getting Wet and Staying Warm

What to expect. . .

Even young babies will love this pool because the water is bathtub warm at 91 degrees. At least two lifeguards are on duty at all times, and there can be as many as six when the pool gets crowded. In addition to the indoor pool, the Lakewood Link Recreation Center has a basketball court, a fitness center, a rock climbing wall, and dozens of classes, including swim classes for children as young as six months old. There is a small outdoor playground with a covered picnic bench to the east of the main entrance.

The Lakewood Link Indoor Pool is divided into two sections. The first features a fabulous pirate ship play structure, complete with slides, water cannons, and a pirate flag. This section of the pool has a zero-depth (beach) entry and is 3.5 feet at its deepest point. A giant pirate ship mural on one wall and fish sculptures hanging from the ceiling create a fun and stimulating atmosphere. The second section is a larger pool that is seven feet at its deepest point in the middle. A full-size dragon slide sends you into this pool, out through its mouth. The splashdown area for the slide is 3.5 feet deep, and is roped off from the deeper section. The slide is designed for children six and older, but you can ride down the slide with a younger child on your lap.

Lakewood Link does not have mandatory safety breaks. In addition to men's and women's locker rooms, two family locker rooms are located adjacent to the pool, each with a toilet, sink, shower, bench, and diaper-changing table. Lockers are available in the area surrounding the pool but you must provide your own lock. Plenty of benches and towel hooks are conveniently placed near the pirate ship area of the pool.

Annual Events . . .

The Climbing Competition is for all ages and skill levels and is held late January or early February.

Easter Eggstravaganza is the weekend before Easter.

Freaky Friday takes place on the Friday before Halloween.

Other destinations within 5 miles . . .
White Fence Farm (Site 178) - 1½ miles
Casa Bonita (Site 165) - 4 miles

Scales 'n' Tails - Lakewood (Site 139) - 4 miles
Sloan's Lake Park (Site 122) - 4½ miles

Longmont Recreation Center Leisure Pool

Courtesy Longmont Recreation Services

310 Quail Road
Longmont, 80501
(303) 774-4800
www.ci.longmont.co.us

Hours:	9:00 AM - 9:30 PM, Monday - Friday 9:00 AM - 5:30 PM, Saturday and Sunday
Admission:	Under 2: Free; Age 2-10: $4; Age 11-17: $4.50; Age 18-54: $5.75; Age 55+: $4.50. American Express, Discover, MasterCard, Visa, cash, and checks accepted.
Parking:	Free parking lot.
Food:	Food and drink other than water are not permitted in the pool area. You may bring your own food and eat at the tables in the lobby overlooking the pool. A reasonably-priced café sells a variety of food, ranging from burritos and corn dogs to yogurt and bagels. Hours for the café vary by season. Picnic tables are also located overlooking the pond.
Discounts:	Discounted pricing is available to residents of Longmont. A 20-visit punchcard can be purchased at a discount. Family Swim is the first Thursday of every month from 6:00 PM - 9:30 PM. Family admission is $12.50 ($10 for residents).

Getting Wet and Staying Warm

What to expect. . .

The Longmont Recreation Center has a large leisure pool with activities for children of nearly every age. The water is maintained at a comfortable 86 degrees. At least two lifeguards are on duty at all times, and there can be as many as six when the pool gets crowded. In addition to the leisure pool, the Recreation Center has a separate lap pool, an indoor running track, a fitness center, a rock climbing wall, coin-operated foosball and air hockey tables in the lobby, and scores of classes, including swim classes for children as young as six months old. A man-made lake in front of the building has a paved walking path encircling it and a deck with safety rails for admiring the view. A skate park is open daily from sunrise to sunset.

Courtesy Longmont Recreation Services

The leisure pool has a zero-depth (beach) entry play area with geysers and a small slide that splashes down into six inches of water so even very small children can ride. An activity structure sprays water out in every direction. Wheels control the flow of water coming out of pipes. Next to the play pool is a very small lazy river that is 3.5 feet deep. Two tall water slides, a body slide and a tube slide, are available for anyone 42 inches or taller. Parents may ride with their child on their lap if they are too small to ride alone. The water slides are not turned on until 10:00 AM, and all water features are turned off during swim lessons. The Longmont Recreation Center leisure pool does not have mandatory safety breaks.

Men's and women's locker rooms both have diaper-changing tables. Additionally, a family locker room has five private cabanas, each with a toilet, sink, shower, bench, and diaper-changing table. Lockers are provided at no charge but you must provide your own lock.

Admission to the Rec Center also grants daily admission to St. Vrain Memorial Center, Centennial Pool, Sunset Pool, Roosevelt Pool (Site 88), and Kanemoto Pool (Site 86) provided you have your paid receipt.

Note: On the website click on Recreation and Culture, *then* Longmont Recreation Facilities.

Other destinations within 5 miles . . .

Kanemoto Park and Pool (Site 86) - ½ mile
B&C BounceTown (Site 42) - 2 miles
Itty Bitty City (Site 47) - 2 miles

Sunflower Farm (Site 132) - 2 miles
Roosevelt Activity Pool (Site 88) - 2½ miles

North Boulder Recreation Center Pool ☆☆☆☆☆

Courtesy Boulder Parks & Recreation

3170 Broadway Street
Boulder, 80304
(303) 413-7260
www.BoulderParks-Rec.org

Hours:	Open daily and hours vary seasonally; visit the website for current schedule.
Admission:	Under 3: Free; Age 3-18: $4.25; Age 19-59: $6.75; Age 60+: $5. Admission includes full access to the recreation center. MasterCard, Visa, checks, and cash accepted.
Parking:	Free parking lot.
Food:	Other than plastic water bottles, food and drink are not allowed in the pool area. You may bring in your own food and eat at the tables provided in the lobby area. Vending machines sell snacks and drinks.
Discounts:	Punchcards for 10, 20, or 40 visits are available for purchase at a discounted rate.

Getting Wet and Staying Warm

What to expect. . .

Although it is rather small, the North Boulder Recreation Center leisure pool area has something for everyone. The water is maintained at a very warm 88 degrees. At least two lifeguards are on duty at all times. In addition to the leisure pool, the North Boulder Recreation Center has a lap pool, racquetball courts, outdoor tennis courts, weight and fitness rooms, a gymnastics center, and hundreds of classes, including swim classes for children as young as six months old.

The leisure pool has a zero-depth (beach) entry play area that is 2.5 feet at its deepest point. Geysers and an activity center with wheels, small dumping buckets and pipes gives children something to play with and explore, and an underwater bench on the side gives parents a place to sit and stay very close to their children. In one corner of this play area is a short, wide slide so friends can slide down together side by side. This slide is ADA and toddler accessible. A connected pool area has basketball nets and some room to swim and is three feet deep. A water slide sits in the corner. Children must be 48 inches tall or be able to swim to ride alone, but lap riding is permitted.

Children under 6 must be within arm's reach of an adult, and the adult must be actively engaged with the child. Safety breaks are taken for the last 10 minutes of each hour. Men's, women's, and family locker rooms are provided. The family locker room has three private cabanas, each with a toilet, sink, shower, bench, and diaper-changing table. Lockers are available at no charge but you must provide your own lock. The North Boulder Recreation Center leisure pool is one of the smallest ones in the Denver metro area, but it is a great place for families with young children who live in or are visiting the Boulder area.

Other destinations within 5 miles . . .

Tebo Train (Site 160) - 1 mile
Boulder Museum of Contemporary Art (Site 4) - 1½ miles
Colorado Music Festival Children's Concerts (Site 25) - 1½ miles
Boulder History Museum (Site 3) - 2 miles
CU Museum of Natural History (Site 7) - 2 miles
Fiske Planetarium (Site 169) - 2 miles

Storybook Ballet (Site 36) - 2½ miles
Scott Carpenter Park (Site 121) - 3 miles
Rocky Mountain Theatre for Kids (Site 34) - 4½ miles
Boulder Reservoir Swim Beach (Site 81) - 5 miles
Celestial Seasonings (Site 166) - 5 miles
Kids Kabaret (Site 31) - 5 miles

Getting Wet and Staying Warm

Paul Derda Recreation Center Indoor Pool ☆☆☆☆☆

Courtesy Paul Derda Recreation Center Indoor Pool

Paul Derda Recreation Center
13201 Lowell Boulevard
Broomfield, 80020
(303) 460-6900
www.ci.broomfield.co.us/recreation

Hours:	The pool opens daily at 9:00 AM. Closing time varies. Water slides open at 10:00 AM Monday - Friday.
Admission:	Under 4: Free; Age 4-12: $4; Age 13-17: $4.50; Age 18-59: $6; Age 60+: $4.50. Admission includes full access to the recreation center. American Express, MasterCard, Visa, checks, and cash accepted.
Parking:	Free parking lot.
Food:	Vending machines sell snacks and drinks. You may bring your own food and drink. Eating is allowed inside the pool area; tables and chairs are provided. In the warmer months, you can also eat outside on the patio that connects to the pool area.
Discounts:	Discounted pricing is available for residents of Broomfield.

What to expect. . .

The Paul Derda Recreation Center is very family-oriented. In addition to the leisure pool, the Recreation Center has a 35-foot climbing wall, Kids Zone Indoor Playground (Site 52), a fitness area, a gymnastics center, a game room, a preschool, and scores of classes to enjoy, including swimming classes for children as young as six months old. The leisure pool is located on the lower level. The water temperature is maintained at 88 degrees. Three lifeguards are on duty during the day, and as many as nine are on duty in the evenings and on weekends.

The play area has steps on one side and zero-depth (beach) entry on the other. A toddler play structure has a small alligator slides, dumping buckets, and wheels to turn. Other features include lemon drop fountains and an underwater bench. A small current pool is located on one end of the play area. A body slide and a tube slide are available. Lap riding is permitted; children must be 46 inches or taller to ride alone. Single and double tubes are provided for the tube slide. The pool also has an adult spa kept at a steamy 103 degrees, and a family spa maintained at 98 degrees.

Paul Derda Recreation Center does not have mandatory safety breaks. Diaper-changing tables are available in both the men's and women's locker rooms. Additionally, the Recreation Center has a family locker room with six private cabanas. Each cabana has a toilet, sink, shower, bench, and a diaper-changing table. Lockers are provided at no charge, but you must provide your own lock.

Other destinations within 5 miles . . .

Kids Zone (Site 52) - same location
The Bay Aquatic Park (Site 79) - 2½ miles
Little Monkey Bizness - Westminster (Site 53) - 4 miles
Skate City - Westminster (Site 175) - 4½ miles

Boondocks Fun Center (Site 151) - 4½ miles
The Butterfly Pavilion (Site 134) - 5 miles
Krispy Kreme (Site 172) - 5 miles
Scales 'n' Tails - Northglenn (Site 139) - 5 miles

HELPFUL TIP - If you ride down a water slide with a child on your lap, you will go underwater when you reach the end of the slide. This may be obvious to most people, but I was surprised by this. So was my 3-year-old.

Ridge Recreation Center Activity Pool

Courtesy Foothills Parks & Recreation District

6613 South Ward Street
Littleton, 80127
(303) 409-2333
www.ifoothills.org

Hours:	10:30 AM - 9:00 PM, Monday - Friday (opens at 11:00 in summer months) 12:00 PM - 5:30 PM, Saturday 10:00 AM - 5:30 PM, Sunday Water features are turned off from 4:30 - 6:30 PM Monday through Thursday.
Admission:	Not yet walking: Free; Age Walking-17: $5.25; Age 18-61: $7.25; Age 62+: $6.25. Admission includes full access to the recreation center. Discover, MasterCard, Visa, checks, and cash accepted.
Parking:	Free parking lot.
Food:	Vending machines sell chips, candy, soda, and bottled water. You may bring in your own food and drink. Tables and chairs are provided around the perimeter of the pool, as well as in other areas of the recreation center. Picnic tables are located outside.
Discounts:	Discounted pricing is available for residents of the Foothills Park & Recreation District. Household daily admission is $21 ($13.50 for residents). $2 Tuesday is available at all facilities in the Foothills Park & Recreation District. Seasonal passes and multi-visit cards are available.

What to expect. . .

Ridge Recreation Center is a bright facility with a large activity pool that has something for children of all ages. The water temperature is maintained at a comfortable 87 degrees. Two to six lifeguards are on duty at all times, depending on the crowd. In addition to the Activity Pool, the Ridge Recreation Center has racquetball courts, a climbing wall, a lap pool, a fitness area, a Clay Arts studio, a dance and aerobics studio, and plenty of classes, including swimming classes for children as young as six months old. A small playground section near the main (west) entrance offers a nice view of the foothills.

The Activity Pool has zero-depth (beach) entry with geysers and a movable pipe system in the very shallow part. This area gradually gets as deep as 3.5 feet. A toddler play structure with a tot slide, wheels that turn, and lots of water spraying out is located in the center. Children must be at least 48 inches tall or pass a swim test to ride the 150-foot body slide. At one end of the pool is a current channel for walking, swimming, or floating. A bubble bench, like a jacuzzi tub without the hot water, is in here too. The current channel is four feet deep.

Ridge Recreation Center does not have mandatory safety breaks. In addition to men's and women's locker rooms, there are five cabanas in the family locker area. Each cabana has a toilet, sink, shower, and a bench that can double as a diaper-changing area. A diaper-changing table is also located in the public area where lockers are provided at no charge (but you must provide your own lock). Children 6 and older must use the gender-appropriate locker room or the family locker area.

Note: When visiting the website click on Programs and Facilities, then Ridge Recreation Center.

Other destinations within 5 miles . . .

Jump Street (Site 48) - 2½ miles
Fun City (Site 153) - 2½ miles
My Art Workshop (Site 54) - 3 miles
Deer Creek Pool (Site 84) - 4½ miles

Robert F. Clement Park (Site 117) - 4½ miles
Weaver Hollow Park and Pool (Site 92) - 5 miles
Audience of One -Burgundy Theater (Site 23) - 3 miles

Getting Wet and Staying Warm

Utah Pool ☆☆☆☆☆

Courtesy City of Aurora

1800 South Peoria Street
Aurora, 80012
(303) 696-4303
www.auroragov.org

Hours:	Hours vary by season. Visit the website for current hours.
Admission:	Under 2: Free; Age 2-17: $3.50; Age 18-61: $4.25; Age 62+: $3.50 American Express, Discover, MasterCard, Visa, checks, and cash accepted.
Parking:	Free parking lot.
Food:	A concession stand sells hot dogs, pizza, nachos, and other snack foods. You may bring your own food, but no glass or alcohol. A large eating area is next to the concession stand. Several picnic tables are located in the sand play area outside.
Discounts:	Multi-visit cards and monthly passes can be purchased at a discounted rate.

What to expect. . .

Utah Pool has a lap pool, a leisure pool with a water slide, a large indoor sprayground, and an outside sandbox area. The lap pool features a diving board, a high dive, and a plunge slide, and is maintained at 83 degrees. The leisure pool is a rectangular pool that is 60 feet long and three feet deep throughout. The water is kept at 87 degrees. A 140-foot water slide drops into the leisure pool. Children must be 48 inches tall or pass a swim test to ride the water slide; lap riding is not permitted. Next to the leisure pool is a large indoor sprayground with a a slide, pipes and fountains spraying water, dumping buckets, and geysers shooting up from the ground. Like the leisure pool, the water in the sprayground is quite warm. An outdoor patio with picnic tables and a sandbox is open during the summer. The only way into the patio is through the pool area.

Men's and women's locker rooms are available, as well as a family locker room with a toilet, sink, shower, dressing area, and a diaper-changing table. Lockers are provided at no charge but you must bring your own lock. Generally, six to eight lifeguards are on duty. Safety breaks occur during the last 10 minutes of every hour; adults may continue to swim during this time. Utah Pool offers swim lessons for children as young as six months old.

Note: Click on Residents, then Recreation, then Aquatics, then Utah Pool to get on the pool's website.

Other destinations within 5 miles . . .

Cinema Grill (Site 167) - 3 miles
Todd's Tropical Fish (Site 140) - 3½ miles
Aurora History Museum (Site 1) - 4 miles

Cherry Creek State Park Swim Beach (Site 82) - 4 miles
Skate City - Aurora (Site 175) - 4 miles
Wings Over the Rockies Museum (Site 163) - 5 miles

Courtesy City of Aurora

Courtesy City of Golden

Getting Wet and Staying Warm

Wheat Ridge Recreation Center Pool ☆☆☆☆☆

Courtesy Wheat Ridge Parks & Recreation

4005 Kipling Street
Wheat Ridge, 80033
(303) 231-1300
www.ci.wheatridge.co.us

Hours:	Varies depending on season and class schedules; call for current hours.
Admission:	Under 3: Free; Age 3-5: $4.50; Age 6-17: $6; Age 18-64: $6.50; Age 65+: $6. Admission includes full access to the recreation center. Discover, MasterCard, Visa, checks, and cash accepted.
Parking:	Free parking lot.
Food:	Vending machines are in the lobby. You may bring in your own food. Eating is permitted in the pool area at the tables provided. An outside patio connects to the pool area.
Discounts:	Jefferson County residents receive discounted pricing. A daily family admission is available to Jefferson County residents for $13 and Wheat Ridge residents for $10. Punchcards for 20 visits can be purchased at a discount.

What to expect. . .

The Wheat Ridge Recreation Center leisure pool is fairly large and has something for everyone. The water temperature is kept between 86 and 88 degrees. Two to four lifeguards are on duty at all times, depending on the size of the crowd. In addition to the leisure pool, the Recreation Center has racquet-ball courts, a climbing wall, a lap pool, a fitness area, a Wii game room, and scores of classes, including swimming classes for children as young as six months old.

The leisure pool has zero-depth (beach) entry that gradually slopes to reach a depth of three feet. Although it is beach entry, there is a small lip so watch your step when you first enter the water. This area has geysers, lemondrop fountains on the side, and dumping buckets, but your child will probably spend most of her time sliding on the frog slide — its long tongue is the slide. Next to the play area is a Lazy River that is 3.5 feet deep and has a water curtain. Inner tubes are provided but you may also walk the river if it isn't crowded. The water curtain can be avoided if you are walking, but it would be more difficult floating in a tube. A 120-foot water slide is available for children who are 48 inches or taller; lap-riding is permitted for smaller children.

Mandatory safety breaks take place at pool manager's discretion depending on the size of the crowd. They take place every 90 minutes for 15 minutes. In addition to men's and women's locker rooms, the Recreation Center has six cabanas in the family locker area. Each cabana has a toilet, sink, shower, and a diaper-changing table. You must get a key from the front desk to get into one of the cabanas. When you get to the pool, turn the key into one of the lifeguards. Lockers are provided but you must bring your own lock. A bathroom with a diaper-changing table is located in the pool area so you don't have to return to the locker room.

The Wheat Ridge leisure pool generally opens to children at 10:00 AM, but the fountains are turned on at 11:00 AM, and the water slide is turned on at 3:30 PM in the winter and noon in the summer.

Note: Click on Department, then Parks and Recreation, then Pools and Swimming on the website.

Other destinations within 5 miles . . .

Rising Curtain Theatre Academy (Site 33) - 2½ miles
Fish Den (Site 138) - 3½ miles
Lakeside Amusement Park (Site 155) - 4 miles
Scales 'n' Tails - Lakewood (Site 139) - 4 miles
Casa Bonita (Site 165) - 4½ miles

Majestic View Nature Center (Site 112) - 4½ miles
The Arvada Center (Site 22) - 5 miles
Squiggles Playground (Site 123) - 5 miles
The Bookery Nook (Site 59) - 5 miles
Secrest Pool (Site 89) - 5 miles

Getting Wet and Staying Cool

Many Coloradans take their vacations during spring, fall, or winter because our summers really can't be beat. Because of the low humidity, even the hottest days are better than many parts of the country. If you think Denver doesn't have beaches, you'd be mistaken, and ours come with a mountain view. Add in the plethora of water parks and outdoor pools, and there are more than a dozen places for you and your child to beat the heat. All of the places in this chapter allow you to bring your own food so you can save money by packing a lunch. None of the destinations permit glass and most prohibit alcohol as well. Also, keep in mind when planning your visit that afternoon summer showers are not uncommon.

A special note: the term "safety breaks" is used throughout this chapter. It refers to a time when everyone must get out of the pool for a specific period of time (adults are sometimes permitted to continue swimming). Plan your visit carefully, as it is no fun to start playing in the water, only to be told a few minutes later to exit the pool!

Boulder Reservoir

Reservoir and AWQUA Lounge ☆☆☆☆☆

Photo by Linda Strand
Courtesy City of Aurora Parks & Rec

5800 South Powhaton Road
Aurora, 80016
(303) 690-1286
www.auroragov.org/reservoirs

Hours:	The swim beach is open during reservoir hours, Memorial Day till Labor Day. Reservoir hours vary by month throughout the year.
Admission:	$10 vehicle pass American Express, Discover, MasterCard, Visa, checks, and cash accepted.
Annual Pass:	$65. Residents and employees of Aurora receive a discount.
Parking:	No additional charge for parking.
Food:	A concession stand is open in the summer from 10:00 AM - 6:00 PM. The stand accepts MasterCard, Visa, checks, and cash. You may bring your own food, but no glass. Several picnic pavilions are near the swim beach and one picnic pavilion is at the boat launch. Picnic shelters are available on a first come, first serve basis unless they are reserved.

What to expect. . .

Aurora Reservoir is a multi-use aquatic recreational facility that offers fishing, sailing, non-motorized boating, and windsurfing on the 860-acre reservoir. A paved 8.5-mile path encircles the reservoir. The swim beach has beach sand, volleyball nets, and covered picnic tables. Several sun sails provide some shade. Lifeguards are on duty during high-use hours. A large playground behind the beach offers slides and climbing structures for both younger children and older kids. The playground is made of plastic and has no shade, so the equipment gets very hot in the heat of the summer sun. An abundance of Canada geese live near the playground, so I would recommend closed-toe shoes at the playground.

The AWQUA Lounge is an educational facility located between the concession stand and the playground. The entrance is made to look like a drainpipe, and once inside you'll be immersed in an underwater scene, complete with the sounds of bubbles in the background. Children can dress up like a fish, play AWQUA Bingo, view a water sample under a microscope, or get a closer look at a live aquatic animal. The AWQUA Lounge is open from noon till 4:00 PM, Wednesday through Sunday in the summer. On Friday mornings, the Lounge opens at 9:00 AM and offers a variety of activities for toddlers and preschoolers.

Bathrooms at the beach have diaper-changing tables, showers, sinks, toilets, and dressing areas. Bathrooms are also located on the side of AWQUA Lounge building but do not have diaper-changing tables. My GPS didn't recognize the address at all. Aurora Reservoir is two miles east of Quincy and E-470, near the Arapahoe County Fairgrounds. Turn at the sign that says "Welcome to Aurora Reservoir" and then keep driving till you reach the entrance gate.

DID YOU KNOW? Because swimming gives babies free movement, they can develop actions they wouldn't otherwise have the opportunity to experience. Additionally, some studies indicate that regular swimming can improve eating and sleeping patterns in infants.

KIDS AREN'T DROWN PROOF (TM)

Drowning is quick and silent. A child can drown in less than two minutes. There is usually no warning, such as screams or splashing.

TAKE PREVENTATIVE STEPS.
SAVE A LIFE.

SAVE A LIFE!

DROWNING PREVENTION FOUNDATION

A Partial List of **Safety Guidelines**

1 Never leave a child alone near water to answer the phone, the doorbell, go to the bathroom, attend to another child or attend to household chores, even for a few seconds.

2 Keep a constant eye on young children playing in or near any body of water, wading pool, public pool, bathtub or lake.

3 At large gatherings, designate an adult to watch children at play, and while in pool.

4 Fence your pool on all four sides with a barrier that is at least 5 feet high.

5 Move lawn chairs, tables and other potential climbing aids away from the fence to help keep children out.

6 Any gate or door leading to the pool area should be self-closing and self-latching, opening outward, with the latch placed on the pool side out of reach.

7 Install panic alarms on all house doors and windows leading to the pool area and automatic safety cover over the pool.

8 Completely remove cover before children are allowed in pool.

9 Drain off water that accumulates on top of the pool cover.

10 A child can drown in as little as two inches of water.

11 Keep reaching and throwing aids, such as poles and life-preservers, on both sides of the pool.

12 All non-swimmers should always wear approved personal flotation devices when they are near water.

13 Swimming lessons do not insure safety. A child who falls into water unexpectedly might panic and forget his swimming skills.

Photo courtesy of Starfish Swim School

CPR It is crucial that you and all of your child's caregivers can swim and know how to perform cardiopulmonary resuscitation (CPR) in an emergency. Immediate CPR could prevent death or massive brain damage.

www.drowningpreventionfoundation.org

Getting Wet and Staying Cool

The Bay Aquatic Park ☆☆☆☆☆

The Bay Aquatic Park
Courtesy City County of Broomfield

250 Lamar Street
Broomfield, 80020
(303) 464-5520
www.ci.broomfield.co.us

Hours:	10:00 AM - 6:00 PM, Monday - Thursday 10:00 AM - 8:00 PM, Friday 10:00 AM - 6:00 PM, Saturday and Sunday Open Memorial Day weekend through Labor Day.
Admission:	Under 4: Free; Age 4-17: $6; Age 18-59: $8; Age 60+: $6 American Express, MasterCard, Visa, checks, and cash accepted.
Summer Pass:	$75, available only to Broomfield residents.
Parking:	Free parking lot.
Food:	A cash-only concession stand is available. You may bring in your own food and drink, no glass or alcohol. Picnic tables and ample lawn space are available.
Discounts:	Discounted pricing is available for Broomfield residents with a residency card. Family Night is every Friday from 4:00 PM - 8:00 PM, and the entire family can come for $10.

What to expect. . .

The Bay is an affordable water park ideal for families with young children. The Bay has three main sections:

The Tot Pool ranges in depth from 6-18 inches. A wide slide with three lanes is made of a special material that isn't very slippery, so children don't go too fast. A ledge at the bottom of a rock structure juts out over the pool, providing a small amount of shade.

The Leisure Pool has zero-depth (beach) entry and gradually gets as deep as 3.5 feet. A five-lane slide is positioned at the deep end. Children must be at least 46 inches tall to ride alone. Smaller children can ride on a parent's lap. The shallow section features an interactive water play structure with a tube slide and water spraying out from virtually every side.

There are two **Serpentine Water Slides** for those who want a faster ride. As with the leisure pool, children must be 46 inches tall to ride alone or sit on a parent's lap.

An Innertube Slide can be ridden with single or double tubes. Children must be 46 inches tall to ride alone or sit on a parent's lap.

A section of concrete between the edge of the toddler area of the leisure pool and the splashdown area of the water slides allowed me to keep an eye on both my children at the same time.

Awnings situated around the pool provide some shade, but you'll have to arrive early to get one. Three large umbrellas in the grass area provide additional shade. Complimentary lockers are available, but you need to provide your own lock. The locker rooms have toilets, sinks, showers, diaper-changing tables, and dressing areas. There is not a family locker room, and children age 6 or older must use the same-gender locker room. The water is maintained at about 84 degrees, and the sun does the rest. Generally, about 15 lifeguards are on duty. A 20-minute safety break is taken every day around 2:00 PM.

Note: When visiting the website click on A-Z Index, then Bay Aquatic Park.

Other destinations within 5 miles . . .

Paul Derda Indoor Pool (Site 74) - 2½ miles
Kids Zone (Site 52) - 2½ miles
Rock Creek Farm U-Pick-Em Pumpkin Patch (Site 130) - 3½ miles

The Butterfly Pavilion (Site 134) - 4 miles
Skate City - Westminster (Site 175) - 4½ miles
Kids Crossing Play Area (Site 50) - 5 miles

Bear Creek Lake Park Swim Beach ☆☆☆☆☆

Bear Creek Lake Park Swim Beach
Courtesy City of Lakewood

15600 West Morrison Road
Lakewood, 80465
(303) 697-6159
www.lakewood.org

Hours:	8:00 AM - 8:00 PM daily (Swim Beach) The swim beach is open from Memorial Day weekend through Labor Day. The park itself is open year-round, with hours varying each season.
Admission:	$5 for general vehicle pass; $4 for seniors 62 or older MasterCard, Visa, checks and cash accepted.
Annual Pass:	$45; $35 for seniors 62 or older
Parking:	Parking areas are located throughout the park. Near the swim beach, a large parking lot is located by the playground and an overflow lot is nearby.
Food:	You may bring in your own food and drink (no glass allowed in the park, and no alcohol at the Swim Beach). Picnic tables are located throughout the park. Covered picnic tables are located at the swim beach. A concession stand is open from 10:00 AM - 6:00 PM.

Getting Wet and Staying Cool

What to expect. . .

Bear Creek Lake has 2,600 acres of parkland and 15 miles of dirt trails for biking and hiking, but we go for the swim beach at Big Soda Lake. Only non-motorized watercraft is allowed on Big Soda Lake. The swimming section is roped off from the rest of the lake. The sand is gravelly, not like actual beach sand, but you get a view of the mountains that most beaches can't offer. A loaner station lets you borrow life jackets. Plastic buckets and shovels were scattered along the beach, probably left behind by others. Volleyball courts and a playground with slides are also at the swim beach. A marina with non-motorized boats for rent is located in the parking lot past the playground.

The men's and women's bathrooms both have diaper-changing tables. No lifeguard is on duty at the swim beach. The water is checked weekly to ensure it is safe for swimming. Call ahead to make sure the beach is open. Other amenities in the park include a campground, archery range, horseback riding stables, waterski school, fishing, a Visitor Center, and environmental education programs.

Annual Events . . .

Volunteer Service events take place on **Earth Day, National Trails Day, and National Public Lands Day.**

The Grin and Bear It family adventure race is held in July.

A **Summer Concert** is at the Swim Beach in July.

Note: Click on For Residents, then Parks and Recreation, then Parks and Trails on the website.

Other destinations within 5 miles . . .

Bandimere Speedway (Site 142) - 1 mile
Morrison Natural History Museum (Site 15) - 1½ miles
Dinosaur Ridge (Site 103) - 3 miles

Red Rocks (Site 115) - 4 miles
Weaver Hollow Park and Pool (Site 92) - 4½ miles

DID YOU KNOW? Every natural water body contains diverse microorganisms, some of which, if ingested, could cause illness. This includes creeks, lakes, and reservoirs. Teach your child to avoid letting any water into his mouth.

Site
81
Boulder

Getting Wet and Staying Cool (sidebar)

Boulder Reservoir Swim Beach ☆☆☆☆☆

Courtesy Boulder Parks Recreation

5565 51st Street
Boulder, 80306
(303) 441-3461
www.boulderrez.org

Hours:	10:00 AM - 6:00 PM, Monday - Thursday 10:00 AM - 7:00 PM, Friday - Sunday The swim beach is open from mid-May through Labor Day. The reservoir is open year-round with varying hours.
Admission:	Under 3: Free; Age 3-12; $3; Age 13-18: $4; Age 19-59: $6; Age 60+: $4 MasterCard, Visa, checks, and cash accepted.
Annual Pass:	$300 for two adults and two children ($240 for Boulder residents)
Parking:	Free parking.
Food:	The Rez Grill is open daily till 10:00 AM - 5:00 PM and serves a variety of food from breakfast burritos to grilled items (cash only). You may bring in your own food and drink; no glass.

What to expect. . .

The swim beach at the Boulder Reservoir is roped off into four sections. The sections in the front get deeper gradually to about three feet. The farthest section can get as deep as 15 feet, and you have to pass a swim test to go into that section. The sand is a little more gravelly than regular beach sand but gets smoother toward the water. The view from the swim beach is beautiful. The boathouse, east of the swim beach, rents non-motorized water craft and charcoal grills. You may bring in a propane grill as long as you also bring a fire extinguisher.

Children under five must be with an adult in the water at all times. Generally, two to six lifeguards are on duty, depending on how busy the reservoir is. A small lifeguard station and first aid center is located near the water. Closer to the parking lot is a two-story building. The lower level has locker rooms with showers, toilets, sinks, and dressing areas. There are no diaper-changing tables, but benches in the dressing area will do in a pinch. The Rez Grill and a covered pavilion with plenty of picnic tables are located on the upper level.

Other destinations within 5 miles . . .

Celestial Seasonings (Site 166) - 3½ miles
Leanin' Tree Museum of Western Art (Site 13) - 4½ miles
North Boulder Recreation Center Pool (Site 73) - 5 miles
Storybook Ballet (Site 36) - 5 miles

Cherry Creek State Park Swim Beach ☆☆☆

Courtesy Colorado State Parks

4201 South Parker Road
Aurora, 80014
(303) 690-1166
www.parks.state.co.us/Parks/CherryCreek

Hours:	Sunrise to sunset daily from Memorial D end through Labor Day. The park itself is open 5.00 AM - 11:00 PM daily.
Admission:	$9 daily vehicle pass. MasterCard, Visa, checks, and cash accepted.
Annual Pass:	$73. The annual park pass which gives access to all 42 Colorado State Parks is $70, and a specific Water Basin Authority sticker for access to Cherry Creek must be added for $3 more.
Parking:	Free parking.
Food:	Concessions are available at the marina and a campground store sells drinks and snacks. Vending machines with snacks, drinks, and occasionally beach toys are located at the swim beach. You may bring in your own food; no glass. Picnic tables are available throughout the park.

What to expect. . .

Cherry Creek State Park offers campgrounds, picnic areas, trails for walking or horseback riding, a shooting range, fishing, a marina and more, but our favorite feature is the swim beach. The sand is perfect for building sandcastles so bring along buckets and shovels. The swimming section is roped off from the rest of the reservoir, which is 880 surface acres. While you swim, you can also watch the motor boats and jet skis racing around the water. On the weekends, the beach can reach full capacity so go during the week if you can.

Bathrooms are near the parking lot at the top of the beach area, and include showers and changing areas. A first aid station is available, but there are no lifeguards on duty. Pets are prohibited on the swim beach.

My GPS was a little off with the address. The turn into Cherry Creek State Park is one mile south of I-225 on Parker Road at Lehigh.

Other destinations within 5 miles . . .

Skate City - Aurora (Site 175) - 2 miles
Todd's Tropical Fish (Site 140) - 3½ miles

Utah Pool (Site 76) - 4 miles
Flapjacks and a Flick (Site 170) - 4½ miles

HELPFUL TIP - Fill a beach pail with half sand and half water. Pour the wet sand through a funnel to build a drip sand castle. It's easier for little ones to make than a typical sand castle.

Cherry Creek State Park Swim Beach Courtesy Colorado State Parks

Cook Creek Pool ☆☆☆☆☆

Courtesy South Suburban Parks and Recreation

8711 Lone Tree Parkway
Lone Tree, 80124
(303) 790-7665
www.ssprd.org

Hours:	11:00 AM - 7:00 PM, Monday - Friday 10:00 AM - 6:00 PM, Saturday and Sunday Open from Memorial Day weekend through Labor Day; a modified schedule starting in mid-August.
Admission:	Under 2: Free; Age 2-17: $5.50; Age 18-64: $6.50; Age 65+: $5.75. Discover, MasterCard, Visa, checks, and cash accepted.
Summer Pass:	$475 for 2 adults and 3 children ($330 for residents). The season pass grants admission to all pools in South Suburban Parks and Recreation.
Parking:	Free parking lot.
Food:	A concession stand sells hot dogs, pizza, nachos, and the like. You may bring in your own food; no glass or alcohol. Picnic tables, beach chairs, and lawn space are available.
Discounts:	Residents of the South Suburban Parks and Recreation District receive discounted pricing with an ID card. Discounted multi-visit punchcards are available. Household admission for 2 adults and 3 children is $23.50 ($10 for residents).

What to expect. . .

Cook Creek Pool has a play area, a water slide, and a separate lap pool with a diving board. The play area has zero-depth (beach) entry and a large play structure with slides and wheels that control the flow of water. A 70-gallon bucket is perched on top of the structure and empties every few minutes. It is impossible to play on or near the structure without getting dumped on. Although most children seem to love getting dumped on, Cook Creek is not the pool for you if you think your child won't like it, as there is nothing else for a toddler to play with or on. The play area connects to

Courtesy South Suburban Parks and Recreation

a swimming pool that is 3.5 feet deep. An underwater bench gives parents a place to sit or children a place to jump from. The splashdown area for the water slide is separate from the play area and swimming pool. Children must be at least 48 inches tall or pass a swim test to ride the slide. Lap riding is not permitted. Children under 7 must be within arm's reach of an adult at all times.

The water is heated to 84 degrees and the sun does the rest. Safety breaks occur for 10 minutes at the top of each hour. In addition to men's and women's locker rooms, there are two family locker rooms, each with a toilet, sink, shower, and a diaper-changing table. Lockers are available at no charge but you must provide your own lock. Your admission is good for the entire day so you may leave and come back. Cook Creek Pool is next door to the Lone Tree library, which can provide a nice quiet break if needed. Daily admission is nearly twice as much for non-residents as residents. A South Suburban Parks and Recreation ID is required to qualify for the resident rate.

When visiting the website click on Facilities/Parks, then Outdoor Pools.

Other destinations within 5 miles . . .

Little Monkey Bizness - Lone Tree (Site 53) - 2½ miles
The Wildlife Experience (Site 19) - 3½ miles

Deer Creek Pool ☆☆☆☆☆

Hours:	10:30 AM - 6:30 PM, Monday - Thursday 10:30 AM - 5:00 PM, Friday - Sunday Open Memorial Day weekend through late August.
Admission:	Not yet walking: Free; Age Walking-17: $5.25; Age 18-61: $7.25; Age 62+: $6.25 Discover, MasterCard, Visa, checks, and cash accepted.
Summer Pass:	$219 for two household members ($169 for district residents) $30 for each additional person. Summer pass is good for all pools and recreation centers in the Foothills Parks and Rec District.
Parking:	Free parking lot.
Food:	A cash-only snack bar is open daily from 11:00 AM - 5:00 PM. You may bring your own food and drink; no glass or alcohol. Picnic tables, beach chairs, and lawn space are available.
Discounts:	See below for all available discounts.

Courtesy of Foothills Parks and Recreation District

8637 South Garrison Street
Littleton, 80128
(720) 981-8393
www.ifoothills.org

What to expect. . .

The Deer Creek Pool play area has zero-depth (beach) entry and gradually deepens to 3.5 feet. A bright blue line is painted across the bottom at a depth of two feet, so it is easy to see whether or not your child is in the shallowest part of the pool. The shallow end has geysers, dumping buckets, and a movable pipeline with water flowing through it. A tube slide splashes down into a separate area that is 3.5 feet deep. Children must be at least 48 inches tall or pass a swim test to ride the slide. Lap riding is not permitted. The lap pool is five feet deep.

The pool is heated to about 82 degrees and the sun takes care of the rest. Deer Creek Pool has mandatory safety breaks for the last 10 minutes of the hour. Both the men's and women's bathrooms have diaper-changing tables. A family locker room is available; see a staff member to get the key. Lockers are provided at no charge but you must bring your own lock. Your admission is valid for the whole day, so you may leave and come back. Just get a hand stamp when you leave or keep your wristband on.

Residents of the Foothills Park & Recreation District receive discounted pricing. Household daily admission is $21 ($13.50 for residents). $2 Tuesday is available to everyone. Seasonal passes and multi-visit cards may be purchased at a discount. Twilight hours are 4:30 PM - 6:30 PM, Monday through Thursday, when admission is $2 per person or $8 for a household. Dads get in free on Father's Day.

Note: Click on Programs and Facilities, then Aquatics, then Outdoor Pools when visiting the website.

Other destinations within 5 miles . . .

Denver Botanic Gardens at Chatfield (Site 102) - 2½ miles
Fun City (Site 153) - 3½ miles
Jump Street (Site 48) - 4 miles
My Art Workshop (Site 54) - 4 miles

Ridge Recreation Center Activity Pool (Site 75) - 4½ miles
Robert F. Clement Park (Site 117) - 5 miles
Audience of One - Burgundy Theater (Site 23) - 4 miles

Getting Wet and Staying Cool

H2O'Brien Pool ☆☆☆☆☆

Courtesy Town of Parker

10795 Victorian Drive
Parker, 80138
(720) 851-5873
www.parkeronline.org

Hours:	10:00 AM - 6:00 PM, daily (Friday till 9:00 PM) Open daily from Memorial Day weekend through mid-August, then weekends only through Labor Day. The pool is closed during the Parker Country Festival in mid-June.
Admission:	Under 52": $4.50; Over 52": $5.50 MasterCard, Visa, Town of Parker gift cards, checks, and cash accepted.
Summer Pass:	$185 for a family of four ($175 for residents); $25 for each additional person.
Parking:	Free parking lot.
Food:	A concession stand sells a variety of snack foods, including healthful choices. You may bring in your own food and drink; no glass or alcohol. Beach chairs, picnic tables, and lawn space are provided.
Discounts:	Discounted pricing is available to residents of the 80134 or 80138 zip codes.

What to expect. . .

H2O'Brien Pool is larger than your typical outdoor public pool but not quite a water park, and is great fun for children of all ages. The water is heated to 85 degrees but further warmed by the sun. Because it is so big, 10 to 12 lifeguards are on duty at any given time. The play area has zero-depth (beach) entry and gets as deep as three feet. In this section, you'll find geysers, lemondrop fountains, dumping buckets, and an enormous play structure with two slides and water spraying everywhere. H2O'Brien also has a circulation/lap pool and two 182-foot water slides

Courtesy Town of Parker

with a splashdown area of 3.5 feet deep. Children must be at least 48 inches tall to ride the red slide and at least 52 inches tall to ride the blue slide. Height restrictions are strictly enforced. A sprayground next to the pool has colorful circles that the children love to run through and a mushroom fountain spraying water down.

From 9:00 AM - 10:00 PM Monday through Friday, H2O'Brien Pool offers "Little Squirts," a time for children under 48 inches tall and their grown-ups to come to the pool prior to opening. This time is less crowded and less noisy than the rest of the time. Regular admission applies, but you may stay for open swim. No minors taller than 48 inches will be allowed in during "Little Squirts."

H2O'Brien Pool does not have safety breaks. Inflatables and floaties are not permitted. For safety reasons, only three children under the age of 7 are allowed per adult. Diaper-changing tables are available in both the men's and women's locker rooms. Lockers are provided at no charge but you must bring your own lock. The pool is part of H2O'Brien Park, which has a softball field, a basketball court, and a very large playground.

Note: When visiting the website click on Recreation, then Facilities, then H2O'Brien Pool.

Other destinations within 5 miles . . .

Audience of One - Parker (Site 23) - 3 blocks
CYT Denver - Parker (Site 27) - 3 blocks
Little Monkey Bizness - Parker (Site 53) - 1 mile

Party On (Site 55) - 1 mile
Pump It Up - Parker (Site 56) - 1 mile

Kanemoto Park and Pool ☆☆☆☆☆

Courtesy Longmont Recreation Services

1151 South Pratt Parkway
Longmont, 80501
(303) 651-6934
www.ci.longmont.co.us

Hours:	10:00 AM - 5:00 PM, Monday - Saturday (till 7:00 PM on Tuesday and Thursday) 12:00 PM - 5:00 PM, Sunday Open Memorial Day weekend through Labor Day.
Admission:	Under 1: $0.75; Age 1-5: $3; Age 6+: $3.75 American Express, Discover, MasterCard, Visa, cash, and checks accepted.
Summer Pass:	$275 for two adults and their children under 21 ($220 for residents). The pass grants admission to all pools in the district.
Parking:	Free parking lot.
Food:	You may bring in your own food and drink, no glass or alcohol. The pool area has one picnic table, beach chairs, and some lawn space.
Discounts:	Discounted pricing is available to residents of Longmont. Sunday is Family Day, when admission is $7.50 for the entire family ($6 for residents).

What to expect. . .

Kanemoto Pool is only a little larger than your average backyard swimming pool and heated to 85 degrees, which makes it the perfect place for babies and early swimmers. The pool has zero-depth (beach) entry and reaches a maximum depth of about 3.5 feet. Fountains and geysers are located on the beach side. A rock structure with a short slide is on the opposite side of the pool. About half the pool, including the splashdown area for the slide, is less than 18 inches deep.

Kanemoto Park has a small playground with picnic tables, volleyball nets, a basketball court, a baseball field, and a super-cute dragonfly bicycle rack. The playground has regular swings, baby swings, and a climbing structure with monkey bars and a slide.

Kanemoto Pool does not have mandatory safety breaks. Four unisex bathrooms with diaper-changing

Courtesy Longmont Recreation Services

tables are available and are large enough to serve as changing rooms. One is only accessible from inside the pool area, but the other three can be entered from the park. Kanemoto Pool may be small, but it is also very inexpensive, especially on Sunday. It is a great swimming pool for families with young children who live in or near Longmont.

Note: When visiting the website click on Recreation and Culture, then Recreation Services, then Swimming Pools.

Other destinations within 5 miles . . .

Longmont Recreation Center Leisure Pool (Site 72) - ½ mile
B&C BounceTown (Site 42) - 1½ miles
Itty Bitty City (Site 47) - 1½ miles

Sunflower Farm (Site 132) - 2 miles
Roosevelt Activity Pool (Site 88) - 2½ miles

Pirates Cove Family Aquatic Center ☆☆☆☆☆

Courtesy City of Englewood Parks and Recreation

1255 West Belleview Avenue
Englewood, 80120
(303) 762-2683
www.piratescovecolorado.com

Hours:	10:30 AM - 6:30 PM daily Open daily from Memorial Day weekend through mid-August, then weekends only through Labor Day.
Admission:	Under 2: Free; Age 2-17: $8; Age 18-54: $9.25, Age 55+: $8 Discover, MasterCard, Visa, checks, and cash accepted.
Summer Pass:	$329 for three or more people ($263 for residents)
Parking:	Free parking lot.
Food:	The Barnacle Café provides snack foods and drinks at reasonable prices. Stands sell shaved ice and Dippin' Dots. You may bring in your own food. No glass, alcohol, tobacco products, pizza, or outside food delivery. Picnic tables, beach chairs, and grassy lawns are available throughout the park.
Discounts:	Discounted pricing is available for individuals with a current Englewood or South Suburban Recreation ID. Coupons can be found in the Entertainment Book and on their website. Join their E-club for special promotions.

What to expect. . .

Pirates Cove is an affordable water park ideal for families with young children. Upon entering, you are greeted by a talking bronze pirate statue. From there, you can choose from four different sections:

The Lagoon is the primary focus of the park and is designed with the young child in mind. There is a shallow (six inches) circular wading pool with a mushroom fountain in the center of it. Next to that is a sprayground where water squirts and sprays from a variety of water sculptures. The zero-depth entry lagoon has a giant play structure resembling a pirate ship. This structure has three separate sections connected by bridges. It includes slides, ropes and wheels that control the spray of water, and spray guns that can be shifted toward the people below (my kids got get a kick out of spraying me). Perched atop the middle section is a 750-gallon Dump Bucket that slowly fills with water and then tips and dumps on the people below every five minutes. A bell sounds before it dumps, so you have time to get under the dump zone, or away from it, whichever you prefer.

The River uses a current to send you around in an inner tube. Small children may sit on their parents' laps, but you must be in an inner tube while in the river. More adventurous children will have fun in the Swirling Vortex. The River also features a 35-foot tower with one open water slide and two tube water slides ranging in length and speed (the red one is the shortest and fastest). You must be at least 48 inches tall to ride the slides.

The Beach is a sand play area where kids can build castles. It is large enough for more than 20 children to play without getting in each other's way, but most of the children I observed were work-ing together to create a giant moat running around several castles. There are many shovels, rakes, and buckets for your child to play with. A couple of outdoor showers are at the entrance to The Beach for rinsing off the sand or filling buckets.

The Bay is a great place for older children and younger children who are strong swimmers. It features a plunge slide, a diving board, a lap lane, and lots of room to play and swim.

Bathrooms with changing tables are available near each water section. Near The Lagoon are family changing rooms, outdoor showers, and lockers. Lockers are available for 25 cents each time you lock it. Picnic tables and beach chairs are available free of charge but are occupied quickly, so get there early if you want a chair. You may leave the park and return the same day if you get a stamp upon departure. No refunds are given if the weather turns sour, but you can get a stamp for re-entry later that day. If the park closes for the day due to weather, you can get a stamp to return another day during the season.

Other destinations within 5 miles . . .

Belleview Park (Site 94) - next door
Cornerstone Park (Site 100) - ½ mile
Littleton Museum (Site 14) - 1½ miles
The Town Hall Arts Center (Site 38) - 1½ miles
Hudson Gardens (Site 108) - 2 miles
Skate City - Littleton (Site 175) - 2½ miles
CYT Denver - Aspen Academy (Site 27) - 3 miles

Scales 'n' Tails - Englewood (Site 139) - 3 miles
Younger Generation Players (Site 40) - 3 miles
Museum of Outdoor Arts (Site 18) - 3½ miles
Carson Nature Center and South Platte Park
(Site 95) - 4 miles
Robert F. Clement Park (Site 117) - 4½ miles
The Hop - Littleton (Site 46) - 5 miles

HELPFUL TIP - Take baby powder with you if your child will be playing in the sand. Dry her off with a towel, then liberally sprinkle baby powder all over her body. The sand will brush right off.

Courtesy City of Englewood Parks

Getting Wet and Staying Cool

Roosevelt Activity Pool ☆☆☆☆☆

Courtesy Longmont Recreation Services

903 8th Avenue
Longmont, 80501
(303) 774-4455
www.ci.longmont.co.us

Hours:	10:00 AM - 4:00 PM daily. Open from early June through Labor Day.
Admission:	Under 1: $0.75; Age 1-5: $3; Age 6+: $3.75 American Express, Discover, MasterCard, Visa, cash, and checks accepted.
Summer Pass:	$275 for two adults and their children under 21 ($220 for residents). The pass grants admission to all pools in the district.
Parking:	Free parking lot and free street parking.
Food:	Vending machines sell snacks and drinks. You may bring in your own food or drink; no glass or alcohol. Awnings set over the lawn provide shade.
Discounts:	Discounted pricing is available to residents of Longmont. Saturday is Family Day, when admission is $7.50 for the entire family ($6 for residents).

What to expect. . .

Roosevelt Pool is a heated outdoor pool geared for children under 8. The pool has zero-depth (beach) entry and reaches a maximum depth of about 2.5 feet. Dumping buckets and geysers are located in the beach area. A small sprayground with fountains of various heights is next to the pool; one sprays water up nearly 10 feet high. Just outside the pool is a huge pavilion that can be rented in the summer and is used for ice skating in the winter.

On the opposite corner of the park is the Longmont Memorial Rose Garden and a playground. Paths winding through the garden allow you to see and smell the differences between the many varieties of roses. The playground has regular swings, baby swings, a toddler climbing structure with a tunnel, and a larger climbing structure with slides and monkey bars. A pavilion with several picnic tables is next to the playground.

Roosevelt Pool does not have mandatory safety breaks. The men's and women's bathrooms in the pool area both have diaper-changing tables and dressing areas. A unisex bathroom without a diaper-changing table is near the playground. Paved paths run through Roosevelt Park, connecting the pool, playground, and rose garden.

Note: On their website click on Recreation and Culture, then Recreation Services, then Swimming Pools.

Other destinations within 5 miles . . .

Itty Bitty City (Site 47) - 3 blocks
Kanemoto Park and Pool (Site 86) - 2½ miles
Longmont Recreation Center Leisure Pool (Site 72) - 2½ miles

B&C BounceTown (Site 42) - 3 miles
Rocky Mountain Pumpkin Ranch (Site 131) - 4 miles
Sunflower Farm (Site 132) - 4 miles

GO ONE STEP FURTHER
Water World

Water World, a Denver legend, has more than 45 attractions on 64 acres, making it one of the largest water parks in America. Although its size may be overwhelming for very young children, Water World has themed water rides, wave pools, family tube rides, a 1,000-foot lazy river, and a miniature water park called Wally World for little tykes. It's a great destination for families with a wide range of ages, and a must-do for older kids. Visit **www.waterworldcolorado.com** for more information.

Secrest Pool ☆☆☆☆☆

Courtesy Apex Parks and Recreation

6820 West 66th Avenue
Arvada, 80003
(303) 403-2538
www.apexprd.org

Hours:	12:30 PM - 6:00 PM, Monday - Friday 12:00 PM - 6:00 PM, Saturday and Sunday Open Memorial Day weekend through late August.
Admission:	Under 1: Free; Age 1-3: $1.25; Age 4-18: $4; Age 19-61: $5; Age 62+: $3.25 American Express, Discover, MasterCard, Visa, checks, and cash accepted.
Summer Pass:	$294 for two adults and two children ($236 for residents). Additional family are $25 each. Passes are also good at Lake Arbor Pool and Meyers Pool.
Parking:	Free parking lot.
Food:	A vending machine sells chips and candy. You may bring in your own food and drink. Picnic tables, beach chairs, and lawn space are provided.
Discounts:	Residents of the Apex Park and Recreation District receive discounted pricing. Punchcards for 10 or 20 visits may be purchased at a discount.

What to expect...

Secrest Pool has four separate sections. A toddler play area has zero-depth (beach) entry, geysers, an umbrella fountain, and a large play structure. The toddler area is separated from a swimming area by a rope. The swimming area reaches four feet at its deepest point. Two plunge slides drop into a pool that is five feet deep. The 90-foot water slide drops into 10 feet of water. Children must be six years old and know how to swim in order to ride the slide. Lap riding is not permitted.

The water is heated to 84 degrees and the sun does the rest. Generally four to six lifeguards are on duty. There are no safety breaks. Men's and women's locker rooms are available but do not have diaper-changing tables. Your admission is good for the entire day so you can leave and return; get your hand stamped upon departure. Secrest Pool has swim lessons for children as young as six months old. A playground with slides and a large climbing structure is next door. You must have an Apex resident card to receive the resident discount; cards can be obtained at the Apex Center (Site 65).

Note: When visiting the website click on Facilities, then Secrest Youth Park.

Other destinations within 5 miles . . .

The Arvada Center (Site 22) - 1 mile
Squiggles Playground (Site 123) - 1 mile
Majestic View Nature Center (Site 112) - 2 miles
The 73rd Avenue Theatre Company (Site 21) - 3½ miles
Lakeside Amusement Park (Site 155) - 3½ miles
Fish Den (Site 138) - 4 miles

Apex Center Indoor Pool (Site 65) and Clubhouse
Adventure Playground (Site 41) - 4½ miles
The Bookery Nook (Site 59) - 4½ miles
Rising Curtain Theatre Academy (Site 33) - 4½ miles
Wheat Ridge Recreation Center Pool (Site 77) - 5 miles

Water World

Hours:	10:00AM - 6:00PM
Admission:	Under 40" free; 40" to 47": $30.99; 48" and above: $35.99; Seniors 60+: $6.99 (tax not included).
Summer Pass:	40" to 47": $103.99; 48" and above: $109.19
Parking:	Free parking lot.
Food:	The park is filled with refreshment stands. You may bring in your own food and drink.
Discounts:	Residents of Hyland Hills or Westminster receive discounted tickets. Other discounts may be found at King Soopers, Colorado Parent Magazine online, and participating Beau Jos's pizza restaurants.

Splash at Fossil Trace ☆☆☆☆☆

Courtesy City of Golden

3151 Illinois Street
Golden, 80401
(303) 277-8700
www.splashingolden.com

Hours:	10:00 AM - 6:30 PM daily Memorial Day weekend till mid-August. 10:30 AM - 6:30 PM weekends only, mid-August till Labor Day.
Admission:	Under 2: Free; Age 2-5: $4.50; Age 6-18: $7.50; Age 19-59: $9; 60+: $7 American Express, Discover, MasterCard, Visa, checks, and cash accepted.
Summer Pass:	Full price for the highest-priced individual pass with a 50% discount for all others in the household.
Parking:	Free parking lot.
Food:	Tippers Grill sells snack foods at a reasonable price and accepts credit cards, checks, or cash. You may bring your own food; no glass or alcohol. Picnic tables are located by Tippers Grill and near the Leisure Pool.
Discounts:	Residents of Jefferson County receive discounted admission. Discounted 10-visit punchcards are available. Twilight hours are weekdays from 4:30 to close; admission is $1, $2, or $3 depending on age. Coupons may be available on their website.

What to expect. . .

Splash at Fossil Trace is a family aquatic park owned and operated by the city of Golden. Although it is smaller than most water parks, Splash still offers quite a bit for families with small children. When you first enter the park, a large 8-lane lap pool is available for anyone simply wanting to swim. Beyond the lap pool is the Splash Pad, where the fun begins.

The Leisure Pool is a zero-depth (beach) entry area that reaches a maximum depth of 2.5 feet. In the center of the Splash Pad is an enormous climbing structure with tunnels, bridges, two long water slides, fountains, and pipes spraying water in every direction. Atop the structure is a 500-gallon dumping bucket that empties every three minutes. Two tot slides on one side of the Splash Pad give smaller children a place to play and avoid the dumping bucket.

Courtesy City of Golden

The Splash Pad is a small sprayground with fountains of varying heights.

Two 150-foot **Water Slides** have no height restrictions; riders just need to be able to swim. The yellow slide is a body slide. The pink slide is a body or a tube slide. Tubes are provided, including several double tubes so people can ride together.

The Sandbox is partially shaded by a large umbrella and has plastic troughs and running water.

Several sun sails next to the Splash Pad provide some shade over the beach chairs. Generally, 8 to 10 lifeguards are on duty. Safety breaks are taken for the last 10 minutes of every hour; adults may continue to swim and use the water slides during this time. A bathhouse near the entrance of the park has two family locker rooms, each with a toilet, sink, shower, dressing area, and diaper-changing table. Unisex bathrooms by the Splash Pad also have diaper-changing tables. Lockers are provided at no charge in the bathhouse but you must bring your own lock.

Other destinations within 5 miles . . .

Heritage Square Amusement Park (Site 154) - 1½ miles
Heritage Square Music Hall (Site 30) - 1½ miles
Clear Creek Books (Site 62) - 2½ miles
Clear Creek History Park (Site 98) - 2½ miles

Foothills Art Center (Site 12) - 2½ miles
Dinosaur Ridge (Site 103) - 4 miles
Golden Community Center Leisure Pool (Site 70) - 4 miles
Lions Park (Site 109) - 4 miles

Thornton City Pool ☆☆☆☆☆

Courtesy City of Thornton

2141 East 95th Avenue
Thornton, 80229
(303) 538-7318
www.cityofthornton.net

Hours:	1:00 PM - 6:00 PM Monday - Friday (till 7:30 PM on Wednesday) 12:00 PM - 5:00 PM, Saturday and Sunday Open early June through late August.
Admission:	Under 3: Free; Age 3-12: $3; Age 13-17: $3.75; Age 18-54: $4.75; Age 55+: $3.25
Summer Pass:	MasterCard, Visa, checks, and cash accepted. $165 for four family members; available to Thornton residents only.
Parking:	Free parking lot.
Food:	You may bring in your own food; no glass or alcohol. Beach chairs and tables are provided.
Discounts:	Residents of Thornton with a Resident Recreation ID card receive discounted pricing and get free admission on Independence Day.

What to expect. . .

Your child will immediately like Thornton City Pool because it looks like a rainbow. Nine brightly-colored sun sails are set up around the pool to provide shade. The zero-depth (beach) entry has a play structure with fountains, slides, and wheels that control the flow of water. Perched atop the play structure is a large 300-gallon dumping bucket that empties every 15 minutes. A bell rings for two minutes before it tips so you have plenty of time to get out of the dumping zone, which is clearly marked. Anyone staying in the dumping zone must be sitting down when the bucket empties. The toddler zone slopes and reaches a maximum depth of three feet. Two water slides, a 241-foot body slide and a 231-foot tube slide, empty into a splashdown area that is 3.5 feet deep. Riders must know how to swim or be able to touch the bottom with their head above water. Lap riding is not permitted. A small lazy river has an arch that sprays water. Small children may sit on an adult's lap in the inner tube.

The pool is maintained at 85 degrees and then is heated more by the sun. Generally, four or more lifeguards are on duty. In addition to men's and women's locker rooms, two family locker rooms are provided, each with a toilet, sink, shower, and diaper-changing table. The family locker rooms are kept locked; you may borrow a key from the front desk. Lockers are provided but you must bring your own lock. Complimentary life jackets are available for loan from the front desk. Swim lessons are offered in the morning for children as young as six months old. Thornton City Pool is located in Thornton City Park, which also features a baseball field, a skate park, and two playgrounds.

Note: When visiting the website click on Leisure, then Recreation, then Pools and Swimming, then City Pool.

Other destinations within 5 miles . . .

Jungle Quest (Site 49) - 1 mile
Scales 'n' Tails - Northglenn (Site 139) - 3½ miles

Boondocks Fun Center (Site 151) - 4 miles
Krispy Kreme (Site 172) - 4½ miles

Weaver Hollow Park and Pool ☆☆☆☆☆

Courtesy Foothills Park Recreation District

12750 West Stanford Avenue
Morrison, 80465
(720) 981-3108
www.ifoothills.org

Hours:	10:30 AM - 6:30 PM, Monday - Thursday 10:30 AM - 5:00 PM, Friday - Sunday Open Memorial Day weekend through late August.
Admission:	Not yet walking: Free; Walking-17: $5.25; Age 18-61: $7.25; Age 62+: $6.25 Discover, MasterCard, Visa, checks, and cash accepted.
Summer Pass:	$219 for 2 household members ($169 for district residents) $30 for each additional person. Summer pass is good for all pools and recreation centers in the Foothills Park & Recreation District.
Parking:	Free parking lot.
Food:	A cash-only snack bar is open daily from 11:00 AM - 5:00 PM. You may bring your own food and drink; no glass or alcohol. Picnic tables, beach chairs, and lawn space are available.
Discounts:	Residents of the Foothills Park & Recreation District receive discounted pricing. Household daily admission is $21 ($13.50 for residents). $2 Tuesday is available to everyone. Seasonal passes and multi-visit cards may be purchased at a discount. Twilight hours are 4:30 PM - 6:30 PM, Monday through Thursday, when admission is $2 per person or $8 for a household. Dads get in free on Father's Day.

What to expect. . .

The Weaver Hollow Pool play area has zero-depth (beach) entry. It only gets to about 2.5 feet deep, until it reaches the splashdown area for the water slide, where it reaches 3.5 feet deep. The lap pool, also attached, is five feet deep. The play area has geysers, a fountain, and a small slide designed to look like a ship-wrecked pirate ship. Next to the play area is a sprayground with colored arches to run through. A water slide is available for children who are at least 48 inches tall or can pass a swim test. Lap riding is not permitted.

The pool is heated to 82 degrees and the sun takes care of the rest. Safety breaks occur for the last 10 minutes of every hour. Both the men's and women's locker rooms have diaper-changing tables. A family dressing room is available; see a staff member to get the key. Lockers are provided at no charge but you must bring your own lock. Your admission is valid for the whole day, so you may leave and come back. Just get a hand stamp when you leave or keep your wristband on. Weaver Hollow Pool is located in Weaver Hollow Park, which also features a playground and a skate park.

Note: When visiting the website, click on Programs and Facilities, then Aquatics, then Outdoor Pools.

Other destinations within 5 miles . . .

Jump Street (Site 48) - 4 miles
Bandimere Speedway (Site 142) - 4½ miles
Bear Creek Lake Park Swim Beach (Site 80) - 4½ miles

My Art Workshop (Site 54) - 4½ miles
Ridge Recreation Center Activity Pool (Site 75) - 5 miles

See Also

The Great Outdoors

According to the Green Hour website, children who regularly spend unstructured time outside play more creatively, have lower stress levels, have more active imaginations, develop stronger immune systems, and experience fewer symptoms of ADD and ADHD. Additionally, children who play outdoors have greater respect for themselves, for others, and for the environment. The Denver area offers a wide variety of choices for you and your child to enjoy the great outdoors. This chapter includes nature centers, gardens, state parks, and some of the more unique playgrounds.

Denver Botanic Gardens at Chatfield   ©Scott Dressel-Martin   Courtesy Denver Botanic Gardens

Barr Lake State Park ☆☆☆☆☆

Courtesy Barr Lake

**13401 Picadilly Road
Brighton, 80603
(303) 659-6005
www.parks.state.co.us/parks/barrlake**

Hours:	8:30 AM - 4:00 PM, Wednesday - Saturday (Nature Center) 11:00 AM - 4:00 PM, Sunday (Nature Center) The Park is open daily 5:00 AM - 10:00 PM. Hours for the Nature Center vary seasonally, with longer hours in the summer.
Admission:	$7 vehicle pass. Checks and cash accepted for self-service check-in. Discover, MasterCard, Visa, checks and cash accepted if entrance is staffed.
Annual Pass:	$70 for access to all 42 Colorado State Parks.
Parking:	Free parking.
Food:	The Nature Center sells trail mix and drinks. You may bring your own food and drink. Plenty of picnic tables, some covered, are available.

What to expect. . .

More than 350 species of birds have been spotted in Barr Lake's wildlife refuge. Numerous bald eagles live here during the winter, including a pair that stays to nest and raise its young. Raccoons, beavers, and skunks may occasionally be seen as well. Near the Nature Center is the start of Niedrach Nature Trail, a walking loop that is less than a mile long. The trail is mostly crushed gravel, but also has a boardwalk that takes you up to a lookout area with a fantastic view of the lake and mountains. Hundreds of birds were flying around on both sides of the boardwalk when we made our trek. Benches are stationed along the trail to provide an opportunity to rest or simply sit and watch the wildlife. To the northeast of the Nature Center is the Prairie Welcome Trail, which is mostly flat and approximately one mile. If you want a longer walk, the path around the lake is 8.8 miles and has several wildlife viewing stations along the way.

The Nature Center has a Family Room with comfortable couches, displays about the park's wildlife, aquariums and terrariums, puzzles, and a learning center with horns, shells, and pelts that may be touched. Kids Corner has books, drawings, and animal costumes. Naturalists will take the time to talk with you and your child, and answer any questions you may have. Near the entrance to the Nature Center is a small bookstore with books for all ages about wildlife and nature. In here, a couch sits in front of a large picture window with a bird feeder. Binoculars are provided for some indoor bird-watching.

"Every child is born a naturalist. His eyes are, by nature, open to the glories of the stars, the beauty of the flowers, and the mystery of life." ~ Anonymous

Courtesy Barr Lake

Belleview Park ☆☆☆☆☆

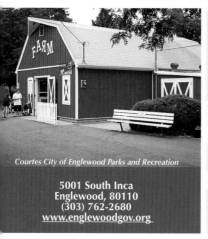

Courtes City of Englewood Parks and Recreation

5001 South Inca
Englewood, 80110
(303) 762-2680
www.englewoodgov.org

Hours: 6:00 AM - 11:00 PM daily
The miniature train and children's farm are open from Memorial Day through Labor Day. Both are closed on Monday, except for opening and closing days. Hours for the train and farm are 10:00 AM - 4:00 PM Tuesday - Saturday, and 11:00 AM - 4:00 PM on Sunday.

Admission: The Park is free!
The train and farm are $1.50 each per person on a cash-only basis.

Parking: Limited parking on Inca Street. Continue west on Belleview past Inca to get to the main parking lot.

Food: You may bring in your own food and drink.

What to expect. . .

One of the largest parks in Englewood — your child will want to spend the entire day here, particularly in the summer. The east side of the park has a large area with two playgrounds separated by a covered pavilion. The larger playground, built for older kids, has swings, monkey bars, and climbing structures. The smaller playground has climbing structures and slides sized for toddlers, plus a few rocking rides. Plenty of picnic tables are under the pavilion, and several grills are nearby as well.

Courtesy of City of Englewood Parks & Rec

The train, farm, and creek are all located on the west side of the park. Running only in the summertime, the train follows a half-mile loop around the park. It costs $1.50 per person per ride, and children under 2 are free. The Children's Farm is also $1.50 per person (no bills larger than $10) and has pigs, goats, cows, miniature horses, ducks, and chickens on loan for the summer from local farms. Feeding the animals is not allowed, but you may gently pet them if they'll let you. A sink with soap and paper towels is provided as you leave the farm. The creek is shallow enough for wading and is filled with families on a hot, summer day. Large trees provide plenty of shade, but not directly over the creek. Picnic benches and grills are also located in this area.

Wear closed-toe shoes if you plan to visit the farm. However, you may want to bring water shoes or sandals for wading in the creek, as some of the rocks can be sharp. If you are not comfortable wading in the creek but your child wants to cool off in the water, Cornerstone Park (Site 100) has a sprayground and is virtually across the street and Pirates Cove (Site 87) is next door. Bathrooms are located near the playground but do not have diaper-changing tables. The park is beautifully maintained and is large enough to not feel crowded even on very busy days.

Note: Click on Englewood Happenings, then Parks, then Park Locations.

Other destinations within 5 miles . . .

Pirates Cove Family Aquatic Center (Site 87) - next door
Cornerstone Park (Site 100) - ½ mile
The Town Hall Arts Center (Site 38) - 2 miles
Hudson Gardens (Site 108) - 2½ miles
Littleton Museum (Site 14) - 2½ miles
Scales 'n' Tails - Englewood (Site 139) - 3 miles

Skate City - Littleton (Site 175) - 3 miles
Younger Generation Players (Site 40) - 3 miles
Museum of Outdoor Arts (Site 18) - 4 miles
Carson Nature Center (Site 95) - 4½ miles
Robert F. Clement Park (Site 117) - 5 miles

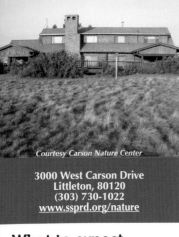

Carson Nature Center and South Platte Park ☆☆☆☆☆

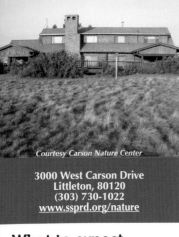

Courtesy Carson Nature Center

3000 West Carson Drive
Littleton, 80120
(303) 730-1022
www.ssprd.org/nature

Hours:	12:00 PM - 4:30 PM, Tuesday - Friday (Nature Center) 9:30 AM - 4:30 PM, Saturday and Sunday (Nature Center) The Nature Center is closed New Year's Day, Independence Day, Thanksgiving, the day after Thanksgiving, and Christmas. South Platte Park is open daily from Sunrise to Sunset.
Admission:	FREE!
Parking:	Free parking lot. Overflow parking available at the nearby RTD lot.
Food:	Eating is discouraged inside the Nature Center, but you may bring your own lunch and eat on the front porch with a scenic overlook.

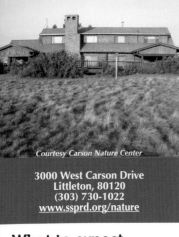

The Great Outdoors

What to expect. . .

The Carson Nature Center seems to be designed especially for children. Aquariums hold trout, bass, and perch. Terrariums with live turtles, salamanders, and snakes are positioned lower to the ground so children can easily see in. Near the terrariums, you'll discover a microscope with pre-pared slides of snakeskin, feathers, seeds, and other items you might find in nature. A section on critical wildlife areas has display cases with drawers that open and panels that lift for interactive exploration; pelts and snakeskin are available to touch. A special corner with puppets and books is near a large window with a bird feeder hanging in front of it. Perhaps the most special feature of the Carson Nature Center is the River Room. A 12-foot long sloped table with flowing water, sand, and a variety of props give your child the chance to create a town or a forest, build dams, or flood different areas, modeling the actions of a real river. Stools put the table in reach of smaller children. Join in — you just might have as much fun building as your child does!

Explorer Packs can be rented for a nominal fee to guide your outdoor exploration. The packs are geared toward school-age children but younger children may benefit too with an adult's assistance. Trails begin in front of the classroom building next door to the Nature Center. The paths are wide, clearly marked, and easy to walk on, but offer no shade at the beginning of the walk. Follow the East Trail from the classroom building to the left. You'll reach a bicycle path and a bridge. Go through the gap in the gate at the bridge and you can follow the trail along the South Platte River. The trail goes under Mineral Avenue. Look up! Cliff swallows build mud nests under this bridge. We continued to follow the trail and found a shady spot where we could sit near the river and played the "Will it Sink or Will it Float" game with sticks, rocks, leaves, and blades of grass. The East Trail is just over two miles round trip. Another trail, the Northern Wildlife Trail, also begins from the Nature Center and is a three-quarter mile loop. Whichever trail you take, be sure to pick up a Trailside Guide from the Nature Center, which points out special features of the trail along the way.

There are two ways to get into Carson Nature Center: through the door marked "Restrooms" on the side of the building near the parking lot or through the front door, which is on the opposite side of the building from the parking lot. The restrooms did not have diaper-changing tables when we visited, but they had plans to install them in both the men's and women's bathrooms.. The Carson Nature Center offers a variety of educational programming for people of all ages; some are free while others charge a fee. Programs change seasonally so check the website regularly. A very small gift shop sells puppets, books, t-shirts, postcards, and drinks to help support the education and outreach programs.

Annual Events . . .

The Stampede for Open Space is part of Littleton's Western Welcome Week, usually the second weekend in August, and offers a "Trail through Time" with a tipi, farm games, goldpanning, and more.

Other destinations within 5 miles . . .

The Hop - Littleton (Site 46) - 1½ miles
Hudson Gardens (Site 108) - 2 miles
Redstone Park (Site 116) - 3 miles
The Town Hall Arts Center (Site 38) - 3 miles
Cornerstone Park (Site 100) - 4 miles
Littleton Museum (Site 14) - 4 miles

Pirates Cove Family Aquatic Center (Site 87) - 4 miles
Skate City - Littleton (Site 175) - 4 miles
Tattered Cover - Highlands Ranch (Site 63) - 4 miles
Belleview Park (Site 94) - 4½ miles
Civic Green Park (Site 97) - 4½ miles
Denver Botanic Gardens at Chatfield (Site 102) - 5 miles

Courtesy Carson Nature Center

The Great Outdoors

City Park ☆☆☆☆☆

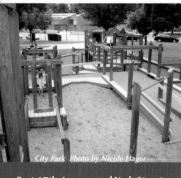

City Park Photo by Nicole Hager

East 17th Avenue and York Street
Denver, 80206
(720) 913-1311
www.denvergov.org/parks_recreation

Hours:	5:00 AM - 11:00 PM daily
Admission:	FREE!
Parking:	Free parking in the lot on the east side of the museum. Free street parking is also available but there is a 2-hour limit.
Food:	You may bring your own food and drink. Picnic tables and pavilions are widely available.

What to expect. . .

Home to Denver Zoo (Site 136), Denver Museum of Nature and Science (Site 11), two lakes, a boathouse, a lily pond, two playgrounds, a rose garden, a public golf course, and more, this 320-acre park is the most popular in the city. A memorial to Martin Luther King Jr. and the Shakespeare Elm are also located in the park. City Park is surrounded by York Street, 17th Avenue, Colorado Boulevard, and 23rd Avenue. Entrances to the park are available on each street. We entered the park at 17th Street and Esplanade.

Although the map shows two playgrounds, we only found one (remember, this park is more than 300 acres). It was a huge wooden structure with regular swings, baby swings, monkey bars, slides, rocking rides, and plenty of things to climb. The toddler section in this playground had a rail all the way around and benches at the entrance of it; children can not get out of this section without passing their parents sitting on the bench. A port-a-potty is next to the playground.

Paddleboats and boats shaped like waterfowl are available to rent in the summer at Ferril Lake, the larger of the two lakes. Hundreds of geese live here. Lots of geese means lots of geese poop, so wear closed-toe shoes. City Park has a summer concert series and a wide variety of other events throughout the year. Bathrooms are located in various areas of the park; some are flushing and some are port-a-potties but we never found any with diaper-changing tables.

Note: Click on Find a Park on the website.

Other destinations within 5 miles . . .

See Appendix I - Downtown Destinations
Kids Kourt (Site 51) - 2½ miles

The Bookies (Site 60) - 4½ miles
Four Mile Historic Park (Site 106) - 4½ miles

Courtesy City and County of Denver

Civic Green Park ☆☆☆☆☆

Courtesy Highlands Ranch Metro District

9370 Ridgeline Boulevard
Highlands Ranch, 80129
(303) 791-2710
www.highlandsranch.org/civicgreen

Hours:	5:00 AM - 11:00 PM daily The fountains run from 10:00 AM - 8:00 PM, from mid-May through Labor Day.
Admission:	FREE!
Parking:	Free street parking and a free lot across the street.
Food:	You may bring in your own food and drink. Several covered picnic shelters are available, as well as plenty of lawn space.

What to expect. . .

Located just south of the Highlands Ranch Library, Civic Green Park has become a favorite place to spend a summer evening. Free musical concerts and movies take place in the amphitheater throughout the summer. In front of the stage, children can be seen dancing and staying cool in the pop-up water fountains, which run from mid-May through Labor Day (although they may be turned off for special events). On the opposite side of the park is a playground with a variety of climbing, bouncing, and spinning structures, including a large, web-like structure. On one side of the playground is a garden oasis surrounded by a very shallow running creek, and on the other side is another fountain for water play. More kids will be found cooling off in these spots as well. Several gardens and walking paths are maintained throughout the five-acre park.

Courtesy Highlands Ranch Metro District

In addition to summer concerts and movies, art shows, dance performances, and special events take place at Civic Green (events are posted on the website). Public bathrooms with diaper-changing tables are located near the playground, behind the garden oasis and creek.

Annual Events . . .

KidFest, usually the third weekend in June, has interactive games, performances, and service providers.

Other destinations within 5 miles . . .

Tattered Cover - Highlands Ranch (Site 63) - ½ mile
Redstone Park (Site 116) - 2½ miles
The Hop - Littleton (Site 46) - 3½ miles

Pump It Up - Littleton (Site 56) - 3½ miles
Carson Nature Center (Site 95) - 4½ miles

"Whatever they grow up to be, they are still our children, and the one most important of all the things we can give to them is unconditional love. Not a love that depends on anything at all except that they are our children." ~Rosaleen Dickson

Clear Creek History Park ☆☆☆☆☆

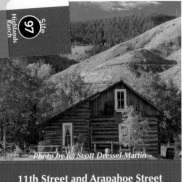

Site 97 Highlands Ranch

Photo by (c) Scott Dressel-Martin

11th Street and Arapahoe Street
Golden, 80401
(303) 278-3557
www.goldenhistorymuseums.org

Hours:	Sunrise to Sunset daily
Admission:	FREE!
Parking:	A small parking lot is at 11th and Arapahoe. Free street parking is also available nearby.
Food:	You may bring your own food and drink. A few picnic tables are located in Clear Creek History Park. More picnic tables and benches are located around the creek. Several restaurants and cafés line the creek as well.

What to expect...

Standing in the parking lot at 11th and Arapahoe and facing Clear Creek, the entrance gate to the park will be on your left. However, I would recommend that you turn right (east) and follow the paved walking path along the creek. Turn left at the corner, cross the bridge at Washington Street, turn left again, and take the path upstream. Along the way, you'll encounter several beautiful bronze sculptures, some life-sized. Benches offer a cool place to sit and admire the view. On warm days, people in rafts or inner tubes can be spotted floating down the creek. A rose garden and the Golden Library will be on your right. Eventually you'll reach another bridge that will take you to the top of Clear Creek History Park, marked by a sign that says "Welcome to the Frontier."

Courtesy Golden History Museums

Clear Creek History Park is home to many of the original buildings from the Pearce Ranch, brought here log by log and carefully rebuilt. Peering into the cabins, two-seater outhouse, blacksmith shop, one-room schoolhouse, and smokehouse will give you an idea of what life was like in Colorado in the late1800s. Many of the buildings will be open during some of the City of Golden's special events, so you can step inside and get a closer look. Visit the Events calendar on the website. A real vegetable garden and chicken coop with Dominique chickens further set the scene. Continue past the garden and you will reach the parking lot at 11th and Arapahoe, completing the loop.

The Golden Visitor Center is on the northwest corner of Washington and 10th. Stop in to see if they have any discounts or passes to any of the other Golden attractions. The creek is lined with trees, but there is very little shade in Clear Creek History Park so wear a hat or plenty of sunscreen. The only bathroom is a port-a-potty near the gate by the parking lot. Before your trip, print a free walking guide from the Clear Creek History Park page.

Other destinations within 5 miles . . .

Clear Creek Books (Site 62) - 4 blocks
Foothills Art Center (Site 12) - ½ mile
Golden Community Center Leisure Pool (Site 70) - ½ mile
Lions Park (Site 109) - ½ mile

Colorado Railroad Museum (Site 156) - 2 miles
Splash at Fossil Trace (Site 90) - 2½ miles
Heritage Square Amusement Park (Site 154) - 3 miles
Heritage Square Music Hall (Site 30) - 3 miles

Confluence Park ☆☆☆☆☆

Courtesy City and County of Denver

**2200 15th Street
Denver 80202
(720) 913-1311
www.denvergov.org/parks_recreation**

Hours:	5:00 AM - 11:00 PM daily
Admission:	FREE!
Parking:	Metered street parking is available on 23rd Street. A paid lot is north of REI.
Food:	A hot dog vendor is usually on site in the warmer months. You may also bring your own food. Bring a picnic blanket too.

What to expect. . .

Confluence Park marks the area where gold was discovered in 1858 and led to the founding and development of Denver. The park includes paved walking trails, some grassy areas, a few benches and picnic tables, and river overlooks. The main attraction, however, is where Cherry Creek meets the South Platte River. The waters rushing together create rapids and small waterfalls. You get picturesque views of nature and Downtown at the same time. From the parking areas, cross two pedestrian bridges to get to the east bank, which is shallow enough that even very young children can

Courtesy City and County of Denver

wade easily. A couple of grassy knolls near this bank, one with a small but well-kept flower garden, provide ample room for a picnic, although there is very little shade. Kayakers and inner tubers can be spotted riding the small rapids on most days. On warm Sunday nights, you might even see performers practicing fire spinning to the beat of a drum circle. Outdoor concerts and movies sponsored by the Greenway Foundation take place in the summer.

Unfortunately, there are no bathrooms in this section of the park (REI is nearby though), but it's still a great place to play and cool off in the water on a hot summer day. We spent nearly two hours at this park, and when it was time to leave, both my children begged me to stay.

Note: On their website, click on Find a Park.

Other destinations within 5 miles . . .

See Appendix I - Downtown Destinations
The Bookery Nook (Site 59) - 3 miles
Sloan's Lake Park (Site 122) - 3½ miles

Fish Den (Site 138) - 4 miles
Rising Curtain Theatre Academy (Site 33) - 4 miles
Kids Kourt (Site 51) - 4½ miles

DID YOU KNOW? With 200 parks within city limits and 14,000 acres of parks in the nearby mountains, Denver boasts the largest city park system in the nation.

The Great Outdoors

Cornerstone Park ☆☆☆☆☆

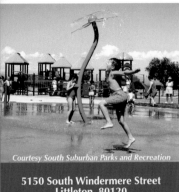

Courtesy South Suburban Parks and Recreation

**5150 South Windermere Street
Littleton, 80120
(303) 798-5131
www.ssprd.org**

Hours:	6:00 AM - 11:00 PM. The sprayground runs from 10:00 AM - 8:00 PM daily (seasonally)
Admission:	FREE!
Parking:	Free parking lot.
Food:	You may bring your own food and drink. A small picnic pavilion is next to the playground.

What to expect. . .

Cornerstone Park has a space-themed playground with a sprayground. As you drive into the park, you'll see parking at Colorado Journey, a miniature golf facility. Continue past Colorado Journey to the end of the road and you'll arrive at Cornerstone Park. The playground has a huge climbing structure with monkey bars, several slides, swings, rockets, and a mission control. Planets and stars are patterned into the rubber base. Next to the playground is a fairly large sprayground with geysers coming up from the ground and a flower showering water down. The sprayground operates daily from Memorial Day weekend through Labor Day. A shallow cement pit next to the sprayground has plenty of dirt for making mud pies. Another playground with baby swings, a teeter-totter, and smaller slides is right-sized for toddlers.

Basketball courts, a baseball field, multi-purpose fields, and a skate park are also here at Cornerstone Park on the east edge of the park. A bike path connects to Progress Park. Bathrooms are next to the picnic pavilion but do not have diaper-changing tables.

Note: Click on Facilities/Parks, then View District Parks under Parks and Trails on the webiste.

Other destinations within 5 miles . . .

Belleview Park (Site 94) - ½ mile
Pirates Cove Family Aquatic Center (Site 87) - ½ mile
Littleton Museum (Site 14) - 1½ miles
The Town Hall Arts Center (Site 38) - 1½ miles
Hudson Gardens (Site 108) - 2 miles
Skate City - Littleton (Site 175) - 2½ miles
Younger Generation Players (Site 40) - 2½ miles

Museum of Outdoor Arts (Site 18) - 3 miles
Scales 'n' Tails - Englewood (Site 139) - 3 miles
CYT Denver - Aspen Academy (Site 27) - 3½ miles
Carson Nature Center (Site 95) - 4 miles
The Hop - Littleton (Site 46) - 5 miles
Robert F. Clement Park (Site 117) - 5 miles

Denver Botanic Gardens ☆☆☆☆☆

Scott Dressel-Martin Courtesy Denver Botanic Gardens

1007 York Street
Denver, 80206
(720) 865-3500
www.botanicgardens.org

Hours:	**Winter Hours (October 1 through April 30):** 9:00 AM - 5:00 PM, daily. Closed New Year's Day, Thanksgiving, and Christmas. **Summer Hours (May 1 through September 30):** 9:00 AM - 9:00 PM, daily
Admission:	Under 4: Free; Age 4-15: $9; Age 16-64: $12.50; Age 65+: $9.50. Add $1 to each admission during Summer Hours. American Express, Discover, MasterCard, Visa, cash.
Membership:	$80 for up to six family members and includes admission to Denver Botanic Gardens at Chatfield (Site 102).
Parking:	Free parking structure across the street.
Food:	In the main building, Offshoots sells a variety of healthful choices and has tables inside. Vending machines in this building sell snacks and drinks. You may bring in your own food. Benches and picnic tables are located throughout the park.
Discounts:	Coupons can be found in the Entertainment Book. Several free days occur each year; check the website for the current year's days.

What to expect. . .

Denver Botanic Gardens, one of the top-ranked botanical gardens in the United States, is an immense 23 acres with 45 gardens and more than 32,000 plants. Plan to spend the whole day, as there is so much to see. The main building houses the three-level, jungle-like Boettcher Memorial Tropical Conservatory and the Greenroof Rooftop Garden. Throughout the rest of the property, you'll discover distinctive themed gardens, such as an ornamental grasses garden, a woodlands mosaic, and a water-smart garden. Although often busy in the summer or on free days, it is large enough that you can still find secluded, quiet spots. The pathways are very stroller-friendly and most of them are paved.

The three-acre Mordecai Children's Garden represents six different Colorado environments. Children can dig in the dirt with shovels, climb a kid-sized mountain, or splash in a creek. A miniature amphitheater, similar to Red Rocks, hosts a variety of activities, including storytimes and puppet shows. The Children's Garden has a wide, paved walking path, its own entrance, a gift shop, family-friendly bathrooms with diaper-changing stations, and a covered picnic pavilion. There is very little shade, however, so bring your sunscreen and have your child wear water-friendly shoes for creek play.

Seedlings classes, designed for children age 3 to 5, include hands-on activities, nature walks, stories, and crafts to offer a way for young children to explore the plant world. Classes are Tuesday mornings at 9:30 AM and 11:00 AM, year-round. The cost is $12; well-behaved younger siblings may attend for free.

Located in the Bonfils-Stanton Visitor Center, the large gift shop sells books, t-shirts, planters, watering cans, and other gardening items, as well as merchandise that corresponds with the current year's special exhibit (e.g., the store was stocked with dinosaur toys and books the year the special exhibit was Jurassic Gardens). Bathrooms with diaper-changing tables are located in the Visitor Center and also in the Main Building. Visit the website before your visit to see highlights of what's in bloom.

Note: Click on Our Gardens, then York Street when visiting the website.

Annual Events . . .

The Summer Concert Series is June through August. Additional fees apply.

Ghost Tours take place in October.

Blossoms of Light runs from early December till the day after New Year's Day.

Other destinations within 5 miles . . .

See Appendix I - Downtown Destinations
Kids Kourt (Site 51) - 1½ miles
Four Mile Historic Park (Site 106) - 3½ miles
The Bookies (Site 60) - 4 miles
Family Arts at DAVA (Site 44) - 5 miles

Denver Botanic Gardens at Chatfield ☆☆☆☆☆

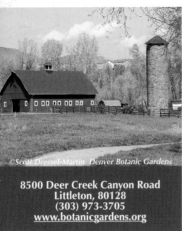

©Scott Dressel-Martin Denver Botanic Gardens

**8500 Deer Creek Canyon Road
Littleton, 80128
(303) 973-3705
www.botanicgardens.org**

Hours:	9:00 AM - 5:00 PM daily. Closed Thanksgiving Day and the day after, Christmas, and New Year's Day.
Admission:	$5.00 vehicle pass. Checks and cash accepted.
Membership:	$80 for up to six family members and includes admission to Denver Botanic Gardens at York Street (Site 101).
Parking:	Free parking lot.
Food:	You may bring your own food and drink.
Discounts:	The first Friday of most months is free.

What to expect...

Denver Botanic Gardens at Chatfield is a 750-acre nature preserve along the banks of Deer Creek. There are a number of nature trails (many of which are stroller-friendly), a wildlife observation area, and a historical farm. From the parking lot, take the path past the one-room schoolhouse and follow it to the right, and to the right again after you cross the bridge and you will come to the Deer Creek Discovery children's area. The Discovery area has a treehouse for climbing, a shallow water feature with a rock

©Scott Dressel-Martin

path across it, and a space where children can set up logs tipi-style. There are no swings or slides here, just a chance for your child to run and play outdoors in a natural setting. Follow the path beyond the treehouse and you will arrive at the historical farm. There are few animals and most of the buildings are locked, but this section can provide an educational opportunity for older children. Because of its enormous size, Denver Botanic Gardens at Chatfield is used primarily as an events venue. Quiet and spacious, it provides a peaceful forum for exploring nature.

Bathrooms are located on the side of the parking lot and do not have diaper-changing tables.

Annual Events...

The Summer Concert and Movie Series is June through August. Additional fees apply.

The Corn Maze is available for exploring on weekends in September and October. Additional activities, such as hay rides, are usually available for an additional fee.

The Pumpkin Festival occurs one weekend in October.

The Trail of Lights illuminates the garden from mid-December through early January.

Note: Click on Our Gardens, then Chatfield.

Other destinations within 5 miles...

Deer Creek Pool (Site 84) - 2½ miles
The Hop - Littleton (Site 46) - 4 miles
Fun City (Site 153) - 4 miles
Audience of One - Burgundy Theater (Site 23) - 5 miles
Carson Nature Center and South Platte Park (Site 95) - 5 miles
My Art Workshop (Site 54) - 5 miles
Redstone Park (Site 116) - 5 miles
Robert F. Clement Park (Site 117) - 5 miles

Dinosaur Ridge ☆☆☆☆☆

Courtesy Friends of Dinosaur Ridge

**16831 West Alameda Parkway
Morrison, 80465
(303) 697-3466
www.dinoridge.org**

Hours:	**Winter Hours (November through April):** 9:00 AM - 4:00 PM, Monday - Saturday 11:00 AM - 4:00 PM, Sunday **Summer Hours (May through October):** 9:00 AM - 5:00 PM daily
Admission:	FREE!
Membership:	Shuttle tickets can be purchased directly from the driver with cash, or in the gift shop with American Express, Discover, MasterCard, Visa, checks, or cash. Admission to the Exhibit Hall can be purchased at the door with cash or through the gift shop.
Parking:	Free parking lot by visitor center and free street parking near the trailhead.
Food:	The Stegosaurus Snack Shack sells delicious burritos and a variety of snack foods but is only open in the summer. You may bring in your own food and drink. Picnic tables are available near the Visitor Center.

What to expect. . .

Dinosaur Ridge is a long mountain rib that is the site of dinosaur fossils discovered in 1877. Then, dinosaur tracks were discovered in 1937 during the construction of West Alameda Parkway. In 1989, Friends of Dinosaur Ridge was established to preserve the fossils and educate the public about the natural history of the area. Dinosaur Ridge Trail has over 15 marked fossil sites, including a site with more than 300 dino footprints. The trail is paved and stroller-friendly, but it is quite steep. Round trip, the hike is about two miles and would probably take one to two hours to complete. My recommendation is to take the shuttle tour, which lasts 30-40 minutes. The knowledgeable tour guide stops at three of the fossil sites, points out fossils that you can touch, and provides more information than is posted. The shuttle is $4 per person six years and older, four- and five-year-olds are $2, and three years and under are free. Shuttles run every 40 minutes in the summer and every hour or as needed in the winter, with the last shuttle leaving an hour before the Visitor Center closes. You may also ride the shuttle to the top and walk down.

Inside the Visitor Center is a large gift shop with dinosaur-themed apparel, toys, and a huge number of books for people of all ages. A large sandbox filled with "fossils" is set up outside so children can go on their own paleo dig. Behind the Visitor Center is the Exhibit Hall, a small indoor educational museum with a variety of hands-on activities. Admission to the Exhibit Hall is only $1 per person six years and older, four- and five-year-olds are $0.50, and three years and under are free.Like the shuttle guides, the docents in the Hall are extremely knowledgeable and can offer more information than what is posted at each exhibit. The Exhibit Hall closes 30 minutes before the Visitor Center.

Wear sunscreen and comfortable shoes, especially if you plan to walk some or all of the trail. Unisex outhouses are next to the parking lot but do not have diaper-changing tables.

Annual Events . . .

Dinosaur Days take place monthly during the summer (usually the first or second Saturday).

Other destinations within 5 miles . . .

Bear Creek Lake Park Swim Beach (Site 80)- 3 miles
Bandimere Speedway (Site 142) - 3½ miles
Morrison Natural History Museum (Site 15) - 4 miles

Splash at Fossil Trace (Site 90) - 4 miles
Heritage Square Amusement Park (Site 154) - 5 miles
Heritage Square Music Hall (Site 30) - 5 miles

GO ONE STEP FURTHER - Walk Triceratops Trail, a half-mile hiking trail with footprints and other impressions left by dinosaurs, mammals, birds, and beetles maintained by Friends of Dinosaur Ridge. It is located off 6th Avenue and 19th Street in Golden. For more information, visit www.dinoridge.org/tritrail.html.

E.B. Rains Jr. Memorial Park ☆☆☆☆☆

11701 Community Center Drive
Northglenn, 80233
(303) 450-8800
www.northglenn.org/p202.html

Hours:	5:00 AM - 11:00 PM daily
Admission:	FREE!
Parking:	Free parking lot.
Food:	Happy Herbie's Hot Dogs and Brats is on site year-round (weather permitting) except for Monday. You may bring your own food and drink. Plenty of picnic tables are provided, including many right on the lake. Picnic pavilions are on a first-come, first-served basis unless they have been reserved.

What to expect. . .

Named for a fallen police officer, E.B. Rains Jr. Memorial Park truly has something for everyone. The enormous Sensory Playground has regular swings, baby swings, and even a reclining chair swing. Both the toddler play area and the play area for older children have climbing structures with bridges, ramps, tunnels, and slides. The toddler structure is shaded by a sun sail. The park also has a wavy walkway for a fun ride in a stroller or wagon, a small sprayground, hopscotch and four-square courts painted onto the sidewalk, and basketball courts.

In the center of the park is Webster Lake, an 11-acre man-made pond with a large fountain of water in the middle of it. Go fishing, take a stroll on the half-mile paved path around the lake, watch the ducks and geese swimming around, or rent a paddleboat in the summer time.

The memorial area has a triangle of flower beds and a plaque that has "Principles of Character," which is definitely worth reading. The entire park is beautifully landscaped and maintained with wide walking paths. Bathrooms are located near the playground but do not have diaper-changing tables.

Other destinations within 5 miles . . .

D.L. Parsons Theatre (Site 29) - across the street
Boondocks Fun Center (Site 151) - less than ½ mile
Krispy Kreme (Site 172) - 1 mile
Skate City - Westminster (Site 175) - 1 mile

The Hop - Thornton (Site 46) - 1½ miles
Scales 'n' Tails - Northglenn (Site 139) - 2½ miles
Jungle Quest (Site 49) - 4 miles
Little Monkey Bizness - Westminster (Site 53) - 4½ miles

Eldorado Canyon State Park ☆☆☆☆☆

Hours:	The State Park is open sunrise to sunset daily The Visitor Center is open 9:00 AM - 5:00 PM virtually every day.
Admission:	$8 vehicle pass $3 walk-in pass MasterCard, Visa, checks, and cash accepted.
Annual Pass:	$70 for access to all 42 Colorado State Parks.
Parking:	Parking included with the purchase of a vehicle pass. Parking is available at the Visitor Center and near the head of most trails.
Food:	A vending machine with drinks is located in the Visitor Center. You may bring in your own food and drink. Picnic tables are provided along the bank of South Boulder Creek and near the Visitor Center.

**9 Kneale Road
Eldorado Springs, 80025
(303) 494-3943**
www.parks.state.co.us/parks/eldoradocanyon

What to expect. . .

Eldorado Canyon State Park includes nearly 1,500 acres in a zone between the plains and the foothills. Lichen and moss live abundantly on the rock outcrops and cliffs, giving the canyon its golden hue. The park is truly stunning and quite unlike other state parks we have visited. Two of the trails in this park are particularly child-friendly. Streamside Trail, the first trail you'll come to when you enter, is an easy half-mile hike (one way) along South Boulder Creek. Fowler Trail is probably the most popular trail. It is an easy, fairly flat hike that is just under one mile (one way), the first three-quarters of a mile offers a self-guided nature walk. The brochure for the nature walk is available from the Visitor Center. The Fowler Trail connects to other trails for those who are able to do a longer hike.

The Visitor Center is located about a mile past the entrance to the park. It has a small gift shop with a variety of books and knickknacks and a wall with the Legacy and History of Eldorado Canyon. On Sundays in the summertime, puppet shows take place in the picnic area near the Visitor Center at about noon. Diaper-changing tables are available in both the men's and women's bathrooms.

The drive into the canyon is a bit odd. Artesian Drive ends where Kneale Road begins. A sign that says "El Dorado Springs" marks this road. You'll be driving on a dirt road through a small neighborhood. Keep driving; you will reach the entrance to the canyon. Eldorado Canyon is very popular in the summer months, and the picnic area usually reaches full capacity before noon. The park may also reach full vehicle capacity, in which case vehicles are not allowed into the park until space becomes available.

Climbers abound in the canyon, enjoy the show. Photo by Jim Thornburg

GO ONE STEP FURTHER If you and your child enjoy hiking, purchase *Best Easy Day Hikes Denver* and *Best Easy Day Hikes Boulder* by Tracy Salcedo. Each book offers more than 20 hikes in the area, ranked from easiest to hardest, varying from a short half-hour stroll to a full-day trip. The books are usually available for purchase in the Visitor Center of Eldorado Canyon, and can also be found online or ordered through your local bookstore.

Four Mile Historic Park ☆☆☆☆☆

Photo by Steve Crecelius Wonder Works Studio
Courtesy Four Mile Historic Park

**715 South Forest Street
Denver, 80246
(720) 865-0800
www.fourmilehistoricpark.org**

Hours:	**Winter Hours (October through March):** 12:00 PM - 4:00 PM, Wednesday - Sunday **Summer Hours (April through September(:** 12:00 PM - 4:00 PM, Wednesday - Friday 10:00 AM - 4:00 PM, Saturday and Sunday
Admission:	Under 7: Free; Age 7-17: $3; Age 18-64: $5; Age 65+: $4 American Express, Discover, MasterCard, Visa, checks, and cash accepted.
Membership:	$50 for two adults and their children under 18.
Parking:	Free parking lot.
Food:	You may bring in your own food and drink. Picnic tables are available.

What to expect. . .

Four Mile Historic Park is home to Denver's oldest standing house, and the 12-acre site serves as a window to Denver's pioneer past. The house is the centerpiece of the park, but other buildings include a carriage barn, a miner's and trapper's cabin, a re-creation of a one-room schoolhouse, a tipi, a root cellar, and others. Goats, horses, and chickens live on site. School primers and readers from the early 1900s and a reproduction of a Civil War flag with 35 stars are among the historical artifacts you will see. Weekends tend to have more activity. You can pan for gold or may get to see candles being made. My children were fascinated by the outdoor summer kitchen. I tried to explain that people used to have outdoor kitchens because they didn't have air conditioning and it would get too hot if they cooked inside, but I think this concept was lost on them.

The mission of Four Mile Historic Park is to preserve the historic buildings on this unique site. There-fore, some of the buildings are locked and climbing on any of the farm equipment is prohibited. You will still find a variety of places to explore and plenty of room to run around. Four Mile Historic Park has a meadow, a grove, and an orchard. The loop around the park is less than half a mile and, although the path is not paved, most sturdy strollers should be manageable.

Tours of the house are included in the price of admission. The tour lasts approximately 45 minutes and is not entirely stroller-friendly because it is a historic building. Horse-drawn carriage rides are available most weekends throughout the year; adults are $2 and children under 18 are $1. A children's pioneer story time is offered on the first Saturday of the month at 11:00 AM. Living History Days are held on the second Sunday of the month; demonstrations include sewing, quilting, blacksmithing, and more.

Bathrooms are located in the Bee House, the Gate House, and the Grant Family Education Center. Diaper-changing tables are available in the men's and women's bathrooms in the Education Center.

Annual Events . . .

An Old-Fashioned July 4th Celebration includes horse-drawn rides (admission fee applies).

Great Pumpkin Harvest Festival is a free two-day event in early October with scarecrow-making, caramel apples, a pumpkin patch, and wagon rides.

Colorado Christmas gives you the opportunity to roast chestnuts on an open fire in December.

Other destinations within 5 miles . . .

See Appendix I - Downtown Destinations
The Bookies (Site 60) - 1 mile

Kids Kourt (Site 51) - 2 miles
Wings Over the Rockies Museum (Site 163) - 3 miles

Great Plains Park ☆☆☆☆☆

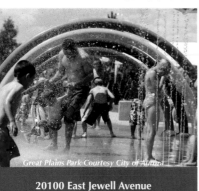

Great Plains Park Courtesy City of Aurora

**20100 East Jewell Avenue
Aurora, 80013
(303) 739-7160
www.auroragov.org**

Hours:	5:00 AM - 11:00 PM daily The sprayground runs from 10:00 AM - 8:00 PM, Memorial Day through early October, weather permitting.
Admission:	FREE!
Parking:	Free parking lot.
Food:	You may bring your own food. Picnic tables are provided.

What to expect. . .

Great Plains is a 50-acre park with a baseball field, a lot of open space, and paved biking/walking trails. There are two separate playgrounds, one for older children and one for younger kids, separated by a picnic shelter that will comfortably seat 16 people. The playground for younger children has baby swings, a climbing structure, and several rocking rides. The one for older kids has swings, a larger climbing structure with lots of dif-

Great Plains Park Courtesy City of Aurora

ferent monkey bars, and a very long "log" that can serve as a balance beam or a seesaw that holds many children at once.

This park would be similar to many neighborhood parks, except that it has a good-sized sprayground. The sprayground has a giant flower design on the floor of it, and each petal has a different water sculpture. A rainbow, water poles, and fountains that shoot up from the ground all give different opportunities for water play. In the very center of the flower, a circle of fountains shoots straight up, surrounding your child with water. A low wall with shade structures surrounds the sprayground. Swim diapers are required in the sprayground for children who are not yet potty-trained.

There are four covered picnic tables at this park, one near the sprayground, two in between the playgrounds, and one to the south of the playground atop a small hill. The main drawback to this park is that the only bathroom is a unisex outhouse. If your child is potty-trained, I would strongly encourage you to have your child use the bathroom before heading to the park.

Note: Click on Departments, then Parks, Recreation & Open Space, then Aurora Parks.

Other destinations within 5 miles . . .
Flapjacks and a Flick (Site 170) - 3½ miles
Plains Conservation Center (Site 114) - 5 miles
Skate City - Aurora (Site 175) - 5 miles

Hudson Gardens ☆☆☆☆☆

6115 South Santa Fe Drive
Littleton, 80120
(303) 797-8565
www.hudsongardens.org

Hours:	9:00 AM - 5:00 PM, Monday - Saturday 9:00 AM - 3:00 PM, Sunday
Admission:	Under 3: Free; Age 3-12: $2; Age 13-59: $5; Age 60+: $3 November through April are "contribution months" where guests choose their own admission price. American Express, Discover, MasterCard, Visa, checks and cash accepted.
Membership:	$50 for two named adults and up to four children.
Parking:	Free parking lot.
Food:	A concession stand near the Garden Railroad accepts Discover, MasterCard, Visa, checks, and cash. You may bring your own food. Tables are available in front of the concession stand and benches are located throughout the gardens.
Discounts:	Free admission on June 15 (Hudson Gardens' birthday) and September 11. Military discounts are available.

What to expect...

The Hudson Gardens has classic regional display gardens, showcasing plant life that grow well in the Rocky Mountain Region. Gardens include a rose garden, ornamental grasses, a wildflower meadow, and more. Be sure to visit the newest garden, the Plant Zoo, which features Porcupine Grass, Ostrich Fern, and other plants with animal names. The Garden Railroad runs from May through October, and features two miniature trains running through an elaborate landscape of bridges, waterfalls, and a variety of plants matching the scale of the trains. Note that this is a model railroad, not a train for

riding. Sit patiently at the Wetlands and you may spot koi, turtles, ducks, and geese. Don't miss the Water Gardens. At the far end of it are hundreds of gigantic lily pads. Sit quietly and you'll spot small frogs jumping, swimming, or resting on a lily pad. Cranes visit this area frequently. The walking path through the gardens is a 1.25-mile loop.

From May through October, you may borrow a Family Explorer Pack from the front desk (it is complimentary but you must leave your ID). There are six different packs available, but I would recommend Frog Hunt or Making Sense for toddlers and preschoolers.

The staff and volunteers at Hudson Gardens are very helpful and knowledgeable and will take the time to answer any questions you may have. Paths are wide and stroller-friendly, although an umbrella stroller would be difficult to maneuver through some sections. The gift shop in the Visitor Center sells gardening supplies, books, candles, and decorative items, as well as a few children's toys and books. Bathrooms are located behind the Visitor Center and near the Garden Railroad. The women's bathroom at the Visitor Center has a diaper-changing table.

Annual Events...

The Summer Concert Series is June through August. Additional fees apply.

Leaf Lookout, from mid-September through October, includes a visit to the pumpkin patch and journey through a straw bale maze.

Garden of Goodies is a free trick-or-treat street around the decorated Oval Garden.

Hudson Holiday is a walk-through display of lights and music in November and December.

Other destinations within 5 miles . . .

The Town Hall Arts Center (Site 38) - less than 1 mile
Skate City - Littleton (Site 175) - 1½ miles
Carson Nature Center and South Platte Park (Site 95) - 2 miles
Cornerstone Park (Site 100) - 2 miles
Littleton Museum (Site 14) - 2 miles
Pirates Cove Family Aquatic Center (Site 87) - 2 miles
Belleview Park (Site 94) - 2½ miles
The Hop - Littleton (Site 46) - 3 miles

Younger Generation Players (Site 40) - 3½ miles
Museum of Outdoor Arts (Site 18) - 4 miles
Robert F. Clement Park (Site 117) - 4 miles
Redstone Park (Site 116) - 4½ miles
Audience of One - Burgundy Theater (Site 23) - 5 miles
CYT Denver - Littleton (Site 27) - 5 miles
My Art Workshop (Site 54) - 5 miles
Scales 'n' Tails - Englewood (Site 139) - 5 miles

The Great Outdoors

Hudson Gardens

The Great Outdoors

Lions Park ☆☆☆☆☆

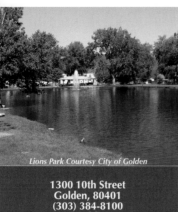

Lions Park Courtesy City of Golden

**1300 10th Street
Golden, 80401
(303) 384-8100
www.ci.golden.co.us**

Hours:	6:00 AM - 10:00 PM daily
Admission:	FREE!
Parking:	Free parking lot.
Food:	You may bring your own food. Picnic tables are available in the pavilions and throughout the park.

What to expect. . .

Located adjacent to the Golden Community Center (Site 70), Lions Park has regular swings, baby swings, a small toddler play structure, and a large play structure designed for older children. The swings are over sand and children can usually be found digging with shovels or trying to build sand castles. A horseshoe pit and a volleyball pit are next to the playground. The view of Lookout Mountain is beautiful from this park, especially if you're looking across the small man-made fishing pond. Across the street is Clear Creek, built for recreational canoeing and kayaking. Flat rock formations along the bank allow you to sit and picnic, fish, skip rocks, or be a spectator. From June through September you will frequently see kayakers, from novice to expert, maneuvering their way down the creek. Bathrooms with diaper-changing tables are located inside the Golden Community Center. Public bathrooms are also next to the baseball fields.

Annual Events . . .

Golden's **Fourth of July Celebration** is usually held at Lion's Park.

Note: On the website, click on Residents & Visitors, then Parks and Trails, then Local Parks, then Lions Park.

Other destinations within 5 miles . . .

Golden Community Center Leisure Pool (Site 70) - next door
Clear Creek Books (Site 62) - ½ mile
Clear Creek History Park (Site 98) - ½ mile
Foothills Art Center (Site 12) - ½ mile

Colorado Railroad Museum (Site 156) - 2½ miles
Splash at Fossil Trace (Site 90) - 4 miles
Heritage Square Amusement Park (Site 154) - 4½ miles
Heritage Square Music Hall (Site 30) - 4½ miles

Lions Park Courtesy City of Golden

Lookout Mountain Nature Center ☆☆☆☆☆

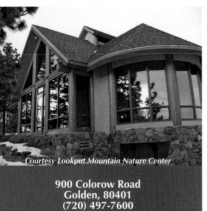
Courtesy Lookout Mountain Nature Center

Hours:	10:00 AM - 4:00 PM, Tuesday - Sunday Weekend hours are extended till 5:00 PM in the summer. The preserve is open daily 8:00 AM till dusk.
Admission:	FREE!
Parking:	Free parking lot.
Food:	Food and drinks are not allowed inside the Nature Center, but picnic tables are available in front of the building.

900 Colorow Road
Golden, 80401
(720) 497-7600
www.co.jefferson.co.us

What to expect. . .

Lookout Mountain Nature Center is located on a 134-acre preserve. The Nature Center has three themes: sustainability of the building itself (e.g., the floors are made from old boxcars), bird migration, and life in the Ponderosa Pine forest. Although the center offers programs for people of all ages, children are their primary audience. A variety of interactive exhibits teach about Colorado plant and wildlife. The Discovery Room is truly fantastic. A large nest with egg-shaped pillows is the perfect spot to cuddle with your child while reading one of the many books available. Bins with animal puppets, different types of tree bark, insects in glass cases, and plaster casts of animal tracks provide an up-close learning experience. An Observation Room has binoculars, headphones with different sounds of the forest, and more books.

Toddler Time takes place on the first and third Thursday and the first Saturday of every month at 10:15 AM and 11:15 AM. Designed for children age 2 to 5, it covers a variety of nature-related topics. Lookout Mountain Nature Center offers a variety of other family programs throughout the month. Programs change seasonally and advance registration is required for all programs, including Toddler Time, unless otherwise noted on the calendar.

The building is the head of two short, child-friendly trails, Meadow Loop and Forest Loop. Each loop is a little over half a mile. The trails connect to create a hike that is approximately 1.5 miles long and allows you to experience both environments. The loop can be followed back to the Nature Center, or taken to the Boettcher Mansion. The Boettcher Mansion was the summer home for Charles Boettcher, a prominent Denver entrepreneur. His granddaughter donated the home and 110-acre property to Jefferson County in 1968. Behind the mansion is a stone gazebo where you can sit quietly and listen to the sounds of nature.

A small gift shop area sells walking sticks, books, and other nature-related items. Bathrooms are located inside the Nature Center and diaper-changing tables are provided in both the men's and women's.

Note: Click on the A-Z index, then scroll down to Nature Center.

Other destinations within 5 miles . . .
Buffalo Bill's Museum and Grave (Site 5) - 1 mile

"As a child, one has that magical capacity to move among the many eras of the earth; to see the land as an animal does; to experience the sky from the perspective of a flower or a bee; to feel the earth quiver and breathe beneath us; to know a hundred different smells of mud and listen unselfconsciously to the soughing of the trees." ~ Valerie Andrews

Louisville Community Park ☆☆☆☆☆

Courtesy City of Louisville Parks & Recreation

**955 Bella Vista Drive
Louisville, 80027
(303) 335-4735
www.louisvilleco.gov**

Hours:	6:00 AM - 10:00 PM daily The dog park is open sunrise to sunset daily. The sprayground operates from 8:00 AM - 8:00 PM in the summer. The park is reserved Labor Day weekend for the city's Fall Festival.
Admission:	FREE!
Parking:	Free parking lot and free street parking.
Food:	You may bring your own food and drink. Pavilions with picnic tables are located near the playground. A child-sized picnic table and benches are in the train structure in the playground.

What to expect. . .

Louisville Community Park features a playground, a sprayground, and an enclosed dog park. The playground has regular swings, baby swings, and a variety of unusual geometrical-looking play equipment, and a rock structure designed to look like the entrance to a mine. The small sprayground, next to the playground, has a few fountains of varying sizes. Three bocce ball courts and a horseshoe pit are also nearby. Additionally, the park has a cemented area where children come to skate or bike, a dirt bike hill, a basketball court, and numerous paved walking paths. Bathrooms are located at the Caranci Pavilion. They do not have diaper-changing tables, but there is some counter space next to the sinks.

The dog park is entirely fenced in and features a man-made pond filled with reclaimed water. We do not have any dogs, so my children especially enjoyed watching the dogs running in and out of the water and playing with each other. The entrance to the dog park is double-gated, making it more difficult for dogs to get out or for children to get in without assistance.

More than 30 different types of trees have been planted at this park. Visit the website and click on the "Virtual Arboretum" link. You can print out a guide that shows where each type of tree is planted and includes a picture of the leaves to help you identify them. Because the park is so new, my GPS didn't recognize the address but it is located at the corner of Bella Vista Drive and County Road.

Note: Click on Services, then choose Parks and Recreation, then Parks Division.

Other destinations within 5 miles . . .
Kids Crossing Play Area (Site 50) - 3½ miles
Waneka Lake Park (Site 124) - 3½ miles
Peanut Butter Players (Site 32) - 4½ miles

Louisville Community Park Courtesy City of Louisville Parks & Recreation

Majestic View Nature Center ☆☆☆☆☆

Courtesy Majestic View Nature Center

7030 Garrison Street
Arvada, 80004
(720) 898-7405
www.arvada.org

Hours:	**Winter Hours (October through May):** 10:00 AM - 3:00 PM, Tuesday, Thursday, and Saturday. **Summer Hours (June through September):** 10:00 AM - 7:00 PM, Tuesday and Thursday 10:00 PM - 5:00 PM, Saturday The park itself is open daily from Sunrise to Sunset
Admission:	FREE!
Parking:	Free parking lot.
Food:	Food and drink are not permitted inside the Nature Center, but picnic tables with a nice view of the mountains are available in front of the Nature Center.

What to expect. . .

Majestic View Nature Center offers a large variety of hands-on activities, all with a nature, wildlife, or environmental theme. Puppets, books, giant floor puzzles, Lincoln Logs, blocks, flashcards, costumes, and other activities will keep your child engaged and entertained for hours. Taxidermy animals and displays on conservation and xeriscaping are also featured inside the 3,000 square foot building. The 82-acre park surrounding the Nature Center includes a lake and wetlands area, prairie grasses, and trails. A new conservation garden was installed in 2009 with the goal of providing elements and information that visitors can recreate in their own gardens. The garden incorporates native and water-wise vegetation, plants that support and attract birds and butterflies, and environmentally sound irrigation practices. A short, paved trail is wide enough for two strollers side by side and leads to Majestic View Community Playground, located on 72nd Avenue just west of Carr. A dirt trail can be followed down to the lake and through other areas of the park. Water fountains are located along the trail.

Although Majestic View is located in the middle of a neighborhood, the park is large enough to offer a lovely retreat from the sights and sounds of the city. Majestic View offers Nature Adventures for preschoolers on the third Saturday of the month from 11:00 - 11:45 AM. Other family-oriented programs are presented throughout the month, but most are for children 6 and older. Bathrooms inside the Nature Center have diaper-changing tables in both the men's and women's. A port-a-potty is available at the playground if you're visiting the park when the Nature Center is closed.

Note: Click on Parks and Recreation, then choose Majestic View under Environmental Education.

Annual Events . . .

Trail Day is the first Saturday in June.

Other destinations within 5 miles . . .

The Arvada Center (Site 22) - 1½ miles
Squiggles Playground (Site 123) - 1½ miles
Secrest Pool (Site 89) - 2 miles
Apex Center Indoor Pool (Site 65) - 3½ miles

Clubhouse Adventure Playground (Site 41) - 3½ miles
The 73rd Avenue Theatre Company (Site 21) - 4½ miles
Wheat Ridge Recreation Center Pool (Site 77) - 4½ miles
Lakeside Amusement Park (Site 155) - 5 miles

The Great Outdoors

Morrison Nature Center at Star K Ranch ☆☆☆☆☆

Creekside Trail
Morrison Nature Center

Courtesy City of Aurora Parks & Recreation

**16002 East Smith Road
Aurora, 80011
(303) 739-2428
www.auroragov.org/nature**

Hours:	**Fall/Winter/Spring Hours:** 12:00 PM - 4:30 PM, Wednesday - Friday 9:00 AM - 4:30 PM, Saturday and Sunday **Summer Hours:** 9:00 AM - 4:30 PM, Wednesday - Sunday The trail system is open daily sunrise to sunset.
Admission:	FREE!
Parking:	Free parking lot.
Food:	You may bring your own food and drink, but no glass. Picnic tables are provided on the patio and benches are positioned in various locations throughout the park.

What to expect. . .

The Morrison Nature Center is the portal to the 200-acre Star K Ranch natural area. Their mission is to teach about nature and wildlife, get children excited about being outdoors, and encourage everyone to be good stewards of nature. The building was the old house and garage on the ranch. Some of its original features have been kept, and you can see interesting historical photos from when it was built.

One room in the center has puppets, a coloring table, wildlife puzzles, and plenty of books for children to read. Other areas have plant and animal costumes for kids to try on, live animals to see, and educational displays. Star K Kids is a program designed specifically for children 5 and under that includes an animal puppet show and other activities. It is held at 9:30 AM and 11:00 AM most Thursdays throughout the year. Each week's theme is centered around a letter of the alphabet. For example, puppets may talk about which animals have fur and why, and then children will be invited to touch fur and feathers if the letter of the week is "F." A variety of other family events occur throughout the month. Events change every three months so check the website regularly. All events other than Star K Kids require registration. Programs may be cancelled due to lack of participants so be sure to register if you plan to attend.

The Wetland Loop Trail begins outside the Nature Center. Follow the wider path that is beyond the white tree stumps. The loop is approximately three-quarters of a mile and is mostly flat. A nice deck overlooking a pond provides a comfortable spot to watch for wildlife. The Star K Ranch is home to mule deer, turtles, beavers, song birds, great-horned owls, red-tailed hawks, and many other animals.

If you intend to walk one of the trails, bring insect repellant in addition to sunscreen, especially after a rain. I also recommend wearing closed-toe shoes. Two unisex bathrooms are located inside the Nature Center. A diaper-changing table is available in the wheelchair-accessible bathroom. A port-a-potty is available near the parking lot for use when the nature center is closed.

Other destinations within 5 miles . . .

Urban Farm (Site 133) - 4 miles
Aurora Fox Theatre (Site 24) - 5 miles

Cinema Grill (Site 167) - 5 miles
Family Arts at DAVA (Site 44) - 5 miles

Plains Conservation Center ☆☆☆☆☆

The Great Outdoors

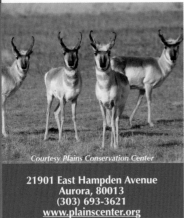

Courtesy Plains Conservation Center

21901 East Hampden Avenue
Aurora, 80013
(303) 693-3621
www.plainscenter.org

Hours:	8:00 AM - 4:00 PM, Monday - Friday 9:00 AM - 5:00 PM, Saturday
Admission:	FREE!
Membership:	$50 for the entire household. Members receive free or reduced admission for PCC classes and activities, as well as other benefits. MasterCard, Visa, checks, and cash accepted.
Parking:	Free parking.
Food:	You may bring your own food and drink. Picnic tables are provided. Bring plenty of water, especially if you are visiting in the summer.

What to expect. . .

When you visit the Plains Conservation Center, you will definitely see prairie dogs. Hundreds of them live here so at least one will be popping its head up in any direction you turn. The purpose of PCC is to reconnect people with the Colorado plains, which are multi-faceted and have changed a great deal over the years. You may visit during the week, but most of the staff will be attending to school groups or working with the Prairie Preschool Companions. Saturday is their big day for the public and you can participate in a variety of activities. Come at 9:00 and your children can take a wagon ride down to the soddies and historic farm to help with chores by watering the garden or feeding the animals. I realize this probably doesn't sound like fun to you, but city kids think it's just great! A wagon ride into the natural area is offered at 10:00 for $3 per person, but members are free. From Memorial Day to Labor Day, Sunset Safari Wagon Rides are every Saturday at 7:00 PM; most end with a marshmallow roast. Sunset Safari Wagon Rides are $5 per person, with members and children under 3 being free.

The Prairie Preschool Companions, a fun and educational program for children age 2 to 5, is every Tuesday and Wednesday from 9:00 AM - 10:00 AM. The program is held in the Front Range Building, which is the building on the left side of the drive just past the yurt (round building). The session introduces a different nature theme each week using puppets, stories, and songs. When the weather permits, the group also takes a walk or wagon ride into the natural area, the tipis, or the farm. Upon returning to the Front Range Building, children can stay and play with stuffed animals, puzzles, and musical instruments, or read a book inside a tipi. Prairie Preschool Companions is $6 per child per session, or five sessions for $25. Reservations are not required, and children must be accompanied by an adult.

Regardless of where you live, the prairie will be hotter in the summer and cooler in the winter, so dress appropriately for the temperature difference and wear closed-toe shoes. Bathrooms are located in the Front Range Building and Prairie View Shelter Center but do not have diaper-changing tables.

Annual Events . . .

Moonwalks take place throughout the year, every month on the night of the full moon.

Harvest at the Homestead is the last Saturday of September and has "the best zuke shoot" in town. The historic farm is alive with people dressed in period clothing from 1887.

Christmas in the Soddie, the first Saturday of December, celebrates Christmas with games, food, and activities from 1887.

Other destinations within 5 miles . . .
Flapjacks and a Flick (Site 170) - 2 miles
Skate City - Aurora (Site 175) - 4 miles
Great Plains Park (Site 107) - 5 miles

Courtesy Plains Conservation Center

The Great Outdoors

Red Rocks ☆☆☆☆☆

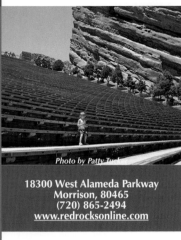

Photo by Patty Tucker

**18300 West Alameda Parkway
Morrison, 80465
(720) 865-2494
www.redrocksonline.com**

Hours:	**Visitor Center and Trading Post** 8:00 AM - 7:00 PM daily from May through September 9:00 AM - 4:00 PM daily from October through April Closed Thanksgiving and Christmas. **Park** 5:00 AM - 11:00 PM daily The amphitheater closes to the public around noon on concert days.
Admission:	FREE!
Parking:	Free parking in designated areas throughout the park. Free parking lots at the Visitor Center and at the Trading Post.
Food:	Ship Rock Grille is open daily from 10:30 AM - 2:30 PM (try a buffalo burger). A concession stand is outside of Ship Rock Grille at the Visitor Center. The Trading Post has a candy counter and a coffee shop. You may bring your own food and drink. Plenty of picnic spots are available.

What to expect. . .

Red Rocks Park is most famously known for Red Rocks Amphitheatre, the only natural geologically formed open-air theater in existence. It was once listed as one of the seven natural wonders of the world. And it does have perfect acoustics. The beautiful setting, breathtaking views, and impressive sandstone monoliths also make it an extraordinary place to spend the day. The Visitor Center has a huge gift shop with a variety of items for sale, a balcony that is perfect for bird-watching, and exhibits about the music history, geology, and paleontology of the park. Follow the road signs to the Visitor Center, then pick up a map to the rest of the park. Trails range in length and degree of difficulty. The Central Garden is paved and stroller-friendly. You can also enjoy the scenery with a drive through the park.

Live performances and outdoor movies take place in the amphitheater throughout the summer months. An additional fee applies to these events. Visit the Red Rocks website for the concert schedule, and **www.denverfilm.org** for the Film on the Rocks schedule. Men's and women's bathrooms located at the Visitor Center and the Trading Post have diaper-changing tables. The Visitor Center has a family restroom as well. Two family restrooms located on either end of the plaza at the top of the amphitheatre are open on concert days.

Other destinations within 5 miles . . .

Morrison Natural History Museum (Site 15) - 2½ miles
Bandimere Speedway (Site 142) - 4 miles
Bear Creek Lake Park Swim Beach (Site 80) - 4 miles

Heritage Square Amusement Park (Site 154) - 4 miles
Heritage Square Music Hall (Site 30) - 4 miles

Photo by Patty Tucker

Redstone Park ☆☆☆☆☆

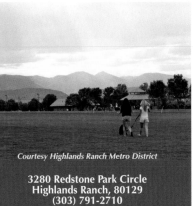
Courtesy Highlands Ranch Metro District

Hours:	5:00 AM - 11:00 PM daily
Admission:	FREE!
Parking:	Free parking lot.
Food:	You may bring your own food and drink. Several picnic pavilions with grills are in the playground area.

**3280 Redstone Park Circle
Highlands Ranch, 80129
(303) 791-2710
www.highlandsranch.org**

What to expect. . .

Expect to get dirty here. Redstone Park has a playground with regular swings, baby swings, a large climbing structure with a slide and monkey bars, strange geometrical climbing equipment, and a teeter-totter that seats four. Next to the playground is a sand and water feature. The water can be turned on to make the sand wetter (and muddier), which makes it easier to build sand castles. Shovels, pails, and other beach toys are often left behind by other children, in case you forget your own. An awning over this area provides some shade. East of the playground is a small man-made lake where you can fish off the dock or follow the dirt path around to feed the ducks.

Bathrooms located next to the playground have diaper-changing tables in both the men's and women's and are well-maintained. Redstone Park also has baseball fields, tennis courts, a batting range, and a skate park with small bowls, ramps, and a snake run. Many children enjoy being spectators for these sports if they are too young to participate.

Courtesy Highlands Ranch Metro District

Note: Once on website, click on Parks and Open Space, then Parks, then Locations, then Redstone Park.

Other destinations within 5 miles . . .

The Hop - Littleton (Site 46) - 2 miles
Tattered Cover Bookstore - Highlands Ranch (Site 63) - 2 miles
Civic Green Park (Site 97) - 2½ miles
Carson Nature Center and South Platte Park (Site 95) - 3 miles
Hudson Gardens (Site 108) - 4½ miles
Denver Botanic Gardens at Chatfield (Site 102) - 5 miles

The Great Outdoors

Robert F. Clement Park ☆☆☆☆☆

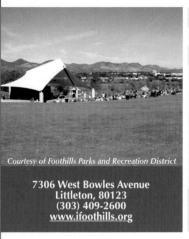

Courtesy of Foothills Parks and Recreation District

7306 West Bowles Avenue
Littleton, 80123
(303) 409-2600
www.ifoothills.org

Hours:	5:00 AM - 11:00 PM daily
Admission:	FREE!
Parking:	Free parking lot.
Food:	A concession stand is usually open in summer months. You may bring your own food and drink. Plenty of picnic shelters are available on a first-come, first-served basis unless they are reserved in advance.

What to expect. . .

Robert F. Clement Park, more commonly referred to as simply Clement Park, offers a beautiful view of the mountains, a 60-acre lake with a 1.4-mile walking path all the way around it, a skate park, tennis courts, baseball fields, batting cages, multi-purpose fields, horseshoe pits, and three separate playgrounds. Several docks with close-set rails around them jut out over the lake. Fishing is allowed with a valid license. A large open area next to the lake is the perfect spot for flying kites on a windy day. This is also where Foothills' Free Summer Entertainment Series takes place annually. On the other side of the lawn is a large playground with two separate areas, one for toddlers and one for older children. The playground has a large climbing structure with slides, tubes, and things that spin. The toddler area has baby swings and a smaller climbing structure with slides. Bathrooms are located in this area but they do not have diaper-changing tables. Across the parking lot are the baseball fields, the skate park, another playground, and more bathrooms. Benches are around the skate park if you want to be a spectator, but many of the skaters smoke cigarettes. Several paved walking paths of varying lengths run through the park, some leading to the Columbine Memorial.

Events other than the concert series take place at this park throughout the summer, so visit the Activities and Events calendar on the website before you go. Jefferson County Library is located near one of the entrances to the park, which is a nice place for a break in the heat of the day or during an afternoon rainshower.

Note: Click on Parks and Trails, then Parks, then Clement Park.

Annual Events . . .

Colorado Irish Festival takes place in July.

The Summerset Festival celebrates the end of summer every September.

Other destinations within 5 miles . . .

Audience of One - Burgundy Theater (Site 23) - 1½ miles
My Art Workshop (Site 54) - 1½ miles
Jump Street (Site 48) - 2 miles
Fun City (Site 153) - 2½ miles
Skate City - Littleton (Site 175) - 3 miles
The Town Hall Arts Center (Site 38) - 3½ miles
Hudson Gardens (Site 108) - 4 miles

Pirates Cove Family Aquatic Center (Site 87) - 4½ miles
Ridge Recreation Center Activity Pool (Site 75) - 4½ miles
Belleview Park (Site 94) 5 miles
Cornerstone Park (Site 100) - 5 miles
Deer Creek Pool (Site 84) - 5 miles
Denver Botanic Gardens at Chatfield (Site 102) - 5 miles
Littleton Museum (Site 14) - 5 miles

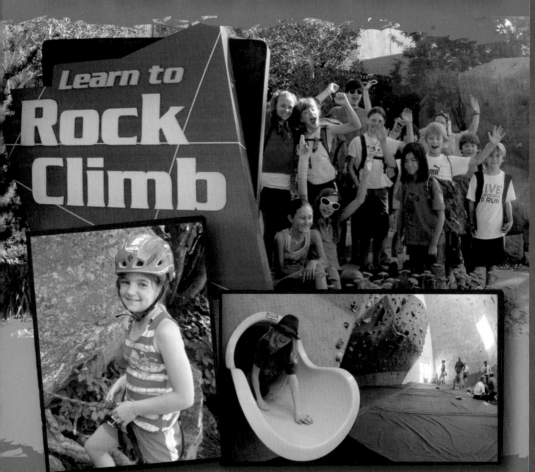

BRC

BOULDER ROCK CLUB
FUN KIDS AND FAMILY PROGRAMS

INDOOR AND OUTDOOR CLIMBING
2829 MAPLETON AVE BOULDR CO 80301
303.447.2804 WWW.TOTALCLIMBING.COM

Rocky Mountain Arsenal Wildlife Refuge ☆☆☆☆☆

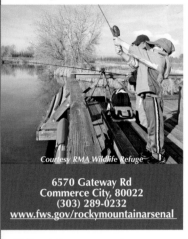
Courtesy RMA Wildlife Refuge

6570 Gateway Rd
Commerce City, 80022
(303) 289-0232
www.fws.gov/rockymountainarsenal

Hours:	7:30 AM - 4:00 PM, Tuesday, Wednesday, Saturday and Sunday (Visitor Center). Refuge hours vary throughout the year.
Admission:	FREE!
Parking:	Free parking lot.
Food:	Eating is not allowed inside the Visitor Center. Picnic tables are available behind the Visitor Center. Because it is a wildlife refuge, be sure to dispose of all your trash and do not feed any animals.

What to expect. . .

This area was once a chemical weapons manufacturing facility, then was leased to a chemical company for the production of pesticides and herbicides. Environmental cleanup began in 1987 and the 17,000 acres of open prairie is now home to nearly 300 species of animals, about 200 of which are birds. On a peak winter's evening, more than 80 eagles can be spotted roosting on the refuge. It may be one of the finest conservation success stories in history and a place where wildlife thrives.

The Refuge caters to the curiosity of children through both permanent exhibits and seasonal ones. The Discovery Room features interactive table top displays, learning stations and an area to make seasonal crafts. Young explorers can find a spot on the colorful childrens' rug to play with natural tree building blocks, seasonal puppets, a wildlife matching game or read a story with mom and dad. In the Exhibit Hall, a dress-up station provides an experience of prairie life along with other hands-on activities. On the back patio, children can "Measure Up" to wildlife by comparing their body size to some of the smallest and largest animals that live on the Refuge.

Tuesday Tots is offered the first and last Tuesday of every month from 10:00 AM - 11:00 AM for children age 3 to 6. The program introduces a different theme each month, usually animal-related and always nature-based. Programs can include hands-on activities, storytelling, puppet shows, hikes, tours, or crafts. For example, our theme was "Eagles," so the naturalist told us some facts about eagles, then read us a story. The weather was nice so we went outside and played an eagle game. Afterward, we returned to the center and each made our own coloring book that we could take home with us. The program is free but reservations are required. To get to the Refuge take I-70 to Quebec Street. Go north on Quebec Street to Prairie Parkway. Turn right and take Prairie Parkway to Gateway Road. Turn left onto Gateway Road and enter the Refuge. Restrooms are available in the newly-built "green" visitor center, and diaper-changing tables are provided in both the men's and women's. The Refuge has more than 9 miles of easy hiking trails including a half-mile hike around Lake Mary, which is great for kids. Wear closed-toe shoes if you intend to explore outside.

If you enjoy your visit to Rocky Mountain Arsenal, you may consider a trip to Two Ponds, a national wildlife refuge in Arvada (**www.fws.gov/twoponds**). It does not have a visitor center or special programs for children, but from May to September everything is in bloom and wildlife may be spotted throughout the refuge.

Annual Events . . .

Wild Walk celebrates Independence Day with a 5K or 1K walk through the Refuge. Strollers are welcome!

Refuge Round-Up celebrates National Wildlife Refuge Week with live performances, historical reenactments, hayrides, bison tours, crafts, and more. It usually takes place in October.

Other destinations within 5 miles . . .
Colorado Rapids (Site 145) - 2 miles
Urban Farm (Site 133) - 2½ miles

Courtesy Rocky Mountain Arsenal National Wildlife Refuge

4751 North Roxborough Drive
Littleton, 80125
(303) 973-3959
www.parks.state.co.us

Roxborough State Park ☆☆☆☆☆

Hours:	9:00 AM - 4:00 PM daily (Visitor Center) The Visitor Center is open till 5:00 PM in the summer months. Roxborough State Park is open daily; hours vary by month.
Admission:	$7 vehicle pass. Checks and cash accepted at the gate or for self-service check-in. A pass can be purchased at the Visitor Center using MasterCard or Visa as well.
Annual Pass:	$70 for access to all 42 Colorado State Parks.
Parking:	Free parking.
Food:	You may bring your own food and drink. Benches and picnic tables are near the Visitor Center.

What to expect. . .

Like Red Rocks (Site 115) and Garden of the Gods (Site 185), Roxborough State Park is filled with spectacular red-rock formations, which are as beautiful in the winter as in the summer. The park is also home to an abundance of birds, fox, and mule deer. The Fountain Valley Overlook, a very short trail that starts at the Visitor Center, offers a beautiful view of several red-rock formations, including the Dakota Hogback and the Lyons formation. The Fountain Valley Trail is a 2.3-mile loop that winds through both prairie and mountain habitats. Although it isn't paved, a sturdy stroller should be able to maneuver through this trail, providing there hasn't been recent rain or snow. Before you start your hike, you may want to stop by the Visitor Center and watch their DVD "Footprints of Past and Present" for information about the plant and wildlife you might see at the park. The Visitor Center also has an interactive geological exhibit with five educational stations.

Every Tuesday at 10:30 AM, Roxborough State Park hosts Kids Hour, a nature-based educational program for preschoolers. Kids Hour is led by volunteers who get to choose what they want to do with their group, so every program will be somewhat different. However, every program includes a short hike or time outside (weather permitting) and an additional activity such as a story, craft, or game. Although the program is generally for preschoolers, older siblings will often be present in the summer months and during school breaks. Kids Hour is free, but reservations are required so the volunteer can prepare for the number of children attending. When you visit, pick up the quarterly Rambles Program Guide that lists all of the programs, hikes, and activities.

The entrance gate is usually only staffed on weekends and during the summer months. A self-service check-in area provides envelopes for payment; envelopes can then be deposited into the painted metal tube next to the trash can. The Visitor Center is approximately two past the entrance gate. A short, paved path leads from the parking lot to the Visitor Center. Diaper-changing tables are provided in both the men's and women's bathrooms.

*"**Just living** is not enough," said the butterfly. "One must have sunshine, freedom, and a little flower." — Hans Christian Anderson*

The Great Outdoors

Samson Park ☆☆☆☆☆

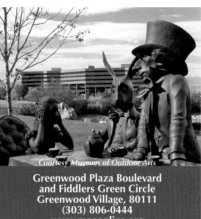

Courtesy Museum of Outdoor Arts

**Greenwood Plaza Boulevard
and Fiddlers Green Circle
Greenwood Village, 80111
(303) 806-0444
www.moaonline.org**

Hours:	Sunrise to Sunset daily
Admission:	FREE!
Parking:	Free parking lot on the east side of the park.
Food:	You may bring in your own food and drink. There are no tables in the park but there is plenty of lawn space so bring a picnic blanket too.

ireat Outdoors

What to expect. . .

Enter Samson Park from the parking lot, follow the path, and you will encounter extraordinary life-size sculptures representing characters from Alice in Wonderland. The White Rabbit, the Caterpillar, a Mad Tea Party, and others are presented in the same order that Alice met them. In another section of the park is StickWorks, large tipi-like structures made from sticks. These pieces are all part of the collection of the Museum of Outdoor Arts (Site 18). A few more of MOA's sculptures are located across the street at MCI Plaza.

The path is stroller-friendly. Some trees provide shade if you are having a picnic lunch here. Public restrooms are located next to the parking lot but do not have diaper-changing tables. Samson Park is adjacent to Comfort Dental Amphitheater (formerly Fiddlers Green), which has outdoor concerts from June through September. Go to **www.livenation.com**, choose Venues, then choose Comfort Dental Amphitheater to make sure you are not going on the same day as a concert.

Note: Click on Collection, Greenwood Village, Art Viewer Samson Park.

Other destinations within 5 miles . . .

Westlands Park (Site 126) - 1½ miles
Family Sports Center (Site 45) - 3½ miles

Little Monkey Bizness - Lone Tree (Site 53) - 3½ miles
CYT Denver - Aspen Academy (Site 27) - 5 miles

Samson Park Courtesy Museum of Outdoor Arts

Scott Carpenter Park ☆☆☆☆☆

Hours:	Sunrise to sunset daily
Admission:	FREE!
Annual Pass:	Free parking lot
Food:	You may bring your own food.

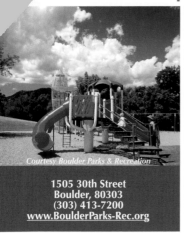

Courtesy Boulder Parks & Recreation

1505 30th Street
Boulder, 80303
(303) 413-7200
www.BoulderParks-Rec.org

What to expect. . .

This park was named to honor astronaut Scott Carpenter, a former Boulder resident. Your child will be delighted by the lunar-themed playground. Enter the park through the echo chamber, two metal discs which will give every voice a tinny sound. However, you may not be able to get your child to pause long enough to try out the echo chamber before he dashes off to the rocket ship, the hallmark of this park. The rocket ship is about four stories tall but has bars that are close together so you don't have to worry about your child falling. A slide from the first level will keep kids active as they slide down, race back up, and then repeat over and over. The playground also includes swings and a red-white-and-blue climbing structure, as well as a picnic shelter with a few benches. There is a very small toddler playground next to the picnic shelter with a space shuttle rocking ride.

The park has a large grassy expanse with plenty of room for running around, having a picnic, or lying down to take a rest. An abundance of trees, including 60 cherry trees, provide ample shade. The hill is a popular winter sledding destination. If you like to bike, paths connect to the Boulder Creek Path that runs west to Central Park and links to the Pearl Street Mall (Site 174). The south side of the park is bordered by Boulder Creek.

Scott Carpenter Pool is part of this park, but it is more suited for older children. Public bathrooms are located on the north side of the pool building. After visiting the playground, head over to the skate park on the other side of the parking lot to watch the older kids on their skateboards and inline skates. The skate park was designed with the help of Boulder skaters and even includes a graffiti wall so people can tag legally. Providing this wall really seems to work, as no graffiti can be found anywhere else in the park.

Other destinations within 5 miles . . .

Rocky Mountain Theatre for Kids (Site 3) - 1½ miles
Kids Kabaret (Site 31) - 2 miles
CU Museum of Natural History (Site 7) - 2 miles
Fiske Planetarium (Site 169) - 2 miles
Pearl St. Mall (Site 174) - 2 miles
Tebo Train (Site 160) - 2 miles

Boulder History Museum (Site 3) - 2½ miles
Colorado Music Festival (Site 25) - 2½ miles
North Boulder Recreation Center (Site 73) - 3 miles
Cottonwood Farm Pumpkin Patch (Site 129) - 4½ miles
NCAR (Site 173) - 5 miles

Sloan's Lake Park ☆☆☆☆☆

Courtesy City and County of Denver

**Sheridan Boulevard and W. 17th Avenue
Denver, 80214
(720) 913-1311
www.denvergov.org/parks_recreation**

Hours:	5:00 AM - 11:00 PM daily
Admission:	FREE!
Parking:	Free parking lots available at the boathouse and at the playground. Free street parking is available around the lake.
Food:	You may bring your own food and drink. A gazebo with picnic tables is located at the playground. More picnic tables are available at the boathouse.

What to expect. . .

Sloan's Lake Park was dry prairie land until the mid 1800s. According to legend, a farmer was beginning to dig a well and apparently dug into an aquifer because he discovered a growing lake the next morning. The lake now covers 177 acres and is a favorite spot for boaters and water skiers in northwest Denver. Swimming is allowed in the lake, but I wouldn't recommend it. The water is fine for boating

Courtesy City and County of Denver

but seemed too dirty for swimming, especially by children. A two-mile paved walking path encircles the lake. The boat launch and ranger's station is on Byron off of Sheridan Boulevard.

The playground is located at 17th and Sheridan, across the lake from the boathouse. It has regular swings, baby swings, a large climbing structure, a teeter-totter, and rocking rides. A small building next to the playground has a water fountain and bathrooms but no diaper-changing tables. Additional bathrooms are located at the ranger's station. The playground has plenty of shade around it and a great view of the lake and mountains.

Sloan's Lake Park is home to hundreds of Canadian geese. Lots of geese means lots of geese poop. The walking paths are pretty clear but it is unavoidable in the grass, so wear closed-toe shoes when you visit this park. If you plan to picnic here, eat at a picnic table. The geese seem to think a blanket on the grass is an open invitation.

Annual Events . . .

Colorado Dragon Boat Festival, held in July, celebrates Asian-American culture.

Note: Click on Find a Park.

Other destinations within 5 miles . . .

See Appendix I - Downtown Destinations
Casa Bonita (Site 165) - 1 mile
Scales 'n' Tails - Lakewood (Site 139) - 2 miles
The Bookery Nook (Site 59) - 2½ miles
Fish Den (Site 138) - 2½ miles
Lakeside Amusement Park (Site 155) - 2½ miles

Rising Curtain Theatre Academy (Site 33) - 2½ miles
Denver Puppet Theater (Site 28) - 3 miles
Lakewood Link Recreation Center Pool (Site 71) - 4½ miles
White Fence Farm (Site 178) - 5 miles

The Great Outdoors

Squiggles Playground ☆☆☆☆☆

The Arvada Center
6901 Wadsworth Boulevard
Arvada, 80003
(720) 898-7200
www.arvadacenter.org

Hours:	Sunrise to sunset daily.
Admission:	FREE!
Parking:	Free parking lot.
Food:	You may bring your own food and drink. A few picnic tables and a lot of benches are provided, or spread a blanket on the lawn.

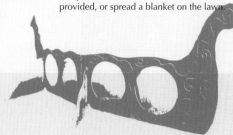

What to expect. . .

Squiggles is not your typical playground. You won't find swings or slides or teeter-totters. Instead, you'll discover a giant artist-designed sculpture named Squiggles the Sea-a-saurus that can be climbed on, crawled under, and explored. The scales are made up of different colors and designs; touch them with your eyes closed and feel the differences. Weather dependent from May to mid-September, Squiggles sprays his magic mist every hour on the hour for 10 minutes from 9:00 AM - 6:00 PM, giving everyone a chance to beat the heat. A stroller-friendly path follows along Squiggles' maze of a body. Next to Squiggles is a large, circular sand area with animal sculptures in it, looking like they're coming up out of the ground. Three of the trash cans will talk or make sounds when you push the flap to throw something away. Your child will be delighted with all the different things to see, hear, and feel.

Mr. Squiggles is the mascot of the playground.

Bathrooms are located inside the Arvada Center (Site 22); most have diaper-changing counters in the men's and women's. An art gallery and a small museum depicting the history of Arvada are also inside. The art on exhibit changes three times per year.

Other destinations within 5 miles . . .

The Arvada Center (Site 22) - same location
Secrest Pool (Site 89) - 1 mile
Majestic View Nature Center (Site 112) - 1½ miles
The 73rd Avenue Theatre Company (Site 21) - 3 miles
Apex Center Indoor Pool (Site 65) - 4 miles
Clubhouse Adventure Playground (Site 41) - 4 miles

Lakeside Amusement Park (Site 155) - 4 miles
Fish Den (Site 138) - 4½ miles
Rising Curtain Theatre Academy (Site 33) - 4½ miles
The Bookery Nook (Site 59) - 5 miles
Wheat Ridge Recreation Center Pool (Site 77) - 5 miles

Waneka Lake Park ☆☆☆☆☆

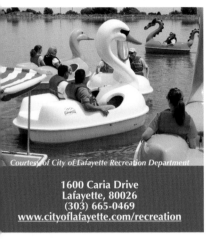

Courtesy of City of Lafayette Recreation Department

1600 Caria Drive
Lafayette, 80026
(303) 665-0469
www.cityoflafayette.com/recreation

Hours:	6:00 AM - 10:00 PM
Admission:	FREE!
Parking:	Free parking lot.
Food:	You may bring in your own food and drink. Picnic tables are provided.

What to expect. . .

This 147-acre park is one of the most popular in Lafayette. The large, shaded playground is a short distance from the lake and has different play structures for older children and for toddlers. The playground has regular swings, baby swings, a teeter-totter, a climbing wall, slides, and some more unusual features like fish stairs, tiki huts, and a two-person alligator rocking ride. Benches surround the playground, making it easy to keep an eye on your child. A small dock with rails around it is located at the front of the boathouse, offering beautiful views of the lake and mountains. Canoes and character paddleboats that look like dragons or swans can be rented from the boathouse in the summer months. The lake has a 1.2-mile walking path all the way around it. It isn't paved, but it is firmly packed dirt so most strollers could manage well. Various recreation equipment creates a Steel Challenge Course along the trail for those looking for a workout.

Waneka Lake Park has two entrances, but the west entrance is the one nearest the playground and boathouse. Public bathrooms with diaper-changing tables in both the men's and women's are located at the boathouse. In addition to a summer concert series, the City of Lafayette holds several events throughout the year at Waneka Lake Park. Current information is available on the website.

Note: Click on Waneka Lake Boathouse.

Other destinations within 5 miles . . .

Bob L. Burger Recreation Center Indoor Pool (Site 66) - 2 miles
Peanut Butter Players (Site 32) - 2 miles
World of Wonder Children's Museum (Site 20) - 3 miles

Louisville Community Park (Site 111) - 3½ miles
Cottonwood Farm Pumpkin Patch (Site 129) - 5 miles

Washington Park ☆☆☆☆☆

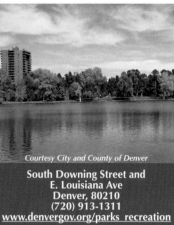

Courtesy City and County of Denver

**South Downing Street and
E. Louisiana Ave
Denver, 80210
(720) 913-1311
www.denvergov.org/parks_recreation**

Hours:	5:00 AM - 11:00 PM daily
Admission:	FREE!
Parking:	Free parking lot, free street parking, and some parking along bike path.
Food:	You may bring your own food and drink. Plenty of picnic tables are provided but very few are in the shade.

What to expect. . .

At 165 acres, Washington Park is one of the three largest parks in the Denver park system. The park is bordered by Virginia Avenue, Downing Street, Louisiana Avenue, and Franklin Street. The entrance at Downing and Exposition takes you to a parking lot near Smith Lake, the playground, and the flower garden. Wash Park, as it is more commonly known, also features a recreation center, a large meadow frequently filled with volleyball nets, a smaller lake, soccer fields, basketball and tennis courts, and walking/biking paths that wind through the park.

Smith Lake has a paved path around it and a cement pier that juts out over the water. You will often see people standing on the pier feeding the ducks and geese. The rails around the pier are wide enough for a small child to fit through, so pay close attention here. Wheel Fun Rentals next to the playground rents pedal boats, kayaks, and canoes. They also rent surreys and other cycles if you prefer to ride around the park on land. Wheel Fun is generally open daily in the summer and weekends the rest of the year if the weather is warm enough.

The large wooden playground is not shaded, but it does have two levels so the lower level is mostly protected from the sun. The playground has a large climbing structure with tunnels and bridges, rocking rides, regular swings, baby swings, and even a tire swing. A stunning garden with over 25,000 annuals is near the playground. The garden is redesigned and replanted every year around Memorial Day. Squirrels and a variety of birds live here at Wash Park, and seem to have lost their fear of people. Don't be alarmed if they join you at your picnic table. The bathrooms on this side of the park are port-a-potties. More bathrooms can be found on the other side of the park near Grasmere Lake.

Note: Click on Find a Park.

Other destinations within 5 miles . . .

See Appendix I - Downtown Destinations
The Bookies (Site 60) - 3 miles
Museum of Outdoor Arts (Site 18) - 4 miles

Scales 'n' Tails - Englewood (Site 139) - 4 miles
Four Mile Historic Park (Site 106) - 4½ miles
Kids Kourt (Site 51) - 4½ miles

Westlands Park ☆☆☆☆☆

Hours:	Dawn to dusk daily. The sprayground runs from Memorial Day weekend through Labor Day.
Admission:	FREE!
Parking:	Free parking lot.
Food:	You may bring your own food and drink. Several picnic pavilions in various areas of the park are available.

**5701 South Quebec Street
Greenwood Village, 80111
(303) 773-0252
www.greenwoodvillage.com**

What to expect. . .

Located in the middle of a business district, you may have driven past Westlands Park without even realizing it. The fun begins as soon as you arrive — enter from the parking lot and you are positioned at the top of a long slide that will take you down into the playground (a ramp and stairs are also available but it's way more fun to slide). The huge playground is separated into three play areas with swings, slides, climbing structures, monkey bars, and more to entertain children from toddlers to teens. The toddler section is mostly shaded and even includes a play house. The playground has four covered picnic tables and large, clean bathrooms with diaper-changing tables in both the men's and women's. The only drawback to the size of the playground is that it is easy to lose track of your children, especially if they are playing on different sides.

When you're ready to explore the rest of the park, you could leave the playground the same way you came in. Or you can climb up the built-in tree climbing structure near the bathrooms. Stairs are next to the tree if the climb proves too difficult for your child. More picnic benches are located at the top next to an enormous grassy field. Head south from here and you will find the lake. Go for a stroll on the paved path that encircles the lake or sit on the bench on the dock. An inline hockey rink, picnic

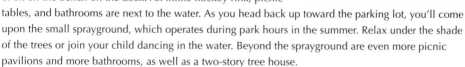

tables, and bathrooms are next to the water. As you head back up toward the parking lot, you'll come upon the small sprayground, which operates during park hours in the summer. Relax under the shade of the trees or join your child dancing in the water. Beyond the sprayground are even more picnic pavilions and more bathrooms, as well as a two-story tree house.

It is easy to see why Westlands Park was featured in *Landscape Architecture Magazine* and the *Denver Post*, and has been named the Top Playground in the Denver metro area by *5280 magazine*. Most of the walking paths are wide enough to accommodate two strollers side by side. The grounds are beautifully landscaped and maintained with lots of flowers and trees.

Note: Click on *Leisure Time*, then *Parks and Open Space*, then *Neighborhood Parks*.

Other destinations within 5 miles . . .

Samson Park (Site 120) - 1½ miles
Little Monkey Bizness - Lone Tree (Site 53) - 4 miles

Family Sports Center (Site 45) - 4½ miles
CYT Denver - Aspen Academy (Site 27) 4½ miles

See Also

Washington Park

Fun on the Farm

Because of the many farms on the outskirts of Denver (and one in the heart of the city), it is possible to expose your child to the positive values of farm life — respect for the environment, appreciation for animals and plants, the satisfaction of hard work leading to a job well done, and an understanding for where food comes from (hint: it's not the grocery store). Besides, it's fun! What child doesn't love dirt, pigs, horses, and the freedom to run around?

Courtesy Sunflower Farm

Anderson Farms Fall Festival ☆☆☆☆☆

Courtesy Anderson Farms

6728 County Road 3 ¼
Erie, 80516
(303) 828-5210
www.andersonfarms.com

Hours:	Fall Festival runs from late-September through the end of October. Hours vary daily, see website for deatils.
Admission:	Under 4: Free; Age 4-12: $10; Age 13-59: $12; Age 60+:$10 American Express, Discover, MasterCard, Visa, business checks, and cash accepted.
Parking:	Free parking lot.
Food:	Concessions such as hot dogs, chili dogs, nachos, bbq sandwiches, candy, cookies, chips, and drinks are available in the gift shop area. You may also bring in your own food and drink. No alcohol.
Discounts:	Coupons for $1-2 off the admission are usually available on their website. $2 discount with military ID.

What to expect...

Family owned and operated, Anderson Farms has been hosting its Fall Festival for well over a decade. Most activities are included in the cost of the admission, but some require an additional fee.

Included are:

Courtesy Anderson Farms

Hayrides to the Pumpkin Patch and Animal Acres
so you can pick out your own pumpkin in the Pumpkin Patch (pumpkins must be purchased) and hand feed the friendly buffalo at Animal Acres. More animal pens holding rabbits, alpacas, mules, or goats are located around the farm. You can purchase a handful of goat feed for a quarter.

The 30-Acre Corn Mazes consists of three separate mazes, ranging from 1.5 to 4 miles. Anderson Farms creates a different design every year, and they provide you with a postcard-sized picture of the maze from the air to help you navigate your way through it.

Hay Bale Maze, designed for very young children, is located next to Kiddie Korral.

Kiddie Korral has a wooden train that kids can climb on, a wooden cow that they can practice milking, a small playground, a tricycle track, and more. It's a great place for children 5 and under.

The Barrel Train is pulled by a riding lawnmower. You can fit your child on your lap if she is too small to ride alone. The ride lasts 5-10 minutes.

The Pumpkin Launcher is exactly what it sounds like and only takes place on weekends.

Additional activities may include the gourd launch, face painting, gem mining, campfire s'mores, and pony rides. Many of these are provided by outside vendors and are only available on the weekend. Other than gem mining, you must pay cash. An ATM machine is located inside the gift shop.

Visit the gift shop for gourds, Indian corn, preserves, and other food items, as well as knickknacks for the home and Halloween decorations. Picnic pavilions in front of the gift shop and in the Kiddie Korral provide some shelter from the sun or rain. Wear closed-toe shoes and bring sunscreen. Bathrooms with changing tables in both the mens and women are located in the gift shop building. Port-a-potties are located at the entrance and just outside the Kiddie Korral. If you arrive early, you may be able to borrow one of their wagons to pull your child around the farm, but bring your ow,n if you can, as they get taken quickly. You should be able to maneuver a sturdy stroller throughout the farm. Additionally, animal pens contain bunny rabbits, alpacas, mules, and goats. You can buy a handful of goat feed for a quarter.

I couldn't figure out how to enter a fraction into my GPS, but directions and a map are available on the website.

HELPFUL TIP - Go to www.pumpkinmasters.com for pumpkin carving patterns and tools, and pumpkin and Halloween links.

Courtesy Anderson Farms

Fun on the Farm

Berry Patch Farms ☆☆☆☆☆

Hours:	8:00 AM - 6:00 PM, Tuesday - Saturday from June through September 10:00 AM - 4:00 PM, Tuesday - Saturday in October 10:00 AM - 4:00 PM, Wednesday and Saturday in November
Admission:	FREE! Discover, MasterCard, Visa, checks, and cash accepted for market purchases.
Parking:	Free parking.
Food:	You may bring in your own food and drink, or purchase from their large produce store. A picnic area is available.

13785 Potomac Street
Brighton, 80601
(303) 659-5050
www.berrypatchfarms.com

What to expect. . .

Berry Patch Farms is a 40-acre family-owned working farm that grows a wide variety of organic fruits and vegetables, from "every day to gourmet." Raspberries, strawberries, carrots, cherries, currants, basil, and fresh flowers are available for picking by you and your child. Many other options are for sale in the produce stand. Check the produce section of the website to see what is currently in season. In addition to dozens of varieties of fruits and vegetables, the store sells organic coffee beans from Ethiopia, organic beef and eggs, and organic fruit brought in from the Western Slope. Jams, teas, caramel corn, salsa bags, and gift items are also available.

Come to the Country Harvest Days on Saturdays in October. They have long hay rides, face-painting, a large mural for children to color, crafts, an educational video about growing pumpkins, and Bacon Bits — the fattest pig I have ever seen. A hay bale maze is set up for kids to go through before picking a pumpkin in the pumpkin patch.

EASY BERRY COBBLER

3 tablespoons butter

8 ounces berries

½ cup sifted flour

1 teaspoon baking powder

½ cup sugar

½ cup milk

¼ teaspoon salt

In your microwave, melt butter in a 1- to 1 ½-quart baking dish. Add fruit but do not stir. In a separate bowl, combine all the remaining ingredients and spoon on top of fruit. Bake at 350° for 30-35 minutes or until golden brown.

Courtesy Berry Patch Farms

Berry Patch Farms is very child-friendly and family-oriented. Tractors with trailers will drive you to the pick-your-own produce sections. If you are picking your own, save the flowers, carrots, and basil for last so they stay fresh and don't wilt. Wear closed-toe shoes and sunscreen. Bathrooms with changing tables are available near the market and port-a-potties are located on the farm.

DID YOU KNOW? Many dentists buy back Halloween candy at $1 per pound and then send it overseas to our troops. To find a participating dentist in your area, visit www.halloweencandybuyback.com.

Cottonwood Farm Pumpkin Patch ☆☆☆☆☆

Hours:	10:00 AM - 6:00 PM daily from late September till Halloween
Admission:	FREE! American Express, Diners Club, Discover, MasterCard, Visa, checks, and cash accepted for pumpkin purchases.
Parking:	Free parking.
Food:	You may bring in your own food and drink. Covered pavilions with hay bales are provided. A barbecue restaurant is located next door. (Please note that they do not host birthday parties.)

1535 North 75th Street
Boulder, 80303
(720) 890-4766
www.cottonwoodfarms.com

What to expect. . .

Get ready for fall and for Halloween with a visit to the Cottonwood Farm Pumpkin Patch. This family-operated farm has hosted a pumpkin patch for the public for more than 10 years. Pumpkins are priced by size, from $1 to $10, so you're sure to find one that fits your budget. Several different farm animals are in pens around the property. You can not feed them, but you may pet them through the fence, if they stay within reach. Information is posted next to the pen so your child can learn a little more about the animal inside. The custom-designed corn maze is only about a mile long, making it a bit more manageable for young children, and a hay bale maze is available for the littlest children. Plenty of fall- and Halloween-themed backdrops provide great photo spots, including a giant pumpkin that says, "How tall this fall?" so you can see your child's growth over the years. The most interesting facet of Cottonwood Farm Pumpkin Patch is the antique farm equipment, including a running 1906 steam tractor engine. Information is provided near each piece of equipment, describing the age of the machine and its function.

Complimentary wagons are provided, but bring your own if you can as there is a limited number available. A produce stand is set up with plenty of pumpkins, gourds, and Indian corn. You may also pick your pumpkin from the pumpkin patch. Tractor-trailer rides are available for $3 per person. Port-a-potties are available at the edge of the parking area.

Other destinations within 5 miles . . .

Kids Kabaret (Site 31) - 2½ miles
Rocky Mountain Theatre for Kids (Site 34) - 3 miles

Scott Carpenter Park (Site 121) - 4½ miles
Waneka Lake Park (Site 124) - 5 miles

HELPFUL TIP - If you visit a corn maze closer to the end of October, more people will have tromped through it, making it easier for you to find your way through.

Rock Creek Farm U-Pick-Em Pumpkin Patch ☆☆☆☆☆

Fun on the Farm

Rock Creek Farm Photo by Gary Thomas

Hours:	9:00 AM - 6:00 PM daily from late September till Halloween
Admission:	FREE! Checks or cash accepted for purchases and for the corn mazes.
Parking:	Free parking.
Food:	You may bring your own food and drink. Drinks, caramel apples, pumpkin bread, and candy are available for purchase.
Discounts:	Coupons for $1 off corn maze admission are available on their website.

2005 South 112th Street
Broomfield, 80020
(303) 465-9565
www.rockcreekfarm.com

What to expect. . .

Follow a dirt road to over 100 acres of field where you can choose the perfect Halloween pumpkin, many of which are still on the vine. Get lost in one of three corn mazes with over five miles of paths, or keep it simple and wander through the hay bale maze. Slide down a giant inflatable slide or take pictures in front of the Halloween backdrops. Visit the goats, ponies, donkeys, and chickens, all penned. Rock Creek Farm partners with Birds of Prey Foundation, which rehabilitates hawks, eagles, and falcons that are injured in the wild. As the season gets busier, Birds of Prey does an educational presentation on these birds. Face painting is usually available on the weekends.

The corn maze has a theme which changes each year. The corn maze is free for children under 6, $5 for children 6-11, and $8 for 12 and up. Wear closed-toe shoes and plenty of sunscreen as there is virtually no shade available. If you want to cut your pumpkin from the vine, borrow shears at the front entrance. Visit their website when you return home for delicious pumpkin recipes. Also, plan to buy some of their family-recipe pumpkin bread and some of the caramel apples that have made them famous. If you are interested in decorative items, gourds and Indian corn are for sale. Port-a-potties are located near the entrance and near the corn maze.

Other destinations within 5 miles . . .
The Bay Aquatic Park (Site 79) - 3½ miles
World of Wonder Children's Museum (Site 20) - 4½ miles

DID YOU KNOW? One cup of pumpkin puree has only 1 gram of fat, 2.5 grams of protein, 7 grams of fiber, and 310% of RDA of Vitamin A!
Visit www.pumpkinnook.com/cookbook.htm for "Pumpkin Recipes and Halloween Recipes Galore!"

Rocky Mountain Pumpkin Ranch ☆☆☆☆☆

Hours:	9:00 AM - 6:00 PM, mid-July through October Days vary throughout the season; check the website.
Admission:	FREE! Discover, MasterCard, Visa, and cash accepted for market purchases.
Parking:	Free parking lot.
Food:	You may bring in your own food for the Fall Festival. Tables and chairs, some with shade umbrellas, are set up during this time.
Discounts:	Coupons for the produce market can be found on their website.

9057 Ute Highway/CO 66
Longmont, 80503
(303) 684-0087
www.rockymtnpumpkinranch.com

What to expect. . .

The Rocky Mountain Pumpkin Ranch is the largest organic farm in Boulder County and the second largest in the state of Colorado. Specializing in farm-fresh, hand-picked, certified-organic produce, Rocky Mountain Pumpkin Ranch grows over 100 different varieties of vegetables. In addition to the fruits and vegetables, the market also sells locally produced honey, juices and ciders, a large variety of canned goods, several different butters (peach, apple, cherry, pumpkin), roasted chilies, and homemade breads. Visit their website to see what is currently available. Rather than visiting their Open Door Market, you can also find their products at the Boulder or Longmont Farmer's Markets.

HEIDI'S EASY MINI PUMPKIN MUFFINS

1 - 15oz can of pumpkin

1 box of dry cake mix (white, chocolate, spice or butter golden work well).

1/2 - 3/4 bag of chocolate chips

Preheat oven to 350°. Mix pumpkin and dry cake mix together. Add chocolate chips to your liking. Spoon into the mini muffin tins, fill them pretty full, as they don't really rise. (regular size muffins don't seem to work as well). Bake for 8-10 min., or until toothpick comes out clean.

Recipe from: www.pumpkinnook.com/cookbook.htm

In the month of October, the Rocky Mountain Pumpkin Ranch is open daily for its Fall Festival, regardless of weather. A visit to the Bee House (morning only), hay maze, petting zoo, pick your own pumpkin, and paint your own pumpkin are available each day. Complimentary wagons are provided. On the weekends, outside vendors offer additional activities like face painting, pony rides, inflatable bouncers, train rides, and more. These additional activities may cost from $1 - $5, generally on a cash basis. Seating and gathering areas are provided for you to enjoy a picnic lunch. Port-a-potties are available in several locations on the farm.

Other destinations within 5 miles . . .

Sunflower Farm ☆☆☆☆☆

11150 Prospect Road
Longmont, 80504
(303) 774-8001
www.sunflowerfarminfo.com

Hours:	10:00 AM - 3:00 PM, Saturdays from May through November 10:00 AM - 1:00 PM, Monday - Friday in September and October 10:00 AM - 3:00 PM, Sundays in September and October
Admission:	Age 1+: $5 Monday - Friday, $6 on Saturday, and $8 on Sunday. Under 12 months is always free. Discover, MasterCard, Visa, checks, and cash accepted.
Parking:	Free parking.
Food:	You may bring your own food and drink. Benches and picnic tables are all over the property. On the weekends, an outside vendor sells hot dogs, brats, and drinks (cash only).
Discounts:	Buy ten passes for $50, good for Saturday admission only.

What to expect. . .

If you were one of the lucky children who got to visit your grandparents' farm in the summer, a trip to Sunflower Farm is a lot like that. Visit llamas, goats, sheep, cows, horses, and mules in their pens. Chickens roam freely. You'll usually find baby animals on the farm too (we saw piglets and baby mules). Near the goat, sheep, and llama pens, you'll discover buckets of corn that you can toss in to feed the animals. Hand sanitizer is also near each pen. Play with shovels, pails, and trucks in the large sand pit. Climb

Courtesy Sunflower Farm

the tractors. Explore the giant treehouse. Climb on or run around in the stacks of hay bales. Lounge in the hammocks, soar on a zipline, or spin on the tire swings. Grab a helmet and skate or ride a tricycle. All these activities and more are included in the admission price. Sunday is slightly more expensive because they have live music and wagon hayrides. Autumn is a great time to visit, as the farm is alive with sunflowers and pumpkins.

Look up into the silo and you may spot the barn owl who lives next to the ladder at the top. Unisex bathrooms are available but they do not have diaper-changing tables. A wood barn has sheltered tables and chairs in case of inclement weather or too much sun. Sunflower Farm t-shirts are available for purchase, and pumpkins are sold in October. My GPS was a little off upon arrival. A stone wall that says Sunflower Farm marks the turn.

Other destinations within 5 miles . . .

Kanemoto Park and Pool (Site 86) - 2 miles
Longmont Recreation Center Leisure Pool (Site 72) - 2 miles
B&C BounceTown (Site 42) - 2½ miles

Itty Bitty City (Site 47) - 3½ miles
Roosevelt Activity Pool (Site 88) - 4 miles

GO ONE STEP FURTHER - Find songs, poems, and activities about farm life at www.kinderkorner.com/farm.html.

FARMERS ARE THE HEART OF HORIZON™

Ever since Horizon® began 20 years ago, farmers have been at the heart of our success. Horizon is proud to partner with over 600 organic family farms across the country.

Griffin Farm, Ferndale, CA

Goelz Family Organic Farm, Maple Lake, MN

Wengerd Farm, Ovid, NY

Learn more at **www.HorizonOrganic.com**

Visit us on Facebook! www.facebook.com/Horizon

Urban Farm ☆☆☆☆☆

Hours:	10:00 AM - 1:00 PM, Saturday if the weather is permitting
Admission:	Children: $5; Adults: Free Checks or cash accepted.
Membership:	$35 for two adults and their children; membership runs the calendar year.
Parking:	Free parking lot.
Food:	You may bring in your own lunch and picnic by the garden.

10200 Smith Road
Denver, 80239
(303) 307-9332
www.theurbanfarm.org

What to expect...

Founded in 1993 as Embracing Horses, an after-school program for 15 inner-city children, The Urban Farm has expanded to provide agricultural and environmental education to thousands of urban children, youth, and their families. During the week, it runs 4H programs, riding lessons, and private educational activities for its members and participants, but the farm is open to the public on Saturdays throughout the year. The family that runs the farm believes it is important for children who live in the city to learn about and understand the role that agriculture plays in the world.

Begin your visit at the office and educational building, where you will be asked to fill out and sign a waiver. Particularly in the winter and early spring, you may find ducklings, chicks, or baby rabbits living inside the building. Tours of the farm are generally self-guided, but they are happy to escort you if they have available staff. You may see riding lessons in progress or people tending to their gardens (The Urban Farm rents plots of land to people who would like to grow their own produce). You will certainly see a variety of farm animals, including alpacas, guinea fowl, cows, horses, chickens, miniature horses and donkeys, and goats. If she's enjoying the outdoors, you'll also meet Miss Piggle Wiggle, the farm's 400-pound pig. The National Weather Service is located on the property; occasionally you will witness their balloons being released into the sky.

A visit to The Urban Farm allows you to experience true farm life without having to drive out of the city. Occasionally, the farm hosts horse shows and family fun days; check the website calendar for the current year's events. The Urban Farm is not stroller-friendly. Some of the animals roam freely around the property; I strongly recommended that you wear closed-toe shoes. Bathrooms are located in the office and educational building, but they do not have diaper-changing tables.

Other destinations within 5 miles . . .

Rocky Mountain Arsenal Wildlife Refuge (Site 118) - 2½ miles
Morrison Nature Center at Star K Ranch (Site 113) - 4 miles
Aurora Fox Theatre (Site 24) - 4½ miles

Colorado Rapids (Site 145) - 4½ miles
Family Arts at DAVA (Site 44) - 4½ miles

See Also

Clear Creek History Park (Site 98)

Ferrara's Happy Apple Farm (Site 183)

Four Mile Historic Park (Site 106)

Littleton Museum (Site 14)

Rock Ledge Ranch (Site 190)

White Fence Farm (Site 178)

Creatures Great and Small

Children seem to be born with a deep love of animals. They lack the judgment and the fears that sometimes develop as we grow older. From insects or water creatures to exotic animals or petting zoos, the Denver area has it all. Choose your favorite and get a membership if one is available. Chances are your child will want to visit again and again and again and . . .

Denver Zoo Courtesy Denver Zoo

The Butterfly Pavilion ☆☆☆☆☆

Courtesy The Butterfly Pavilion

6252 West 104th Avenue
Westminster, 80020
(303) 469-5441
www.butterflies.org

Hours:	9:00 AM - 5:00 PM daily (last entrance at 4:15 PM) Closed Thanksgiving and Christmas.
Admission:	Under 2: Free; Age 2-12: $5.50; Age 13-64: $8.50; Age 65+: $6.50. American Express, Discover, MasterCard, Visa, checks and cash accepted.
Membership:	$65 for two adults and their children up to age 12.
Parking:	Free parking lot.
Food:	Food and drink are permitted inside the building but not in the rainforest conservatory. Picnic tables are located outside.
Discounts:	Coupons can be found in the Entertainment Book, the Chinook Book, and on ColoradoKids.com.

What to expect. . .

The Butterfly Pavilion is an invertebrate zoo that allows you to see and interact with live animals from around the world. They aim to educate the public about the importance of invertebrates, which make up about 97% of the species on our planet, and habitat conservation. It is divided into four main sections:

Crawl-a-See-Em is a room containing dozens of terrariums with beetles, roaches, scorpions, millipedes, leaf insects, and many spiders living in Tarantula Tower. Children (and adults) have an opportunity to hold Rosie, their Chilean Rose Hair tarantula. Several step stools are available so your child has an opportunity to get eye-to-eye with the critters living in here.

Water's Edge features fish, jellies, sea stars, and other sea creatures. Two large tanks make up the petting zoo where you and your child can gently touch horseshoe crabs, sea urchins, and sea stars.

Wings of the Tropics is a 3,000 square foot enclosed rainforest that is home to more than 1,200 live butterflies and moths of all colors and sizes. The chrysalis viewing area is located near the exit of this room. The Butterfly Pavilion receives 600 - 1,200 chrysalides each week from nine sustainable butterfly farms around the world so they are all in different stages of life here. Watch patiently for a few moments and you will see several of them moving; you may even be as lucky as we were and see a butterfly emerge from one of them. Butterfly Encounters, with a live butterfly release, takes place daily at 12:30 PM and 3:30 PM. Although you are not allowed to touch the butterflies, you could have one land on you, especially if you are wearing red.

The Traveling Exhibit Hall changes approximately every six months, and is always bug-themed. The constant in this room are the display cases holding hundreds of varieties of honeybees, scarabs, grasshoppers, cicadas, butterflies, and more.

When the weather is nice, take a walk outside through the Discovery Garden with butterfly gardens, Gazebos, and Nature Trail. The Nature Trail is about a 1.5-mile loop and we saw several prairie dogs along the way. The best time to visit the Discovery Garden is June through September, when everything is in bloom. April and May are also nice, but tend to have a large amount of school groups visiting.

Bathrooms with diaper-changing tables are located next to the Crawl-a-See-Em room and in the back of the Traveling Exhibit Hall. A family restroom is also available in the back of the Traveling Exhibit Hall. The entire facility is stroller-friendly. Visit the large gift shop if you're looking for anything bug-related, from toys to shirts to books to garden decor.

Annual Events . . .

Bug-a-Rhythm, in January, is all about sound and music within the bug world.

Plant Conservation Day takes place in May.

Insectival lasts for two days in July to celebrate the Butterfly Pavilion's birthday.

Bug-a-boo is a Halloween event that takes place the weekend before Halloween.

Living Lights is held in December in celebration of the holiday season.

Other destinations within 5 miles . . .

Scales 'n' Tails - Northglenn (Site 139) - 3½ miles
The Bay Aquatic Park (Site 79) - 4 miles

Paul Derda Indoor Pool (Site 74) - 5 miles
Kids Zone (Site 52) - 5 miles

 **DID YOU KNOW?** For every person on earth, there are nearly 200 million insects. There are more beetles than any other animal. This is actually good news. Without bugs, our ecosystem would shut down: many animals would have nothing to eat, our rivers would become infested with algae, and flowers would go unpollinated.

Courtesy The Butterfly Pavilion

Colorado Horse Park ☆☆☆☆☆

Site 134 Westminster

Halloween with Horses. Photo by Kevin Kertz
Courtesy of Colorado Horse Park

7522 South Pinery Drive
Parker, 80134
(303) 841-5550
www.coloradohorsepark.com

Hours:	Check the website for upcoming events.
Admission:	FREE!
Parking:	Free parking lot by the main building. Limited parking by the arenas.
Food:	You may bring in your own food and drink.

What to expect. . .

The Colorado Horse Park's purpose is to promote amateur equestrian athletics. Additionally, they work to preserve open space and assist in fundraising for a number of charitable organizations. The Colorado Horse Park hosts competitive equestrian shows and events throughout the year, but most activities occur during the summer months. Although the events are for the competitors, they are open to the public.

A covered area, usually set up with tables and chairs, sits between the two arenas. You can see both arenas from this vantage point, and you may also eat in this area. For a closer look, you can sit in the stands, but these are uncovered. The main building has bathrooms without changing tables.

Annual Events . . .

Halloween with Horses is held on a Saturday in mid-October and includes pony rides, face painting, a pumpkin patch, horses in costume, and a costume contest for the guests. Admission fee applies.

SOME OF OUR FAVORITE HORSE BOOKS:

For babies to preschoolers:
Giddy Up! Let's Ride! by Flora McDonnell
Robert the Rose Horse by Joan Heilbroner
The Wild Little Horse by Rita Gray

For early school-age children:
A Horse Named Doodlebug by Irene Brady
Black Beauty by Anna Sewell
My Friend Flicka by Mary O'Hara
Hot on the Range by R.D. Jentsch

For older school-age children:
The Black Stallion by Walter Farley
The Winnie the Horse Gentler series by Dandi Daley Mackall

Courtesy Colorado Horse Park

Denver Zoo ☆☆☆☆☆

Courtesy Denver Zoo

2300 Steele Street
Denver, 80205
(303) 376-4800
www.denverzoo.org

Hours:	10:00 AM - 4:00 PM, daily Nov. 1 through Feb. 28 9:00 AM - 5:00 PM daily from Mar. 1 through Oct. 31
Admission:	Under 3: Free; Age 3-11: $6; Age 12-64: $10; Age 65+: $8 (winter) Under 3: Free; Age 3-11: $8; Age 12-64: $13; Age 65+: $10 (summer) American Express, Discover, MasterCard, Visa, and cash accepted.
Annual Pass:	$90 for two named adults and their children under 18.
Parking:	Free parking.
Food:	The zoo has three restaurants and several concession stands. Samburu Grille seems to have the healthiest options. You may bring your own food and drink. There are plenty of places to picnic.
Discounts:	There are eight free days each year; check the website for the current year's schedule.

What to expect. . .

Denver Zoo houses 3,800 animals representing 650 species from North and South America, Africa, Asia, and Australia. Some of the animals are among the world's rarest and most unusual, such as the Komodo dragon and the okapi. A few of the zoo's special exhibits are:

Bear Mountain was the first natural habitat of its kind in North America.

Predator Ridge has several species from Africa, including lions and hyenas.

Tropical Discovery is an indoor rainforest featuring fish and reptiles.

Primate Panorama is seven acres of natural-like habitat for gorillas and monkeys.

Bird World has nearly 200 species of birds.

Special shows, demonstrations, and feedings scheduled throughout the day in various areas of the zoo offer visitors the chance to get up close and learn more about the featured animals. Near

Courtesy Denver Zoo

the elephants, a nursery is home to newborn animals until they are ready to be returned to their exhibit. During the summer, take a ride on the Pioneer Train and the Endangered Species Carousel. Each is $2 to ride, and children under 3 are free.

Bathrooms are located throughout the zoo, all with diaper-changing tables. Family restrooms near the entrance offer a comfortable, private place for breastfeeding. The gift shop is enormous. In addition to animal-themed gifts, toys, apparel, and novelties, you can also purchase sunscreen, disposable cameras, and batteries.

Annual Events . . .

Earth Day is celebrated in April.

Boo at the Zoo is held over two days the weekend of Halloween.

Zoo Lights is open during most December evenings. Additional fee applies.

Other destinations within 5 miles . . .

See Appendix I - Downtown Destinations
Kids Kourt (Site 51) - 3½ miles
Four Mile Historic Park (Site 106) - 4 miles

The Bookies (Site 60) - 4½ miles
Family Arts at DAVA (Site 44) - 5 miles

DID YOU KNOW? Most large pet stores have fish, birds, and small animals like rabbits and guinea pigs. Visit **www.petco.com** or **www.petsmart.com** to find a store near you, or visit the pet store at the nearest mall (most malls have one). Just be prepared . . . you may come home with a new family member.

Courtesy Denver Zoo

Downtown Aquarium ☆☆☆☆☆

Courtesy of Downtown Aquarium

700 Water Street
Denver, 80211
(303) 561-4450
www.downtownaquariumdenver.com

Hours:	10:00 AM - 9:00 PM, Sunday - Thursday 10:00 AM - 9:30 PM, Friday and Saturday Closed on Christmas Day
Admission:	Under 3: Free; Age 3-11: $9.99; Age 12-64: $15.99; Age 65+: $14.99 American Express, Discover, MasterCard, Visa, and cash accepted.
Annual Pass:	$145 for four people.
Parking:	Paid lots are available next to the aquarium and across the street.
Food:	Dine in the Aquarium Restaurant or at the snack bar. You may bring your own food and eat in the patio area just outside the concession stand. Picnic tables are behind the aquarium near Sharkey's Fun Zone.
Discounts:	Sign up for the Tank E-club on the website or become a fan on Facebook to get special promotions and coupons. Come after 5:00 PM for Friday Family Nights and children under 10 get $5 admission.

What to expect. . .

Downtown Aquarium has over one million gallons of exhibit space containing more than 500 species of fish. It is an immersive, sensory experience with background sounds, animatronic animals, and intricate detailing in every section. Look all around as you follow the path through the aquarium, as you will find tanks over and under you, as well as curves in the glass that allow you to step in and have the sensation that you are in the tank. There are nine themed exhibits, each with a variety of water creatures, as well as other special animals or displays:

North America features creatures found on our continent, including a snapping turtle and otters.

In the Desert has a flash-flood simulator, as well as lizards, snakes, and spiders.

Under the Sea simulates a coral reef habitat. Look for the 250-pound fish in one of the tanks.

At the Wharf is home to sea stars, anemones, and potbelly seahorses.

The Rainforest features piranhas, colorful fish, and tigers.

The Coral Lagoon has colorful fish in low aquariums so children can have a great view.

The Sunken Temple teaches about sharks and conservation and has unusual fish like unicorn fish.

The Shipwreck is where the big sharks live.

At the Beach has stingrays that you can try to feed.

Scheduled feeding times are posted. The archer fish feeding is really entertaining, if you can time it right. Also, the otters spend much of their day napping, so their feeding is when you are most likely to see them active, although it is also the most crowded time to be in the North America section. Between the tigers and the archer fish is a No Bones section, where animals such as sea stars and urchins may be available for gentle touching.

One of the Aquarium's best kept secrets is a separate building located behind the Aquarium. Inside is Sharkey's Fun Zone, a soft foam-molded ocean-themed indoor playground for children under 48 inches. Children can climb over, under, and around an octopus, a shark, a whale, and other water creatures. Sharkey's Fun Zone is open at the same time as the Aquarium. It is completely free of charge — you don't even need to purchase a ticket to the Aquarium to play in here — but it does not have a bathroom. The floor is extra cushioned, and benches and cubbies are installed around the edges of the room. Stroller parking is available outside the entrance. When the weather is warm, Downtown

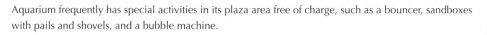
Aquarium frequently has special activities in its plaza area free of charge, such as a bouncer, sandboxes with pails and shovels, and a bubble machine.

The Aquarium Restaurant is on the lower level of the aquarium. A 150,000-gallon tank in the center of the restaurant offers close-up views of black tip reef sharks, groupers, and schooling jacks. Come for Friday Family Nights from 5:00 PM until close and get a $1.99 Kids Meal for children 10 and under with each adult meal purchased. Kids admission for the aquarium is only $5 and adults receive a discounted admission with an Aquarium Restaurant receipt. Parking for the lot across the street is validated after 6:00 PM with a restaurant receipt.

Men's and women's bathrooms with diaper-changing tables are available on the first floor behind the ballroom. A family bathroom is here as well. You may want to visit before you begin, especially if you are potty-training, as the next bathroom is halfway through between *Under the Sea* and *At the Wharf*. It is a unisex bathroom and also has a diaper-changing table. The entire facility is stroller-friendly with wide walking paths.

Other destinations within 5 miles . . .

See Appendix I - Downtown Destinations
The Bookery Nook (Site 59) - 3½ miles
Sloan's Lake Park (Site 122) - 3½ miles

Fish Den (Site 138) - 4 miles
Rising Curtain Theatre Academy (Site 33) - 4½ miles
Kids Kourt (Site 51) - 5 miles

Courtesy of Downtown Aquarium

Creatures Great and Small

Site
138
Denver

Creatures Great and Small

Fish Den ☆☆☆☆☆

Hours:	11:00 AM - 7:00 PM, Monday - Thursday 10:00 AM - 9:00 PM, Friday and Saturday 11:00 AM - 5:00 PM, Sunday
Admission:	FREE!
Parking:	Free parking lot.

5055 West 44th Avenue
Denver, 80212
(303) 458-0376
www.fishdendenver.com

What to expect. . .

For very young children, a trip to a fish store can be just as much fun as a visit to an aquarium. Fish Den is one of the oldest fish stores in Colorado. With over 100 fresh water tanks, 140 salt water tanks, and thousands of fish to look at, your child will have plenty to see. The staff is friendly and knowledgeable. If they are not too busy, your child may even have a chance to ask some questions.

Other destinations within 5 miles . . .

See Appendix I - Downtown Destinations
The Bookery Nook (Site 59) - ½ mile
Lakeside Amusement Park (Site 155) - ½ mile
Rising Curtain Theatre Academy (Site 33) - 1½ miles
Denver Puppet Theater (Site 28) - 2 miles
Sloan's Lake Park (Site 122) - 2½ miles
Casa Bonita (Site 165) - 3½ miles

Wheat Ridge Recreation Center Pool (Site 77) - 3½ miles
Scales 'n' Tails - Lakewood (Site 139) - 4 miles
Secrest Pool (Site 89) - 4 miles
The Arvada Center (Site 22) - 4½ miles
Squiggles Playground (Site 123) - 4½ miles
The 73rd Avenue Theatre Company (Site 21) - 5 miles

DID YOU KNOW?

• Fish have been on the earth for more than 450 million years, long before dinosaurs roamed the earth.

• There are more species of fish than all the species of amphibians, reptiles, birds, and mammals combined.

• The largest fish is the great whale shark, which can reach 50 feet in length.

• The smallest fish is the Philippine goby, which is less than 1/3 of an inch fully grown.

• Tropical fish are one of the most popular pets in the United States.

Scales 'n' Tails ☆☆☆☆☆

www.scalesntails.com

Hours:	10:00 AM - 8:00 PM, Sunday - Thursday
	10:00 PM - 9:00 PM, Friday and Sunday
Admission:	FREE!
Parking:	Free parking at all locations.

Multiple Locations. . .

1695 Wadsworth Boulevard,
Lakewood, 80214
(303) 462-0039

1470 West 104th Avenue,
Northglenn, 80234
(303) 450-6169

3928 South Broadway
Englewood, 80113
(303) 761-5087

What to expect. . .

Scales 'n' Tails is a reptile and exotic animal pet shop that welcomes visitors. Generally, they have between 80 and 150 animals in their stores, including lizards, snakes, turtles, tarantulas, scorpions, and centipedes. They may also have some more unusual animals like hedgehogs, sugar gliders, or dwarf caimans (baby alligators). If the store is not too busy, they will give you a close-up look (and sometimes feel) of some of the animals and tell you little-known facts. The employees were all very knowledge-able, very friendly, and very patient with all our questions. Scales 'n' Tails also offers an educational program, where they will bring some of the animals to a group of children.

Other destinations within 5 miles . . .

See Museum of Outdoor Arts (Site 18) for destinations near Englewood location.
See Casa Bonita (Site 165) for destinations near Lakewood location.
See Boondocks Fun Center (Site 151) for destinations near Northglenn location

*"**Our task** must be to free ourselves . . . by widening our circle of compassion to embrace all living creatures and the whole of nature and its beauty." ~ Albert Einstein.*

Todd's Tropical Fish ☆☆☆☆☆

Hours:	10:00 AM - 6:00 PM, Monday - Saturday 1:00 PM - 5:00 PM, Sunday
Admission:	FREE!
Parking:	Free parking lot.

10015 East Hampden Avenue
Denver, 80231
(303) 338-1331

What to expect. . .

Todd's Tropical Fish is a store that is comfortable with families coming to just have a look. They have over 300 varieties of tropical fish in more than 100 tanks, as well as clams, anemones, water plants, and live rocks.

Other destinations within 5 miles . . .

Cherry Creek State Park Swim Beach (Site 82) - 3½ miles
Utah Pool (Site 76) - 3½ miles
Skate City - Aurora (Site 175) - 4 miles

Wild Animal Sanctuary ☆☆☆☆☆

Wild Animal Sanctuary

Hours:	9:00 AM - 4:00 PM daily Closed all holidays and in the event of bad weather.
Admission:	Under 3: Free; Age 3-12: $5; Age 13+: $10 American Express, Discover, MasterCard, Visa, checks, and cash accepted.
Parking:	Free parking lot.
Food:	You may bring in your own food and drink. Tables and chairs are provided on both observation decks.

1946 County Road 53
Keenesburg, 80643
(303) 536-0118
www.wildanimalsanctuary.org

What to expect. . .

The Wild Animal Sanctuary is America's oldest and, at 320 acres, largest facility of its kind. There is currently a Captive Wildlife in Crisis in our nation and around the world. For example, more tigers are being held captive illegally in the state of Texas than exist in the wild worldwide. The sanctuary provides food, care, and shelter for about 200 large carnivores (bears, tigers, lions, other wildcats, and wolves), most of which have been confiscated from illegal and/or abusive situations. The animals can not be released into the wild, as they have no survival skills.

Wild Animal Sanctuary

When you enter the facility, you will be given a very brief orientation about their purpose. A Tour Guide Handbook with a map of the facility and information about the animals is provided to every party. Then you can choose to go to one of two observation decks. The first is accessible by a stairway that is fairly steep, so proceed with caution if you have younger children with you. (My 3-year-old needed assistance on the descent.) From this area you can view the wolf, bear, and second tiger habitats. The second observation area is accessible via a ramp. Halfway up is an Education Center. Inside you can watch movies showing some of the animals in various stages of rehabilitation. Beneath the Education Center is the Tiger Roundhouse where you can look down and see tigers napping in the sun or swimming in their pool.

Keenesburg is a bit outside the Denver metropolitan area (in fact, portions of County Road 53 are unpaved), but the Wild Animal Sanctuary is so unique and its purpose so important that I wanted to include it anyway. Before your visit, please understand that the sanctuary is not a zoo. The animals are not on exhibit. Instead, it is an opportunity for you to view the animals living in a natural setting and to learn about the importance of facilities like this one and how you can help support them. We really enjoyed our visit and learned a lot in the process.

The wild animal-themed gift shop sells clothing, jewelry, toys, calendars, and postcards to help support the sanctuary. Bring quarters for the coin-operated binoculars available on both observation decks or simply bring your own binoculars. Bathrooms are located in the parking lot and also in the Education Center but do not have diaper-changing tables.

Annual Events . . .

Wild Safari takes place in June and celebrates the anniversary of the sanctuary with a big party.

See Also

Barr Lake (Site 93)

Belleview Park (Site 94)

Cheyenne Mountain Zoo (Site 181)

Denver Museum of Nature and Science (Site 11)

Four Mile Historic Park (Site 106)

Hudson Gardens (Site 108)

Morrison Nature Center at Star K Ranch (Site 113)

Plains Conservation Center (Site 114)

Rocky Mountain Arsenal National Wildlife Refuge (Site 118)

The Wildlife Experience (Site 19)

Fish Den

Take Me Out to the Ball Game

Denver is home to many sports teams and is one of a select group of only thirteen US cities with professional teams from four major sports: baseball, basketball, football, and hockey. If you enjoy attending sporting events, you can continue to do this with children. However, they may not be able to sit through an entire game, so plan to arrive late or leave early.

Coors Field prior to the start of a game. Photo by Heidi Knapp

Bandimere Speedway ☆☆☆☆☆

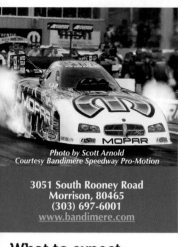

*Photo by Scott Arnold
Courtesy Bandimere Speedway Pro-Motion*

**3051 South Rooney Road
Morrison, 80465
(303) 697-6001
www.bandimere.com**

Schedule:	Season runs from mid-April through mid-October. Races are typically Wednesday, Friday, Saturday, and Sunday. Wednesday and Friday races are in the evening; weekend races start in the morning and can last all day.
Admission:	$10-58, depending on the event. Children 12 and under get junior pricing or free admission at most events. Tickets can be purchased online or at the box office using American Express, Discover, MasterCard, Visa, and cash.
Parking:	Usually free except for large events, when it is $10.
Food:	Two concession stands near each of the main grandstands. You may bring in your own food and drink (no alcohol) as long as your backpack or cooler is no larger than six-pack size (about 12x12x12).
Discounts:	Coupons for adults may be available at various sponsor locations that are involved in a particular event.

What to expect. . .

Drag racing is an acceleration contest between two vehicles. Vehicles that compete on the track can range from 300 MPH Top Fuel Dragsters and Funny Cars to Jr. Dragsters driven by kids age 8-17. Races generally last between 3.9 and 17 seconds. Bandimere Speedway is overseen by the National Hot Rod Association, which sets rules in drag racing for the United States and Canada for over 80,000 drivers. Every ticket to Bandimere includes admission into the Pits so you and your child can get up close to the cars and drivers. If you're not familiar with drag racing, visit Bandimere's website, click on Fan Guide, then Drag Racing 101 for a short tutorial. The website also has a detailed calendar with events, times, and pricing.

Bandimere Speedway has been family owned and operated for more than 50 years. They strive to offer the best motorsport entertainment in Colorado. Drag racing is loud. Very loud. Bandimere Speedway sells a variety of ear protection for children and adults, but if you or your child are very sensitive to noise, that is something to take into consideration. Well-maintained port-a-potties are available.

Annual Events . . .

NAPA Night of Fire and Thunder is part of a "Race to Read" program and takes place in May.

Big O Tires Jet Car Nationals/Family Festival occurs near Independence Day.

Junior Dragster Nationals is a week-long racing event in July; racers are 8-20 years old.

Colorado Bug-In is an all-VW event and takes place in early August.

Cummins Rocky Mountain Truck Fest is an all-truck event that also takes place in early August.

Other destinations within 5 miles . . .

Bear Creek Lake Park Swim Beach (Site 80) - 1 mile
Morrison Natural History Museum (Site 15) - 1½ miles
Dinosaur Ridge (Site 103) - 3½ miles

Red Rocks (Site 115) - 4 miles
Weaver Hollow Park and Pool (Site 92) - 4½ miles

Take Me Out to the Ball Game

Colorado Avalanche ☆☆☆☆☆

Courtesy Colorado Avalanche

Pepsi Center
1000 Chopper Circle
Denver, 80204
(303) 405-1100 • (303) 428-7645 (Tickets)
avalanche.nhl.com

Schedule:	Season runs October through mid-April. Games are typically at 5:00 PM or later and may take place any day of the week. There are a few 1:00 PM games, generally on Saturday or Sunday. There are 41 home games each season.
Admission:	Ticket prices range from $27 - $218. Children under 3 do not require a ticket. Tickets can be purchased online, by phone, or at the Pepsi Center Box Office using American Express, Discover, MasterCard, Visa, or cash.
Parking:	Several paid lots are nearby.
Food:	Permanent concessions accept cash and major credit cards; portable concessions are cash only. Outside food and beverages are not permitted.
Discounts:	Family night tickets include four tickets and four meals with drinks for $99. Season tickets and multi-game tickets are available at a discounted rate.

What to expect. . .

Ice hockey is a fast-paced and highly physical game. The Colorado Avalanche relocated to Denver from Quebec City in 1995. Home games take place at the Pepsi Center, which is designed to offer good views from every seat. Keep an eye out for their mascot, Bernie the Saint Bernard. Hockey games generally last about 2.5 hours. If you have never attended a hockey game, visit the website, click on *Fan Zone*, then *Hockey 101* for a short tutorial. The Colorado Avalanche won the Stanley Cup in their first year in Denver in 1996, and again in 2001.

The Pepsi Center is an indoor arena, but games can be cool so bring a sweater or a jacket. Diaper-changing tables are available in all men's, women's, and family bathrooms. Family bathrooms are located near Sections 130, 238, and 346, as well as near the entrance and by Blue Sky Grill.

The South Suburban Family Sports Center in Centennial (Site 45) is the Avalanche practice facility. Fans are welcome to attend practices during the regular season. Practices typically start at 10:30 AM on non-game days when the team is in town.

Photo by Heidi Knapp

Other destinations within 5 miles . . .

See Appendix I - Downtown Destinations
Sloan's Lake Park (Site 122) - 3 miles
The Bookery Nook (Site 59) - 3½ miles

Kids Kourt (Site 51) - 4 miles
Fish Den (Site 138) - 4½ miles
Rising Curtain Theatre Academy (Site 33) - 4½ miles

Take Me Out to the Ball Game

Colorado Mammoth ☆☆☆☆☆

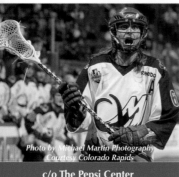

Photo by Michael Martin Photography
Courtesy Colorado Rapids

c/o The Pepsi Center
1000 Chopper Circle, Denver, 80204
(303) 405-1100
(303) 405-1101 (Tickets)
www.coloradomammoth.com

Schedule:	Season runs January through April. Games are typically at 7:00 PM or later on Friday or Saturday. There are 8 home games each season.
Admission:	Ticket prices range from $5 - $38. Children under 3 do not require a ticket. Tickets can be purchased online, by phone, or at the Pepsi Center Box Office using American Express, Discover, MasterCard, Visa, or cash.
Parking:	Several paid lots are available.
Food:	A wide variety of concession stands are available inside the arena. Permanent concessions accept cash and major credit cards; portable concessions are cash only. Outside food and beverages are not permitted.
Discounts:	The Party Pack includes four tickets, four hot dogs, and four drinks for $39, and is available for three games each season. Season and group tickets are available at a discounted price. Coupons can be found in the Entertainment Book.

What to expect. . .

Lacrosse, a hard-hitting sport which derived from the Native Americans, is now one of the fastest growing sports in the world. Denver was recently named the #1 Best Lacrosse City by *Inside Lacrosse Magazine* and is home to the Colorado Mammoth, a professional indoor lacrosse team in the National Lacrosse League. You may be surprised at the size of the crowd (averaging 16,000+ per game) and by how passionate the fans are (painted faces and cowbells galore). You'll hear the entire arena chant "Get in the Box" when an opposing team's player is sent to the penalty box. The meaning of this chant is two-fold: indoor lacrosse is properly called box lacrosse, so it is also an invitation to experience the excitement of the game. Games always include post-game autograph sessions with the entire team. Box lacrosse is an exciting, fast-paced game that a family of four can enjoy for less than the price of going to the movies. The Colorado Mammoth won the NLL Championship in 2006.

If you are unfamiliar with lacrosse, visit the *Fan Center* section of the website and click on *LAX 101*. Mammoth games generally last about 2.5 hours. The Pepsi Center is an indoor arena. Diaper-changing tables are available in all men's, women's, and family bathrooms. Family bathrooms are located near Sections 130, 238, and 346, as well as near the entrance and by Blue Sky Grill. If you attend a Colorado Mammoth game and fall in love with the sport, you can continue to attend games after the National Lacrosse League's season ends in April. The Denver Outlaws (Site 150), professional outdoor lacrosse, starts its season in May.

Other destinations within 5 miles . . .

See Appendix I - Downtown Destinations
Sloan's Lake Park (Site 122) - 3 miles
The Bookery Nook (Site 59) - 3½ miles

Kids Kourt (Site 51) - 4 miles
Fish Den (Site 138) - 4½ miles
Rising Curtain Theatre Academy (Site 33) - 4½ miles

DID YOU KNOW?

According to the LiveStrong website, the advantages of children participating in sports include:

- Joining a sports team helps children reach the 60 minutes of physical activity recommended by the CDC.
- Participating in sports teaches children the importance of teamwork.
- Since part of playing a sport is being both a gracious winner and loser, children learn sportsmanship.
- Sports provide an opportunity for children to socialize and build long-lasting friendships.
- Playing a sport teaches discipline; children must take direction, be dedicated, practice consistently and train hard.
- A child can also learn leadership skills by becoming team captain or leading the team in practice or during games.

Colorado Rapids ☆☆☆☆☆

Photo by Garrett Ellwood Courtesy Colorado Rapids

c/o Dick's Sporting Goods Park
6000 Victory Way, Commerce City, 80022
(303) 727-3500
(303) 825-4625 (Tickets)
www.coloradorapids.com

Schedule:	Season runs March through October. Games are typically in the afternoon or evening on a Saturday or Sunday, although midweek games may be scheduled. There are 15 home games each season.
Admission:	Ticket prices range from $16 - $80. Children under 3 do not require a ticket. Tickets can be purchased over the phone or online using any major credit card, inside any Dick's Sporting Goods store, or at the box office.
Parking:	Parking is included in the price of your ticket.
Food:	A wide variety of food is available inside the stadium. Outside food and drink are not permitted.
Discounts:	Rapids Family Night packs include four tickets, four drinks, and four personal pizzas for $79.

What to expect. . .

Soccer is widely regarded as the most popular sport on Earth, claiming one billion fans worldwide. Only in North America is it called soccer; the rest of the planet recognizes it as football. Dick's Sporting Goods Park, home to the Colorado Rapids, is the largest soccer complex in Colorado. The Colorado Rapids team was founded in 1995 and were the 2010 MLS Champions. They have always been among the top teams in the league, however suffer from average fan attendance, with about 13,000-15,000 people attending each of the 15-16 home games.

A soccer match lasts exactly 90 minutes. Soccer is the only sport with no timeouts or stoppages so there is constant action. Dick's Sporting Goods Park is an outdoor stadium, so dress according to weather. Keep an eye out for the Rapids' four mascots: Edson the Eagle, Marco van Bison, Jorge el Mapache, and Franz the Fox. Plenty of concession stands and bathrooms with diaper-changing tables are located throughout the stadium. If you have never attended a soccer game, visit the website, and click on *Fan Center*.

Other destinations within 5 miles . . .

Rocky Mountain Arsenal National Wildlife Refuge (Site 118) - 2 miles
Urban Farm (Site 133) - 4½ miles

Dick's Sporting Goods Park Photo by Garrett Ellwood Courtesy Colorado Rapids

Take Me Out to the Ball Game

Colorado Rockies ☆☆☆☆☆

Take Me Out to the Ball Game

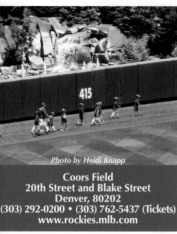

Photo by Heidi Knapp

Coors Field
20th Street and Blake Street
Denver, 80202
(303) 292-0200 • (303) 762-5437 (Tickets)
www.rockies.mlb.com

Schedule: Season runs early April through early October. The regular season has 81 home games. Weekday games are usually in the evening. Weekend games may be mid-day or in the evening.

Admission: Ticket prices range from $4 - $100. Children under 3 do not require a ticket. Tickets can be purchased online or by phone using American Express, Discover, MasterCard, or Visa. The Coors Field Ticket Office also accepts checks and cash.

Parking: Several paid lots are available.

Food: Permanent concessions accept cash and major credit cards; portable concessions are cash only. You may bring your own food in a soft-sided container no larger than 16x16x8". Alcohol, glass, cans, and thermoses are prohibited. Water bottles must be sealed at entry or emptied.

Discounts: The Coca Cola Value Pack includes four tickets, four hot dogs, four drinks, and a Lot B parking permit for $59. Season and mini-plan tickets are available at a discounted rate.

What to expect. . .

For Rockies fans, there is something magical about a baseball game that must be experienced in person. Since it opened in 1995, Coors Field has been a league leader in attendance, and the popularity of the Rockies has continued to grow, especially in recent years. In 2007, the Colorado Rockies (AKA Blake Street Bombers) won 22 of their last 23 games to earn their first trip to the World Series. Coors Field holds 50,000 fans. Look for the ring of purple seats on the highest deck, which marks the spot that is exactly 5,280 feet above sea level. The Rockpile is the bleachers section located behind center field. It is a very popular section because of the low ticket price — children are

only $1 — but it offers no shelter from the sun, rain, or snow. The Rockies mascot, Dinger, is a dinosaur because triceratops fossil remains were discovered on the property during the construction of Coors Field. When he is't entertaining fans on the field, you may find him hanging around the small playground behind Section 147. A concession stand with child-size items is also near this playground.

Games have nine innings and generally last about three hours. However, any game may have extra innings. Coors Field is an outdoor stadium, so dress accordingly and try to get seats in the third base side if you're going to an evening game so the sunset doesn't blind you. Unlike most baseball stadiums, Rocky Mountain Oysters are on the menu of some concession stands. The lower area of Section 342 is a designated "Family Section" and alcoholic beverages are not permitted. Booster seats are available from the Guest Relations Center behind Section 127. All bathrooms have diaper-changing tables; family restrooms are located in Sections 124, 135, 149, 222, 311, 339, and 403.

Other destinations within 5 miles . . .

See Appendix I - Downtown Destinations
The Bookery Nook (Site 59) - 4 miles

Kids Kourt (Site 51) - 4½ miles
Sloan's Lake Park (Site 122) - 5 miles

Colorado Sports Hall of Fame ☆☆☆☆☆

Take Me Out to the Ball Game

Courtesy Colorado Sports Hall of Fame

INVESCO Field at Mile High (Gate 1, West Side)
1702 Bryant Street, Suite 500
Denver, 80204
(720) 258-3888
www.coloradosports.org

Hours:	10:00 AM - 3:00 PM, Tuesday - Saturday from June through August. 10:00 AM - 3:00 PM, Thursday - Saturday from September through May. Hours are subject to change due to stadium events, so call ahead.
Admission:	FREE!
Parking:	Free parking in Lot C on the west side of the stadium.
Food:	Food and drink other than water bottles are not permitted inside the museum. However, you may bring your own food and drink and eat at the picnic tables at the bottom of the stairs outside Gate 1.

What to expect. . .

The Colorado Sports Hall of Fame began with 20 inductees, and five or six more are added each year. Currently, over 200 people who have contributed to sports in Colorado are honored here, from outstanding athletes in every sport to sports writers to excellent coaches. Special displays honor women's role in sports and disabled athletes. A large exhibit of the current year's inductees is located on the wall behind the front desk. A separate room called Kids Zone has a variety of sports uniforms, equipment, and balls. The room is quite small but we were able to gently throw around a couple of the balls. The uniforms and gear are all adult-sized but my children still enjoyed putting everything on and posing for pictures.

Courtesy Colorado Sports Hall of Fame

Guided tours of Invesco Field are available for an additional fee (children under 5 are free). The tours are stroller-friendly but last about 75 minutes and it is not easy to depart the tour once it starts. Reservations are encouraged. Backpacks or large bags are not allowed inside the museum or on the tour; you may check them in at the front desk. Diaper-changing tables are available in both the men's and women's bathrooms.

My GPS took me to a house in a neighborhood rather than Invesco Field at Mile High. This is apparently quite common, as the front desk was able to give me directions from that house to the stadium. To get to the parking lot, enter off Federal Boulevard and turn east on 17th Avenue.

Other destinations within 5 miles . . .
See Appendix I - Downtown Destinations
The Bookery Nook (Site 59) - 3½ miles
Sloan's Lake Park (Site 122) - 3½ miles

Rising Curtain Theatre Academy (Site 33) - 4½ miles
Kids Kourt (Site 51) - 5 miles

Denver Broncos ☆☆☆☆☆

Bronco out at DIA

INVESCO Field at Mile High
1701 Bryant Street
Denver, 80204
(720) 258-3333 (Tickets)
www.denverbroncos.com

Schedule:	Season runs September through January. Games are typically on Sunday or Monday night. Occasionally, a Thursday or Saturday game may be scheduled. There are 8 home games each season.
Admission:	Ticket prices range from $45 - $125. Children under 2 do not require a ticket. Tickets can be purchased online using American Express, Discover, Master-Card, and Visa. The box office also accepts checks and cash.
Parking:	Several paid lots are available.
Food:	Permanent concessions accept cash and major credit cards; portable concessions are cash only. You may bring your own food in a soft-sided container no larger than 12x12x12". Alcohol, glass, cans, and thermoses are prohibited. Water bottles must be sealed at entry or emptied.
Discounts:	2,000 tickets are sold at half-price for every home game; these tickets go on sale in mid-July.

What to expect. . .

The Denver Broncos play in the American Football Conference of the National Football League. although they began as a charter member of the American Football League in 1960. The Broncos have sold out virtually every home game since 1970. Denver is well-known for its die-hard Broncos fans. Games are very exciting and also very loud. Keep an eye out for the Broncos mascots, Miles and Thunder (Thunder is the live Arabian gelding). Listen for the famous "In-Com-Plete" chant every time the opposing team throws an incomplete pass. The Denver Broncos have made six Super Bowl ap-pearances. They won back-to-back in Super Bowl XXXII and Super Bowl XXXIII.

A football game usu-ally lasts about three hours, unless it goes into overtime. The sta-dium is outdoors, so dress according to the weather. All restrooms have diaper-changing tables; family rest-rooms are located at

Courtesy Denver Broncos

sections 105, 122, 305, 324, 341, 508, and 534. Before or after the game, visit the website and click on *Kids*, then *Game Zone* for online coloring pages and games.

Season tickets are available by adding your name to the Waiting List. Current wait time is estimated to be at least 13 years.

Other destinations within 5 miles . . .

See Appendix I - Downtown Destinations
The Bookery Nook (Site 59) - 3½ miles
Sloan's Lake Park (Site 122) - 3½ miles

Rising Curtain Theatre Academy (Site 33) - 4½ miles
Kids Kourt (Site 51) - 5 miles

Denver Nuggets ☆☆☆☆☆

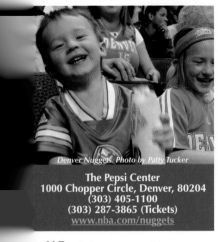

Denver Nuggets. Photo by Patty Tucker

The Pepsi Center
1000 Chopper Circle, Denver, 80204
(303) 405-1100
(303) 287-3865 (Tickets)
www.nba.com/nuggets

Schedule:	Regular season games run November through April. Games are typically evening and can be any day of the week. There are 41 home games each season.
Admission:	Ticket prices range from $10 - $600. Children under 3 do not require a ticket. Tickets can be purchased online, by phone, or at the Pepsi Center Box Office using American Express, Discover, MasterCard, Visa, or cash.
Parking:	Several paid lots are available.
Food:	A wide variety of food is available inside the arena. Permanent concessions accept cash and major credit cards; portable concessions are cash only. Outside food and drink are not permitted.
Discounts:	Season and group discounts are available. Coupons may be found in the Entertainment Book.

What to expect. . .

Basketball originated in 1891 in Springfield, Massachusetts, but has evolved over the years to become a sport that is popular worldwide. The Denver Nuggets have played in the National Basketball Association since the NBA's merger with the American Basketball Association in 1975, and are currently one of only three teams to have advanced to the NBA Playoffs each of the past seven seasons. Over 19,000 devoted Nuggets fans attend each of the team's home games. Keep an eye out for the Nuggets Super-Mascot, Rocky the Mountain Lion. He is famous for his acrobatics, dancing, and skits.

Games generally last about 2.5 hours. Home games take place at the Pepsi Center, which is an indoor arena designed to offer good views from every seat. Diaper-changing tables are available in all men's, women's, and family bathrooms. Family bathrooms are located near Sections 130, 238, and 346, as well as near the entrance and by Blue Sky Grill.

Other destinations within 5 miles . . .

See Appendix I - Downtown Destinations
Sloan's Lake Park (Site 122) - 3 miles
The Bookery Nook (Site 59) - 3½ miles

Kids Kourt (Site 51) - 4 miles
Fish Den (Site 138) - 4½ miles
Rising Curtain Theatre Academy (Site 33) - 4½ miles

HELPFUL TIP - In addition to all the major and minor league sports available, you can also enjoy college games in virtually every sport. Denver University is well-known for its hockey and lacrosse teams (**www.du.edu/live/athleticsandrecreation.html**). Air Force Academy (**www.goairforcefalcons.com**) and CU Boulder football and basketball games (**www.cubuffs.com**) are also very popular. The women's teams offer great opportunities as well for a very reasonable price with availability last minute. Gymnastics, basketball, volleyball, soccer, and lacrosse are some great options. Many of the teams have special family events where the kiddos can meet the players.

Denver Outlaws ☆☆☆☆☆

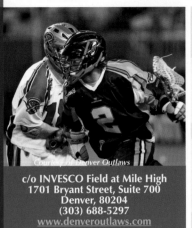

Courtesy of Denver Outlaws

c/o INVESCO Field at Mile High
1701 Bryant Street, Suite 700
Denver, 80204
(303) 688-5297
www.denveroutlaws.com

Schedule	Season runs May through August. Games are typically on Saturday, although Sunday or weekday games may be scheduled. There are 6 home games each season.
Admission:	Ticket prices range from $10 - $40. Children under 2 do not require a ticket. Tickets can be purchased over the phone or through TicketMaster using American Express, Discover, MasterCard, or Visa. The box office also accepts checks and cash and is open on game day.
Parking:	Several paid lots are available.
Food:	Permanent concessions accept cash and major credit cards; portable concessions are cash only. You may bring your own food in a soft-sided container no larger than 12x12x12″. Alcohol, glass, cans, and thermoses are prohibited. Water bottles must be sealed at entry or emptied.
Discounts:	Season and group discounts are available.

What to expect. . .

Field lacrosse is an outdoor team sport that is played using a lacrosse stick to catch, carry, pass, and hurl a small rubber ball into the opposing team's goal. It is sometimes referred to as "the fastest game on two feet." If you attended a Colorado Mammoth (Site 144) game and fell in love with the sport, you can continue to attend games after the National Lacrosse League's season ends in April (although you'll discover some differences between field lacrosse and box lacrosse). Major League Lacrosse, professional outdoor lacrosse, starts its season in May. The Outlaws are an expansion team that began playing in 2006. Their first game beat the previous MLL attendance record, and the team won the Western Conference Championship that year. Look for Stix, the Outlaws mascot. You may even be able to get his autograph.

If you've never attended a lacrosse game, visit the FanZone section of the website and click on Intro to LAX. Games generally last under three hours. The stadium is outdoors, so dress according to the weather. All restrooms have diaper-changing tables; family restrooms are located at sections 105, 122, 305, 324, 341, 508, and 534.

Annual Events . . .

Fourth of July game, usually the highest attended of the season, includes a fireworks display.

Other destinations within 5 miles . . .

See Appendix I - Downtown Destinations
The Bookery Nook (Site 59) - 3½ miles
Sloan's Lake Park (Site 122) - 3½ miles

Rising Curtain Theatre Academy (Site 33) - 4½ miles
Kids Kourt (Site 51) - 5 miles

See Also

Colorado Springs Sky Sox (Site 182)

Family Sports Center (Site 45)

Pro Rodeo Hall of Fame (Site 189)

Faster! Higher!

"Faster, Mommy, Faster!" If you've ever heard your child utter this phrase, it may be time to visit an amusement park. You'll find parks with a variety of outdoor rides, attractions, and indoor activities. Measure your child first; most rides have height restrictions. Then you can choose the facility that is right for your child and for your budget.

Courtesy Lakeside Amusement Park

Faster! Higher!

Boondocks Fun Center ☆☆☆☆☆

Boondocks Fun Center Photo by Nicole Hager

11425 Community Center Drive
Northglenn, 80233
(720) 977-8000
www.boondocksfuncenter.com

Hours:	10:00 AM - 10:00 PM, Sunday - Thursday (till 11:00 PM in summer) 10:00 AM - 12:00 AM, Friday and Saturday Closed Easter, Thanksgiving and Christmas.
Admission:	Unlimited Fun (under 60"): $16.95; General Unlimited Fun: $24.95. Unlimited fun includes miniature golf, bumper boats, laser tag, go-karts, Kiddie Cove, and 10-20 arcade tokens. Activities can be purchased separately. American Express, Discover, MasterCard, Visa, and cash accepted.
Parking:	Free parking lot.
Food:	No outside food or drink are allowed. Vending machines, a snack bar, and a café with a wide variety of food are on site.
Discounts:	$12 Tuesday is available every Tuesday from 4:00 PM - 10:00 PM and all day Tuesday in the summer. Coupons can be found in the Entertainment Book and usually on ColoradoKids.com.

What to expect. . .

Boondocks is an 8-acre indoor/outdoor amusement center that has a wide variety of activities. Attractions can be purchased separately or as part of a package. Most have some height restrictions.

Miniature Golf has two courses, one of which is stroller- and wheelchair-friendly.

Bumper Boats have a height restriction of 36" to ride and 44" to drive.

Go-Karts have a height restriction of 40" to ride and 48" or 60" to drive, depending on the track.

Batting Cages offer slow and fast pitch softball and 40-70 mph hardball.

Laser Tag runs every 10 minutes all day long, with the game lasting about six minutes. It has a height restriction of 40".

Max Flight is a ride simulator with a height restriction of 44".

The **Arcade** has a variety of video games and ticket-dispensing games. Tickets can be redeemed for prizes.

Kiddie Cove is a 32-foot tall climbing structure that will keep your child jumping, swinging, sliding, and climbing. Children must be 48" or smaller to go into Kiddie Cove. It is located in the back corner of the arcade. A miniature air hockey game is near the entrance of Kiddie Cove (tokens required).

Boondocks offers a good value for unlimited all-day fun once your child is at least 40" tall. Under that height and it would probably be more cost-effective to purchase attractions separately. Kiddie Cove is only $3 for all day play, a great price for an indoor playground. A cushioned bench is just inside the gate for parents to sit and relax. $12 Tuesday includes unlimited miniature golf, bumper boats, Kiddie Cove, laser tag, and select video games.

The employees were friendly, helpful, and easy to find when I needed assistance. Tables and chairs are available outside, but seating is limited inside except in the Back Porch Grill. It is easy for children to become over-stimulated here because of all the activity and noise. It is quite loud both inside and outside, between the music, the games, and the sounds of lots of children having a good time. You may leave and your unlimited pass is still good for the day when you return. Diaper-changing tables are available in both the men's and women's restrooms.

Other destinations within 5 miles . . .

D.L. Parsons Theatre (Site 29) - less than ½ mile
E.B. Rains Jr. Memorial Park (Site 104) - less than ½ mile
The Hop - Thornton (Site 46) - 1 mile
Krispy Kreme (Site 172) - 1 ½ miles
Skate City - Westminster (Site 175) - 1 ½ miles
Scales 'n' Tails - Northglenn (Site 139) - 2 miles

Jungle Quest (Site 49) - 3 miles
Thornton City Pool (Site 91) - 4 miles
Little Monkey Bizness - Westminster (Site 53) - 4 ½ miles
Paul Derda Recreation Center Indoor Pool (Site 74) - 4 ½ miles
Kids Zone (Site 52) - 4 ½ miles

Laser Tag Kiddie Cove
Kiddie Go-Karts
Max Flight Bumper Boats

Courtesy Lakeside Amusement Park - Site 155

Elitch Gardens ☆☆☆☆☆

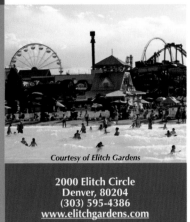

Courtesy of Elitch Gardens

**2000 Elitch Circle
Denver, 80204
(303) 595-4386
www.elitchgardens.com**

Hours:	Hours vary throughout the season from May through Oct. Island Kingdom Waterpark is open from 10:00 AM - 6:00 PM on regular operating days from Memorial Day weekend through Labor Day.
Admission:	Under 4: Free; Under 48": $27.99; 48" and over: $40.99. American Express, MasterCard, Visa, and cash accepted.
Annual Pass:	$79.99 each for three individual passes; $74.99 each for four or more passes. Season passes are usually less expensive if purchased before May 31.
Parking:	Parking is $15, cash only. A season parking pass is $50.
Food:	A wide variety of restaurants and concession stands are available. Most accept credit cards, but some are cash only. Outside food and drink other than water are not permitted inside the park. However, several picnic tables are located in the parking lot. Keep your receipt and have your hand stamped before leaving the Park for a picnic lunch.
Discounts:	Coupons change from year to year. Call for the most current information.

What to expect. . .

Elitch Gardens is the largest amusement park in the Denver metro area and has rides and attractions galore for people of all ages. A ticket to Elitch Gardens includes admission to Island Kingdom Waterpark, which is open Memorial Day weekend through Labor Day. For the sake of space, this section focuses only on those areas that are for young children who are at least 36" tall.

Elitch Gardens has a section called Startoon Studios featuring 13 rides for children under 54" tall. Many are miniature versions of the adult rides, including a roller coaster and tea cups. Parents can ride with their child on four of the rides; the rest are made for little tikes only. In other areas of the park, you'll find eight more "Family Rides" like the giant ferris wheel and Ghost Blasters. You must accompany your child on most of these rides.

Island Kingdom Waterpark has five attractions for children at least 36" tall, including a giant wave pool and a water slide. Perhaps the best section for little ones is Hooks Lagoon, which features pirate ships with slides and tunnels, as well as a five-story climbing structure (enclosed with netting) with water spraying in every direction. You must be under 54" (or accompanied by someone who is) to play in Hooks Lagoon. The water is heated entirely by the sun, so visit during the hottest parts of summer. At least 35 lifeguards are on duty at all times, and complimentary life jackets are available.

For the best value, I recommend visiting on a hot day when Island Kingdom is open so you can enjoy the water park and the amusement park. Everyone entering the park must pay the full admission, so go with another family if you can. One set of parents can watch the little ones in Startoon Studios while the other set enjoys some of the grownup rides. In addition to the rides, Elitch Gardens has three entertainment venues with different shows throughout the day. Also, the Summer Concert Series is free with park admission; seating is on a first-come, first-served basis.

Small lockers may be rented for $12 and large lockers for $17 for the entire day using MasterCard, Visa, or cash. Return the key at the end of your use and you will receive $5 in Elitch Dollars that can be used anywhere in the park and are good for the whole season. Men's and women's bathrooms throughout the park have diaper-changing tables, including those in Island Kingdom.

Annual Events . . .

Kids Fest is a two-day event that is usually the second weekend of August.

Fright Fest takes place weekends in October. It is Family by Day and Fright by Night. Plan to leave by 6:00 PM unless you and your child enjoy being scared.

Other destinations within 5 miles . . .

See Appendix I - Downtown Destinations

The Bookery Nook (Site 59) - 3½ miles

Fish Den (Site 138) - 4 miles

Sloan's Lake Park (Site 122) - 4½ miles

Kids Kourt (Site 51) - 4½ miles

Rising Curtain Theatre Academy (Site 33) - 4½ miles

Courtesy of Elitch Gardens

Fun City ☆☆☆☆☆

Faster! Higher!

9670 West Coal Mine Avenue
Littleton, 80123
(303) 972-4344
www.funcitycolorado.com

Hours:	11:00 AM - 9:00 PM, Sunday - Thursday 11:00 AM - 11:00 PM, Friday and Saturday Bowling is open till 11:00 PM Sunday - Thursday and midnight on weekends.
Admission:	Unlimited Fun Pass ranges from $25 - $40, depending on the number of attractions chosen. Activities can also be purchased separately. American Express, Discover, MasterCard, Visa, and cash accepted.
Parking:	Free parking lot.
Food:	Outside food and drink are not permitted. A bar/restaurant in the bowling alley serves reasonably-priced pizza, burgers, salads, and sandwiches.
Discounts:	Visit the **Offers** link on the website to see current deals. Discount tickets are available at Safeway and King Soopers.

What to expect. . .

Fun City (formerly known as Mr. Biggs) is a 144,000 square-foot indoor amusement facility. Although it is really geared toward older children and teenagers, several attractions are suitable for toddlers and preschoolers.

Little City, for children under 10, is a miniature town with a bakery, auto shop, dress shop, toy store, music room, and police station. It has a soft, padded floor and is connected to the Inflatables section.

Foam Factory is a three-story enclosed area with 20,000 foam balls that can be dropped, shot, or thrown.

Miniature Golf is an indoor 18-hole course.

Laser Jam is an interactive laser tag arena. Players must be able to carry eight pounds on their back.

Grand Prix is a raceway with cars that can reach 40 MPH. Drivers must be at least 48" tall.

Fun City also has an arcade and a 40-lane bowling alley. The section with Little City and the Foam Factory are poorly lit at night, but large windows on one wall keep it nice and bright during the day. The women's bathrooms have diaper-changing tables. The food we ordered was good but the service was terrible. Ultimately, we ordered at the bar because a waitress still hadn't visited our table 20 minutes after we sat down, even though we made eye contact and waved at several of them.

Other destinations within 5 miles . . .

Jump Street (Site 48) - 1½ miles
Audience of One - Burgundy Theater (Site 23) - 2½ miles
My Art Workshop (Site 54) - 2½ miles
Ridge Recreation Center Activity Pool (Site 75) - 2½ miles

Robert F. Clement Park (Site 117) - 2½ miles
Deer Creek Pool (Site 84) - 3½ miles
Denver Botanic Gardens at Chatfield (Site 102) - 4 miles
Skate City - Littleton (Site 175) - 5 miles

DID YOU KNOW? Many Bowling Centers across the state offer free bowling for children in the summer. Visit **www.kidsbowlfree.com** for more details.

Heritage Square Amusement Park ☆☆☆☆☆

Hours:	11:00 AM - 6:00 PM, weekends in April, May, September, and October 10:00 AM - 8:00 PM daily from Memorial Day weekend through Labor Day.
Admission:	Admission is free. Tickets for the rides may be purchased for $1.25 each. An unlimited pass can be purchased for $20. MasterCard, Visa, and cash accepted.
Parking:	Free parking lot.
Food:	Python Pit Grill is a cash-only snack bar. The Garden Grill accepts MasterCard, Visa, and cash and serves a full menu. You may bring in your own food and drink, but no alcohol or glass. Picnic tables are on a first-come, first-served basis.
Discounts:	Coupons are available on their website under **Pricing**, on ColoradoKids.com, and in the Entertainment Book. Discounted unlimited wristbands may be at King Soopers. Join the email list and get coupons bi-weekly over the summer.

18301 West Colfax Avenue
Golden, 80401
(303) 727-8437
www.heritagesquareamusementpark.com

What to expect. . .

Heritage Square is a replica of a Western village, complete with Victorian architecture. The amusement park was designed especially for families with young children. Kiddie Land has eight rides for children at least 36" tall, like a mini coaster, tea cups, and planes. These rides require two tickets, and parents may accompany their children on Kiddie Land rides for free, except for the swings. Heritage Square also has two miniature golf courses (including a "Family Course"), go-karts (children must be at least 40" tall to ride), bumper boats and paddle boats, and an arcade. Pony rides and magic shows are also available weekends in the summer. The Heritage Square Music Hall (Site 30) is also located on the property.

The Heritage Square Alpine Slide is separately owned so you cannot use your tickets for the slide, and it isn't included in the unlimited pass. The slide is $7 for adults and $3 for children under 7. Parents and children can ride together. Take a chairlift to the top of the mountain, grab a sled, and slide down one of two half-mile tracks. The slide keeps approximately the same hours as Heritage Square.

An old-time photo shop and some unique gift shops are on site. Much of the park has been repainted or refurbished in recent years. Both the men's and women's bathrooms have diaper-changing tables. Smoking is not limited to designated areas, but the park discourages smoking around children and in Kiddie Land.

Annual Events . . .

A free **Easter Celebration** includes egg hunts and a visit from the Easter bunny.

An **Annual Corvette Show** for Father's Day is free.

Boo Town is a non-scary family event in October.

Other destinations within 5 miles . . .

Lakeside Amusement Park ☆☆☆☆☆

Courtesy Lakeside Amusement Park

4601 Sheridan Boulevard
Denver, 80212
(303) 477-1621
www.lakesideamusementpark.com

Hours:	Lakeside Amusement Park is open from early May through mid-September. Hours vary throughout the season.
Admission:	Gate admission only: $2.50. **Monday - Friday** Unlimited rides and gate admission: $13.75 **Saturday and Sunday** Unlimited rides and gate admission: $19.75 Tickets for rides may be purchased individually. MasterCard, Visa, checks, and cash accepted.
Parking:	Free parking lot with gate admission.
Food:	Several cash-only concession stands are available. You may bring your own food and drink. Picnic tables and benches are located throughout the park.
Discounts:	Coupons can be found in the Entertainment Book.

What to expect. . .

Lakeside Amusement Park has a beautiful view of the mountains, a train that encircles Lake Rhonda, and 16 kiddie rides for children 6 and under. The park has a total of 40 rides, and several of the rides outside Kiddies Playland are suitable for young children. The carousel is the original one from when the park opened Memorial Day weekend in 1908.

Kiddies Playland has 16 rides for small children, including cars, planes, boats, a roller coaster, and a ferris wheel. Each ride uses one coupon and coupons can be purchased for 50 cents. The ride operators in Kiddies Playland generally run more than one ride, so you may have to wait a few minutes for someone to come to a ride. Lines will usually form at a few of the different rides, then rotate through Kiddies Playland. This area has its own ticket booth, stroller-friendly paths, and is mostly shaded.

Bathrooms are located north of Kiddies Playland, behind the Crystal Palace Maze. They do not have diaper-changing tables but there is a bench that could serve as one. Maps are not available at the park, so print one out online before your visit. The main drawback to Lakeside is that smoking is permitted throughout the park, even in Kiddies Playland. Lakeside Amusement Park seems a bit more rundown than some of the other amusement parks in the Denver area (remember, it is over 100 years old), but it is an affordable choice. Although it will probably be past your child's bedtime, stay till dark if you can. Lakeside is famous for its neon lights.

Other destinations within 5 miles . . .

Fish Den (Site 138) - ½ mile
The Bookery Nook (Site 59) - 1 mile
Denver Puppet Theater (Site 28) - 2 miles
Rising Curtain Theatre Academy (Site 33) - 2 miles
Sloan's Lake Park (Site 122) - 2½ miles
Secrest Pool (Site 89) - 3½ miles
The Arvada Center (Site 22) - 4 miles

Squiggles Playground (Site 123) - 4 miles
Casa Bonita (Site 165) - 4 miles
Wheat Ridge Recreation Center Pool (Site 77) - 4 miles
The 73rd Avenue Theatre Company (Site 21)- 4½ miles
Scales 'n' Tails - Lakewood (Site 139) - 4½ miles
Forney Museum of Transportation (Site 158) - 5 miles
Majestic View Nature Center (Site 112) - 5 miles

See Also

Santa's Workshop at the North Pole (Site 192)

Trains, Planes, Boats, Oh My!

Kids point out other cars driving down the freeway, get excited when they see a school bus, and don't mind a bit getting stuck at the train tracks. Things that go "vroom" are fascinating to young children. The destinations in this chapter afford many opportunities for your child to explore vehicles up close, as well as travel in out-of-the-ordinary ways.

Courtesy Colorado Railroad Museum

Colorado Railroad Museum ☆☆☆☆☆

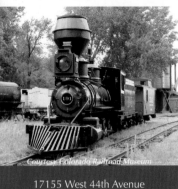

Courtesy Colorado Railroad Museum

17155 West 44th Avenue
Golden, CO 80403
(303) 279-4591
www.coloradorailroadmuseum.org

Hours:	9:00 AM - 5:00 PM daily (till 6:00 PM in June, July, and August) Closed New Year's Day, Thanksgiving, and Christmas.
Admission:	Under 2: Free; Age 2-16: $5; Age 17-59: $8; Age 60+: $7. Discover, MasterCard, Visa, and cash accepted.
Membership:	$50 for two adults and their children under 16.
Parking:	Free parking.
Food:	You may bring your own food and drink. Picnic tables and benches are available all over the property. An outdoor grill selling burgers, hot dogs, grilled cheese sandwiches, and drinks is usually set up in the summer.
Discounts:	Family admission for two adults and up to five children under age16 is $18. AAA and military discounts are also available.

What to expect. . .

The main building at the Colorado Railroad Museum is a replica of an 1880s train depot. Inside you'll find thousands of original photographs, documents, and artifacts covering the history of railroads, particularly in the Rocky Mountain region, for the last 125 years. The lower level of the building has a changing gallery and a huge working model train exhibit. This is a historic building so there is not an elevator to the lower level. Behind the building is a large Garden Railway, created and maintained by members of the Denver Garden Railway Society. The model trains in the garden are usually operating on weekends. The Depot Museum is where daily guided tours begin at 11:00 AM and 1:00 PM from May through September. The tours can last up to an hour, depending on your guide and the number of questions asked.

The exhibits in and around the Depot are interesting and well-designed, but the real fun comes when you enter the Museum Railyard and Grounds. With beautiful Table Mountain as the backdrop, more than 100 rail cars sit on narrow- and standard-gauge tracks. Climb into cabooses, steam engines, a mail car, a private dining car, and many others. Several of the cars have been restored both inside and out to look the way they did when they were in use. Visitors can watch rail cars in the process of being restored in the Restoration Roundhouse. Posted information explains what each car is and what is being done to restore it.

Bring a few quarters to run the train or carnival in the model downstairs, and to start the engine on the Coors Switch Car. Dress comfortably and wear closed-toe shoes, as you'll be walking on dirt and over tracks to get to all the trains. The Depot General Store is a large gift shop that sells any train-related item you can imagine. A diaper-changing station with baby wipes and hand sanitizer is available in the women's bathroom.

Courtesy Colorado Railroad Museum

Annual Events . . .

Bunny Express Train, the day before Easter, includes a train ride and a visit from the Easter Bunny.

Mother's Day Galloping Goosefest, hosted by Mother Goose, has lots of activities to honor mom.

Father's Day Train has free admission for dads.

Junior Railroad Days of Summer with Spike the Railroad Depot Dog is usually the second weekend of August.

Day Out with Thomas is held for several days in September. Yup, that's Thomas the Tank Engine.

Trick or Treat Train takes place the weekend before Halloween.

Santa Express Train is generally the second weekend of December.

Note: The above events feature running trains. Special event admission prices apply.

Other destinations within 5 miles . . .

Clear Creek Books (Site 62) - 2 miles
Clear Creek History Park (Site 98) - 2 miles
Foothills Art Center (Site 12) - 2½ miles

Lions Park (Site 109) - 2½ miles
Splash at Fossil Trace (Site 90) - 5½ miles

GO ONE STEP FURTHER - Colorado is blessed with some of the best scenic railroads in the country. If your child is crazy about trains, take him for a ride on a cog, narrow-gauge, or steam engine.
Go to **www.colorado.com/Train.aspx** for a complete listing of railroads in Colorado.

Evergreen Towne Trolley ☆☆☆☆☆

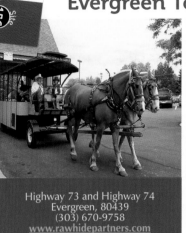

Hours:	1:00 - 4:00 PM, Saturday, from Memorial Day weekend through Labor Day
Admission:	FREE!
Parking:	Free street parking available.
Food:	You may bring your own snacks or drinks on the trolley. A variety of restaurants are available along the trolley route.

Highway 73 and Highway 74
Evergreen, 80439
(303) 670-9758
www.rawhidepartners.com

Photo by Allen Steppler American Frontier Films
Courtesy Evergreen Towne Trolley

What to expect. . .

Patterned after the original horse car that first appeared on the streets of Baltimore, the Evergreen Towne Trolley is drawn by two beautiful Belgian mares. Mr. Forman has been driving horses for 70 years, and has partnered with downtown Evergreen's businesses for four years. Trolley riders receive discount coupons to many of the local merchants. You can hop on the trolley virtually anywhere in downtown Evergreen, but the official starting place is where Highways 73 and 74 meet. There is limited parking in this area; you may be able to find parking along the street.

Round trip, the trolley ride is probably less than a mile, but can take half an hour because it moves at quite a slow pace. There are many standard stops along the way, including Baskin Robbins. Flag him down if you're on the street, or ask him to stop somewhere for you if you're riding. If the trolley isn't crowded, you and your child may be able to ride up front with Mr. Forman and learn more about horses and trolleys.

The Evergreen Towne Trolley is wheelchair-accessible, with a specially designed ramp that they will happily take the time to put down for you. Visiting Evergreen and riding the trolley can be a relaxing way to spend a Colorado summer day.

Other destinations within 5 miles . . .
Buchanan Park Recreation Center Indoor Pool (Site 67) - 4½ miles

DID YOU KNOW?

• The first train was invented in 1822 and was developed as public transportation by 1825.

• The first modern bicycle with pedals and cranks was invented in 1861, although a similar mode of transportation known as the "Laufmaschine" was exhibited in 1818.

• The first gas-engine motorcycle was invented in 1885 — it was simply an engine attached to a wooden bike.

• The first automobile did not have a single inventor, but was instead a process that took place worldwide by many inventors over the course of many decades. Today's modern car has evolved from more than 100,000 patents

• Boats and fixed wheels on carts (the first wheeled vehicle) date back to 3500 BC.

• The horse-drawn carriage was invented in Hungary in the 15th century.

Forney Museum of Transportation ☆☆☆☆☆

Hours:	10:00 AM - 4:00 PM, Monday - Saturday Closed Sundays and major holidays.
Admission:	Under 3: Free; Age 3-15: $4; Age 16-61: $8; Age 62+: $6 Discover, MasterCard, Visa, checks and cash accepted.
Membership:	$50 for four people.
Parking:	Free parking lot.
Food:	Only water bottles are allowed in the exhibition area. You may bring in your own food and drink; an eating area is just inside the entrance to the museum. The gift shop sells snacks and drinks.
Discounts:	Coupons are occasionally on ColoradoKids.com. Visit the website to find out about annual free days such as "Doors Open Denver" and "Night at the Museums."

4303 Brighton Boulevard
Denver, 80216
(303) 297-1113
www.forneymuseum.org

What to expect. . .

The Forney Museum of Transportation began as a private collection in 1955 and has become one of the nation's largest publicly displayed transportation collections. Only about 50-70% of the collection is on display at any one time and pieces are rotated periodically. Classic and antique automobiles, buggies, carriages, motorcycles, bicycles, rail cars, and many other items are housed in the 70,000 square foot facility. The museum is home to several special vehicles, including Amelia Earhart's first car, Denver's only surviving cable car, and one of only eight remaining Big Boy locomotives, the world's largest articulated steam engine. Airplanes hang from the ceiling, and wax figures of historic figures like the Wright Brothers are standing throughout the museum.

A few vehicles are available to sit in, such as a 1914 Model T Ford touring car. The museum is developing more hands-on, interactive exhibits, but currently most of the vehicles may only be viewed. My children were so fascinated by the strange-looking cars and bicycles, the giant steam engine, and the planes suspended overhead, they didn't seem to mind not being able to touch most of them. When you return home, visit the *Fun for Kids* page on their website for coloring sheets of a few of the vehicles you just saw.

The large gift shop has apparel, toys, books, collectors' items, and anything else you can think of related to transportation. Bring a few quarters to drive the model train set up and dimes to ride the vintage wooden horse. A small art gallery is located behind the gift shop. Family bathrooms with diaper-changing tables are down the same hall. There are no bathrooms in the exhibit gallery.

Annual Events . . .

Big Boy Weekend and Model Train Swap, held over Father's Day weekend, is the one time of year when the cab of The Big Boy and other rail cars are opened to the public. Dads get in free when accompanied by a child.

Forney Fall Fest usually takes place on the Saturday before Halloween.

Other destinations within 5 miles . . .
See Appendix I - Downtown Destinations
The Bookery Nook (Site 59) - 5 miles
Lakeside Amusement Park (Site 155) - 5 miles

Platte Valley Trolley ☆☆☆☆☆

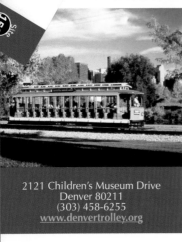

Hours:	12:00 PM - 3:30 PM, Friday through Sunday, from the first weekend in April through the last weekend in October, weather permitting.
Admission:	Under 4: Free; Age 4-12: $2; Age 12+: $4 Tickets may be purchased inside The Children's Museum of Denver, or from the conductor at the Trolley stops (cash only if purchased from the conductor).
Parking:	Parking is available at every stop. Some of it is free and some is metered street parking.
Food:	You may bring your own snacks or drinks on the trolley.

2121 Children's Museum Drive
Denver 80211
(303) 458-6255
www.denvertrolley.org

What to expect...

For 20 years, the Platte Valley Trolley has operated along the scenic South Platte Greenway. The trolley, an open-aired streetcar called a "breezer," runs past Confluence Park (Site 99), REI (Site 57), the Downtown Aquarium (Site 137), the Children's Museum of Denver (Site 6), and Invesco Field at Mile High. REI is the official starting point, but you can get on the trolley at any of the stops.

Platte Valley Trolley
Photos by Darrell T. Arndt
Courtesy Denver Rail Heritage Society

Round trip, the trolley ride lasts about 25 minutes. The Platte Valley Trolley departs from the 15th Street station (REI) on the hour and half hour, with the last run made at 3:30 PM. You may get on or off at any of the stops and complete the trip later. The trolley travels down to Colfax, and then all the seats are flipped (which my children found absolutely fascinating) so you can ride forward-facing in both directions. The trolley is operated by volunteers of the Denver Rail Heritage Society, all of whom are very knowledgeable and provide an Interpretive History Talk of this area as you ride.

The trolley can comfortably hold about 50 people. The engine is located in the back. It is very loud and somewhat obstructs the view of the other side. Strollers can be loaded onboard.

Annual Events...

The Bronco Shuttle operates during all Bronco home games. Visit the website for details.

Other destinations within 5 miles...

See Appendix I - Downtown Destinations
The Bookery Nook (Site 59) - 3 miles
Sloan's Lake Park (Site 122) - 3½ miles

Fish Den (Site 138) - 4 miles
Rising Curtain Theatre Academy (Site 33) - 4 miles
Kids Kourt (Site 51) - 5 miles

GO ONE STEP FURTHER - Although public transportation has never been my idea of a good time, my children are enamored with the big buses and Light Rail trains. Many of the destinations in this book are on an RTD route. Make your next adventure even more exciting by taking public transportation. Visit **www.RTD-Denver.com**.

Tebo Train ☆☆☆☆☆

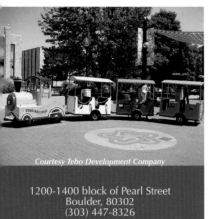

Courtesy Tebo Development Company

1200-1400 block of Pearl Street
Boulder, 80302
(303) 447-8326

Hours:	10:30 AM - 11:45 AM, Monday - Thursday from Memorial Day weekend till Labor Day
Admission:	FREE!
Parking:	Metered street parking and paid lots are available around Pearl Street Mall.

What to expect. . .

Tebo Train is a colorful, four-car mini train for children 10 and under. Adults may ride if accompanied by a child. The train ride begins at 13th Street at the Pearl Street Mall (Site 174) and travels east to 15th Street and back.

Other destinations within 5 miles . . .

Boulder Museum of Contemporary Art (Site 4) - ½ mile
CU Museum of Natural History (Site 7) - 1 mile
Fiske Planetarium (Site 169) - 1 mile
North Boulder Recreation Center Pool (Site 73) - 1 mile
Boulder History Museum (Site 3) - 1½ miles
Colorado Music Festival (Site 25) - 1½ miles

Storybook Ballet (Site 36) - 1½ miles
Scott Carpenter Park (Site 121) - 2 miles
Kids Kabaret (Site 31) - 3½ miles
Rocky Mountain Theatre for Kids (Site 34) - 3½ miles
NCAR (Site 173) - 5 miles

SOME OF OUR FAVORITE TRAIN BOOKS:

For babies to preschoolers:
Two Little Trains by Margaret Wise Brown
Down by the Station by Jessica Stockham
Jiggle Joggle Jee! by Laura E. Richards
Chugga-Chugga Choo-Choo by Kevin Lewis

For preschoolers to early school-age children:
The Little Engine that Could by Watty Piper
The Little Red Caboose by Marian Potter
Smokey and The Caboose Who Got Loose by Bill Peet
Dinosaur Train by John Steven Gurney

For older school-age children:
Train by John Coiley
Seymour Simon's Book of Trains by Seymour Simon

Tiny Town ☆☆☆☆☆

Tiny Town Photo by Patty Tucker

6249 South Turkey Creek Road
Morrison, 80465
(303) 697-6829
www.tinytownrailroad.com

Hours:	10:00 AM - 5:00 PM daily from Memorial Day weekend through Labor Day 10:00 AM - 5:00 PM weekends only in May and September
Admission:	Under 2: Free; Age 2-12: $3; Age 13+: $5 Train rides are $1 per person. MasterCard, Visa, checks, and cash accepted.
Parking:	Free parking lot across the street.
Food:	A concession stand with picnic tables is near the entrance. You may bring your own food and drink and eat at the other picnic area, located near the playground.

What to expect. . .

Tiny Town and its railroad have been open to the public and in operation for more than 70 years. People who once visited Tiny Town when they were children are now bringing their grandchildren. This unique, one-sixth-sized town contains over 100 buildings, each one handcrafted by volunteers. The grocery store, greenhouse, movie theater, saloon, and several other buildings have been decorated with miniatures to create a scene inside. Windows on the top or on the sides of these buildings allow visitors to peer in. Children can even step into a few of the buildings. The Tiny Town Train, powered by a real steam locomotive, carries passengers through Turkey Creek Canyon on a loop that is just over half a mile long. All the cars on the train are open-air except for the caboose, a kids-only enclosed car that is usually filled to capacity. At the far end of Tiny Town is a large playground with swings, monkey bars, and slides.

Tiny Town is nestled in a mountain canyon so it is usually cooler than the rest of the Denver area. The gift shop is fairly small but has train-themed items for sale. Bathrooms are on the outside of the building and have diaper-changing tables in both the men's and women's. A port-a-potty is located halfway through Tiny Town with another near the playground. Adult and kid-sized benches are scattered throughout the town. Most of Tiny Town is stroller-friendly, but I wouldn't recommend using an umbrella stroller.

Tiny Town Photo by Patty Tucker

Cruise In for a Rockin' Good Time!

A Colorado favorite for over 20 years! Take a trip back to the fabulous Fifties with good times and great food for the whole family.

Every Monday is Free Kids Meal day. (11am to close)

Arvada: 7355 Ralston Rd (at Wadsworth) 303-422-1954
Glendale: 4500 E Alameda (at Leetsdale) 303-399-1959
Northglenn: 301 W 104th St (just West of I-25) 303-453-1956
Greenwood Village: 9220 E Arapahoe Rd (just East of I-25) 303-799-1958
Littleton: 8266 W Bowles (at Wadsworth) 303-932-1957
Thornton: 16755 N Washington St. (just E of I-25) 303-451-1950
Colorado Springs: 5794 Palmer Park Blvd (at Powers) 719-570-1952
Colorado Springs: 5490 E Woodmen Rd (at Powers) 719-548-1955

www.gunthertoodys.com

Site 162 Denver

Trains, Planes, Boats, Oh My!

Venice on the Creek ☆☆☆☆☆

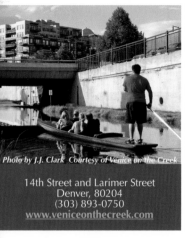

Photo by J.J. Clark Courtesy of Venice on the Creek

Hours:	5:30 PM - 9:30 PM, Friday and Saturday, from June through August
Admission:	$75 per boat for early evening rides (5:30 - 7:50 PM) $100 per boat for candlelight rides (8:00 - 9:00 PM) Pricing is by the boat; each boat can fit up to six people. American Express, Discover, MasterCard, Visa, checks, and cash accepted.
Parking:	Metered street parking and paid lots are available.
Food:	You may bring your own snacks or drinks on the punts.

14th Street and Larimer Street
Denver, 80204
(303) 893-0750
www.veniceonthecreek.com

What to expect...

Venice on the Creek is a slow punt ride down Cherry Creek. A punt is similar to a gondola, but lighter and narrower. It is propelled and steered by a pole operator standing on the back of the punt. Though common in Europe, Venice on the Creek boasts the only known punts in the United States.

Each punt has three benches and two people can fit on each bench. As you ride, the guide will offer a little bit of history about some of the buildings along the creek. To bypass the dams, the engineers created "locks" that use the water level to raise or lower the punt, depending on whether you are headed upstream or down. My children were fearful at first, then became fascinated by this process. The full ride lasts 35-45 minutes roundtrip and will take you down to Confluence Park (Site 99) and back. Rides departing after 8:00 PM are lantern-lit.

The Venice on the Creek kiosk is located on Larimer Street between 14th and Speer. Reservations are required. You will need a credit card to hold your reservation, but your card will not be charged if you need to cancel as long as you call ahead of time to let them know that you won't make it. Because the guides can not control the pace of the current, your scheduled departure time may run a little bit behind, but there is a very nice area with benches and a fountain if you find yourself waiting. Life jackets are not provided (you may bring your own) but it's a steady ride, the creek is shallow, and the only people who have fallen in are the pole operators. There are no bathrooms at Venice on the Creek, but many of the stores and restaurants in the downtown area will allow you to use theirs, especially if you have a desperate look and a toddler in potty-training.

Other destinations within 5 miles . . .

See Appendix I - Downtown Destinations
Sloan's Lake Park (Site 122) - 3½ miles
The Bookery Nook (Site 59) - 4 miles

Kids Kourt (Site 51) - 4 miles
Rising Curtain Theatre Academy (Site 33) - 5 miles

Wings Over The Rockies Air and Space Museum ☆☆

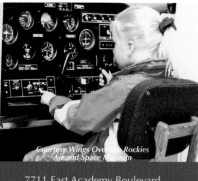

Courtesy Wings Over the Rockies Air and Space Museum

Hours:	10:00 AM - 5:00 PM, Monday - Saturday 12:00 PM - 5:00 PM, Sunday Closed major holidays.
Admission:	Under 4: Free; Age 4-12: $6; Age 13-64: $9; Age 65+: $8. American Express, Discover, MasterCard, Visa, checks, and cash accepted.
Membership:	$50 for everyone living in the same household.
Parking:	Free parking lot.
Food:	Food and drink is allowed in the refreshment center. In warmer weather, picnic tables are usually set up outside.
Discounts:	Military discount is $1 off admission.

7711 East Academy Boulevard
Denver, 80230
(303) 360-5360
www.wingsmuseum.org

What to expect. . .

Housed in a 150,000 square foot airplane hangar, Wings Over the Rockies strives to educate and inspire adults and kids of all ages about aviation endeavors and space. More than two dozen vehicles, airplanes, and bombers spanning over 70 years of aviation history are kept in this museum. Planes are lined up chronologically so you can see the advances made over time. Although you can not climb on or into these planes, many are made so you can stand under the plane and see inside. Other unusual aircraft in here include a replica of a Star Wars X-Wing Fighter and an STOL aircraft built here in Colorado that is literally one of a kind. In addition to aircraft, the museum features rocket engines, a mockup of Lockheed Martin's space station plans, and other space technology. A large display honors the 65 astronauts who have ties to Colorado. Around the perimeter of the hangar are several rooms, each with its own theme. Many of the artifacts have been donated by veterans and retired pilots. You'll find ham radios, a World War II exhibit, pictures of airplane "nose" art, a re-creation of the Eisenhower room, and more. Kids Space is a room with hands-on, interactive activities for children of all ages. Read books about space, build your own robot, put together a giant floor puzzle of the Solar System, or play a computer game.

Cockpit Demo Day is the second Saturday of each month, and it is a unique experience. The B-57 bomber and H21 helicopter are opened for the public to sit inside the cockpits. One or two other aircraft are usually opened and on display as well. Most of the volunteers have flown the aircraft before, so they can tell you what each knob and button does. On Cockpit Demo Day, a runway is set up inside the hangar for children to race pedal-planes. One adult-sized pedal-plane is also available, but you'll probably have to stand in line to ride it. Occasionally, Cockpit Demo Day may be cancelled in a particular month (e.g., if the day before Easter is the second Saturday), so you may want to call ahead.

Courtesy Wings Over the Rockies Air and Space Museum

Wings Over the Rockies has only been professionally run for about five years so it is a work in progress. The museum is working toward having more interactive and hands-on exhibits, but there is still plenty to see, do, and explore. Visit the space and aviation themed gift shop for anything flight related, including flight jackets, models, flyboy t-shirts, and games. Both the men's and women's restrooms have diaper-changing tables.

Other destinations within 5 miles . . .

Aurora Fox Theatre (Site 24) - 2½ miles
Family Arts at DAVA (Site 44) - 2½ miles
Four Mile Historic Park (Site 106) - 3 miles
Kids Kourt (Site 51) - 4 miles
The Bookies (Site 60) - 4½ miles

Cinema Grill (Site 167) - 4½ miles
Little Monkey Bizness - Denver (Site 53) - 4½ miles
Denver Museum of Nature and Science (Site 11) - 5 miles
Utah Pool (Site 76) - 5 miles

GO ONE STEP FURTHER - Visit Blue Sky Bistro in Broomfield (**www.blueskybistro.com**) or The Perfect Landing at the Centennial Airport (**www.theperfectlanding.com**) to get a close up look at the planes as they take off and land. Both of these restaurants are situated next to the runway of a small airport. Breakfast or lunch have more activity than the dinner hour. Or try The Airplane Restaurant (**www.theairplanerestaurant.com**) in Colorado Springs and enjoy your meal inside an actual airplane.

See Also

Bandimere Speedway (Site 142)

Belleview Park (Site 94)

Boondocks Fun Center (Site 151)

City Park (Site 96)

Confluence Park (Site 99)

Denver Firefighters Museum (Site 9)

E.B. Rains Jr. Memorial Park (Site 104)

Fun City (Site 153)

Heritage Square Amusement Park (Site 154)

Lions Park (Site 109)

Sloan's Lake Park (Site 122)

Waneka Lake Park (Site 124)

Forney Museum of Transportation

Hodgepodge

This chapter simply contains all the destinations that didn't seem to fit into any other category. From Skate City to NCAR to Casa Bonita, following are a number of unusual, unique and worthwhile places to visit.

Courtesy Hammond's Candies

Hodgepodge

16th Street Mall ☆☆☆☆☆

16th Street Mall CoMedia Larry Laszlo
Downtown Denver Partnership

16th Street between
Broadway and Market
Denver, 80202
www.denver.com/16th-street-mall

Admission:	FREE!
Parking:	Metered street parking and paid lots available.
Food:	Choose from scores of different restaurants, cafés, and street vendors. Tables and benches are plentiful so you can bring your own lunch as well.

What to expect...

The 16th Street Mall is a pedestrian mall that stretches for 16 blocks through the heart of downtown Denver. Literally hundreds of stores and dozens of restaurants line the mall, from well-known chains to quaint locally-owned businesses. Window-shop or people-watch as you stroll the flower-lined walkway. A free shuttle bus service called MallRide can quickly take you from one end of the Mall to the other. Buses run frequently throughout the day and stop at each intersection. Street performers entertain here in the summer time.

16th Street Mall is stroller-friendly. It can get crowded, especially during rush hour and on the week-ends. Public restrooms can be found at the Tabor Center at 16th and Arapahoe and also at Denver Pavilions at 16th and Glenarm. The larger hotels usually have restrooms in their lobbies. Most other businesses reserve their restrooms for customers only, but some will accommodate you if you have a toddler doing the potty dance.

Other destinations within 5 miles . . .

See Appendix I - Downtown Destinations
Kids Kourt (Site 51) - 3½ miles

Sloan's Lake Park (Site 122) - 4 miles
The Bookery Nook (Site 59) - 5 miles

16th Street Mall CoMedia Larry Laszlo Downtown Denver Partnership

Casa Bonita ☆☆☆☆☆

Hours:	11:00 AM - 9:00 PM, Sunday - Thursday 11:00 AM - 10:00 PM, Saturday and Sunday
Admission:	Free admission, but a meal purchase is required for anyone over 2 years old. Discover, MasterCard, Visa, and cash accepted.
Parking:	Free parking lot.
Food:	No outside food or drink permitted.

6715 West Colfax Avenue
Lakewood, 80214
(303) 232-5115
www.casabonitadenver.com

What to expect. . .

Casa Bonita is a Denver legend. Because they feature live entertainment and they do not charge an admission fee, they require that everyone 2 and older purchase a meal. But no one goes to Casa Bonita for the food anyway. In my opinion, it is mediocre at best, except for the sopaipillas, which are great (but really, how can you go wrong with fried dough covered in honey?). I would recommend the taco salad, because the meat comes on the side. Others have suggested skipping the Mexican food altogether and ordering the chicken fried steak. What makes Casa Bonita such a great spot to visit is the ambiance and the entertainment.

And the entertainment is fantastic, especially for children. The shows vary slightly on weekdays compared with weekends, and also in the afternoon compared with the evening. Whenever you choose to go, expect to see strolling musicians, cliff divers, gunfights, magicians, and dancing gorillas. During the week, puppet shows and piñatas alternate every hour and start at 5:30 PM with a puppet show. On the weekend, the puppet shows and piñatas alternate every half hour and start at 12:30 PM with a piñata. These activities are held in the area near Black Bart's Hideout and are free for children 12 and under. You may want to go through Black Bart's Hideout without your child first, as it may be too scary for younger ones. The restaurant is huge and each area is decorated elaborately with a different theme, ranging from caves to a palace to a jungle. Casa Bonita also has two arcades and artists that paint caricatures and make balloon animals.

If your party has four people or fewer, try to get a table in front the waterfall, as this will afford you the best view of the cliff divers and other entertainment. Larger parties have to sit further from the stage in order to sit together, but there are several tables that still offer a good view. Truthfully, we didn't spend much time sitting anyway, as there is so much to see and do in here. When you need your server for refills on drinks or more sopaipillas, just raise the red flag on your table. If you want to try to avoid the gunfight, arrive early in the afternoon. A gunfight takes place around 1:15 PM and there isn't another one till almost 4:00 PM. Bathrooms are located in several places throughout the restaurant. The wheelchair-accessible bathroom on the upper level next to the bar has a diaper-changing table.

Other destinations within 5 miles . . .

Scales 'n' Tails - Lakewood (Site 139) - 1 mile
Sloan's Lake Park (Site 122) - 1 mile
Rising Curtain Theatre Academy (Site 33) - 3 miles
Fish Den (Site 138) - 3½ miles
The Bookery Nook (Site 59) - 4 miles

Lakeside Amusement Park (Site 155) - 4 miles
Lakewood Link Recreation Center Pool (Site 71) - 4 miles
Denver Puppet Theater (Site 28) - 4½ miles
Wheat Ridge Recreation Center Pool (Site 77) - 4½ miles

Celestial Seasonings ☆☆☆☆☆

Hodgepodge

Photo Courtesy of Celestial Seasonings

4600 Sleepytime Drive
Boulder, 80301
(303) 530-5300
www.celestialseasonings.com/visit-us

Hours:	**Tea and Gift Shop** 9:00 AM - 6:00 PM, Monday - Saturday 11:00 AM - 5:00 PM, Sunday **Tours (depart hourly)** 10:00 AM - 4:00 PM, Monday - Saturday 11:00 AM - 3:00 PM, Sunday
Admission:	FREE!
Parking:	Free parking lot.
Food:	The Celestial Café is open for breakfast and lunch and has a variety of healthful options, including vegetarian items. You may bring your own food and eat at one of the tables set up in the herb garden.

What to expect. . .

Full disclosure: I love tea. I love the smell, I love the taste, and I love the cozy feeling I get when I'm holding a warm cup in my hands. Our visit to Celestial Seasonings was really more for me than for my children, but fortunately they enjoyed themselves as well. Begin your visit in the Tour Center, where several types of tea, including caffeine-free kid-friendly flavors like Sugar Cookie or Tropic of Strawberry, are ready to sample. You may also choose to have a tea prepared for you from a list of nearly 100 different teas. These tastings are complimentary. The Tour Center has an art gallery with original paintings from their tea boxes, as well as a history of Celestial Seasonings.

Photo Courtesy of Celestial Seasonings

For safety reasons, only children 5 and older may go on a factory tour. The tour starts with a 15-minute video about the history of Celestial Seasonings and information on teas and herbs. Even if you are not continuing for the full tour, you may sit and watch the video. I found the video quite interesting, while my children preferred to snuggle with the giant Sleepytime bear sitting in the corner. The room is easy to leave if your child doesn't want to sit through the entire video. If you take a tour, you'll have the chance to step into the famous Mint Room for a potent whiff of peppermint and spearmint.

The Tea and Gift shop is enormous, filled with teapots, cups, toys, every flavor of Celestial Seasonings tea, cozies, jewelry, knick knacks, and natural food items from Haines Celestial. Bathrooms are located in the Tour Center and diaper-changing tables are available in both the men's and women's.

Other destinations within 5 miles . . .

Leanin' Tree Museum of Western Art (Site 13) - less than 1 mile
Boulder Reservoir Swim Beach (Site 81) - 3½ miles
Storybook Ballet (Site 36) - 4½ miles

Kids Kabaret (Site 31) - 5 miles
North Boulder Recreation Center Pool (Site 73) - 5 miles

Cinema Grill ☆☆☆☆☆

Hours:	Movies that are G or PG are generally shown in the morning and afternoon.
Admission:	$4 for evening movies; $2.50 for matinees (starting before 6:00 PM) American Express, Discover, MasterCard, Visa, and cash accepted.
Parking:	Free parking lot.
Food:	No outside food or drink allowed.
Discounts:	Admission is half-price on Tuesday.

13782 East Alameda Avenue
Aurora, 80012
(303) 344-5565 • (303) 344-3456 (Showtimes)
www.cinemagrill.com

What to expect. . .

Cinema Grill features current movies that have been released for a few weeks to a few months, depending on the popularity of the movie. It also offers a large menu with food service at your seat. The menu includes appetizers, burgers, salads, pizzas, and desserts, as well as a kid menu for children 12 and under. Popcorn is the only standard movie fare. No minimum order is required. Instead of rows of seats, the theater has swivel chairs with a tabletop in front of them. Children's movies

are generally shown during the day. The theater is older, but it is clean and stroller-friendly. Restrooms are located in the lobby and diaper-changing tables are in both the men's and women's. We purchased three movie tickets, three drinks, and a popcorn to share and our cost was only about $25, including tax and a tip for our server.

Other destinations within 5 miles . . .

Aurora History Museum (Site 1) - less than 1 mile
Utah Pool (Site 76) - 3 miles
Family Arts at DAVA (Site 44) - 4 miles

Aurora Fox Theatre (Site 24) - 4½ miles
Morrison Nature Center at Star K Ranch (Site 113) - 5 miles
Skate City - Aurora (Site 175) - 5 miles

HELPFUL TIP - Many movie theaters offer inexpensive summer movie programs on weekday mornings. Call or visit the website of the theater nearest you to see if it participates.

Denver Skate Park ☆☆☆☆☆

Courtesy City and County of Denver

2205 19th Street,
Denver, 80202
(720) 913-0700 (Denver Parks & Rec)
www.denverskatepark.com

Hours:	5:00 AM - 11:00 PM daily
Admission:	FREE!
Parking:	Free street parking.
Food:	You may bring in your own food and drink. A covered pavilion with picnic tables is located in the center of the skate park.

What to expect. . .

With 50,000 square feet of bowls, ramps, waves, and pipes, Denver Skate Park is the largest free public skating facility in the nation. Unless it's raining or snowing (and sometimes even then), people come from all over town to skate here. A low wall surrounding the park provides seating space for spectators. Some of the bowls are large and deep, while others are long and shallow. There is also quite a bit of flat space for new skaters. Sadly, we didn't have our skates with us, but my children were quite content running up and down some of the smaller bowls. They also really enjoyed watching the more advanced skaters.

Courtesy City and County of Denver

Tobacco products are not allowed inside the park so it is relatively smoke-free. Those who smoke congregate on the sidewalks. Port-a-potties are available but they do not have changing tables.

Other destinations within 5 miles . . .

See Appendix I - Downtown Destinations
Rising Curtain Theatre Academy (Site 33) - 4½ miles
Sloan's Lake Park (Site 122) - 5 miles

GO ONE STEP FURTHER Support the development of free, quality, public skate parks by making a tax-deductible donation to the Colorado Coalition for Public Skateparks. Visit www.coloradoskateparks.org for more information.

Fiske Planetarium ☆☆☆☆☆

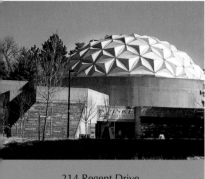

214 Regent Drive
Boulder, 80302
(303) 492-5002
http://fiske.colorado.edu/

Hours:	8:00 AM - 5:00 PM, Monday - Friday 1:30 PM - 4:30 PM, Saturday Closed most federal holidays (depending on CU's schedule).
Admission:	FREE! (Suggested donation of $2 for children over 6 and $3 for adults.) Laser Shows and Star Shows range in price from $3.50 - $6. American Express, MasterCard, and Visa accepted for online purchases. The Ticket Office also accepts personal checks and cash.
Parking:	You may purchase an all-day parking pass for Lot 308 from Fiske. A paid campus lot is at Euclid and Broadway (about a ten-minute walk).
Food:	Food and drink are not permitted inside the planetarium, but there are plenty of places on campus to picnic.

What to expect. . .

Fiske Planetarium is a science museum and a planetarium rolled into one. Several hands-on, interactive exhibits are located in the lobby. An infrared light exhibit has a frozen plastic water bottle. Hold it for a minute or two and compare the way your hands look in the infrared compared with the rest of your body. "View" Jupiter in the cosmos through the huge telescope. Create unusual pictures using the ultraviolet markers under the ultraviolet light. Perhaps the most interesting exhibit is the giant orb located in the center of the lobby. Different images are projected onto it so it is always changing. It may look like Earth, the moon, or another planet in our solar system.

The Fiske Planetarium has live talks, laser shows, and star shows. A Family Star Show takes place every Saturday at 2:00 PM and a Family Laser Show is at 3:15 PM. During Boulder County school breaks, Family Shows are also shown at 10:00 AM and 1:00 PM on Tuesday, Wednesday, and Thursday. For a full description of all shows, visit the website, click on *Events*, then *K12*. From there you can download the School and Group Brochure and choose a show that is most suited for your family. Children under 3 could have a difficult time sitting through an entire show.

The small gift shop sells books, posters, t-shirts, and calendars. Men's, women's, and unisex bathrooms are available but do not have diaper-changing tables.

Note: If you enjoy Fiske, you may also want to visit Gates Planetarium, located inside the Denver Museum of Nature and Science (Site 11).

Other destinations within 5 miles . . .

Boulder History Museum (Site 3) - less than ½ mile
CU Museum of Natural History (Site 7) - less than ½ mile
Boulder Museum of Contemporary Art (Site 4) - less than 1 mile
Colorado Music Festival Children's Concerts (Site 25) - 1 mile
Tebo Train (Site 160) - 1 mile
North Boulder Recreation Center Pool (Site 73) - 2 miles

Scott Carpenter Park (Site 121) - 2 miles
Storybook Ballet (Site 36) - 2 miles
Rocky Mountain Theatre for Kids (Site 34) - 3½ miles
Kids Kabaret (Site 31) - 4 miles
NCAR (Site 173) - 4 miles

Flapjacks and A Flick ☆☆☆☆☆

Courtesy Movie Tavern

Aurora Movie Tavern
18605 East Hampden Avenue
Aurora, 80013
(303) 680-9915
www.movietavern.com

Hours:	9:00 AM, Saturday and Sunday
Admission:	Under 13: $9.00; Age 13+: $10.50 American Express, Discover, MasterCard, Visa, and cash accepted.
Parking:	Free parking lot.
Food:	No outside food and drink permitted.

What to expect. . .

Most people think of Movie Tavern as a great place to go for a date night — dinner, drinks, and a movie all in one location. Movie Tavern is also a great place for families to go on a Saturday or Sunday morning. At 9:00 AM, two to three different G or PG movies are showing. For just a little more than you would pay for a regular movie ticket, you also get all-you-can-eat pancakes and a drink. Bacon can be ordered for an additional 99 cents.

Courtesy Movie Tavern

The theater is stroller-friendly, large, and clean with very comfortable chairs. Buttons that light up are near every seat to call your server over without disturbing other patrons. Men's and women's bathrooms are located in the lobby. A family bathroom with a diaper-changing table is between them. Bring extra cash if you would like to tip your server, or you can order some bacon and add a tip to the charge.

Other destinations within 5 miles . . .

Plains Conservation Center (Site 114) - 2 miles
Skate City - Aurora (Site 175) - 2½ miles

Great Plains Park (Site 107) - 3½ miles
Cherry Creek State Park Swim Beach (Site 82) - 4½ miles

Hammond's Candies ☆☆☆☆☆

Courtesy Hammond's Candies

5735 North Washington Street
Denver, 80216
(303) 333-5588
www.hammondscandies.com

Hours:	9:00 AM - 3:00 PM, Monday - Friday (factory tour) 10:00 AM - 3:00 PM, Saturday (factory tour) Candy store stays open till 4:00 PM.
Admission:	FREE! American Express, MasterCard, Visa, checks, and cash accepted for store purchases.
Parking:	Free parking lot.
Food:	A few picnic tables are near the entrance if you would like to bring your lunch.

What to expect. . .

If you're craving candy — any type of candy — chances are you'll find it at Hammond's Candies. The bulk of the candy inside the store, from ribbon candy to fudge, is handmade daily. They also sell other favorites like Fireballs, Lemonheads, and Gummi Bears, as well as toys, coffee cups, and knickknacks. A great time to visit the store is shortly after a holiday, as they sell leftover holiday-themed candy at drastically reduced prices.

Hammond's Candies has been making candy the same way for nearly a century. They use 1,000 pounds of sugar and 1,000 pounds of corn syrup to hand-make 2,000 pounds of candy every day from Christmas through Easter, and they offer a free tour so you can see just how they do it (no tours are offered on Sunday or national holidays). The tour begins with a short video about the history of Hammond's and the Candy Cane Festival. After the video, the tour group is taken into the factory to see the candy being made. Large windows separate the tour group from the candy makers. Slanted mirrors are positioned above many of the tables so you can get a better look. Steps are placed in front of a few of the windows, but not all of them, so be prepared to lift your child from time to time. Interestingly, the machine still used to make the ribbon candy today was actually built in the late 1800s. Other equipment on display in the tour was built in the 1920s or 1930s. From start to end, the tour lasts about 30 minutes. Free samples of overrun candies are offered at the close of the tour.

Hammond's Candies has been featured on TV shows and in magazines, and people all around the world order their candy. The Candy Cane Festival, held on the second Saturday in December, draws 4,000 to 7,000 visitors. Free tours are offered throughout the day, Christmas candy is for sale in the store, and Santa Claus is hanging out in the parking lot. Crafts, carolers, a train, and outside vendors add to the excitement. Come as early as you can to try to beat the crowds. Avoid some of the crowds by visiting the Friday before for the tour and the candy store, and just spend the day of the festival having fun outside.

The tour and the candy shop are both stroller-friendly. Bathrooms are available but do not have diaper-changing tables.

Other destinations within 5 miles . . .
See Appendix I - Downtown Destinations

Krispy Kreme ☆☆☆☆☆

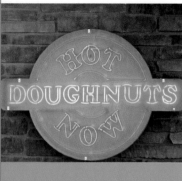

Hours:	5:00 AM - 10:00 PM daily
Admission:	FREE!
Parking:	Free parking lot.
Food:	No outside food or drink.

www.krispykreme.com/home

Multiple Locations. . .

1051 East 120th Avenue Thornton, 80233 (720) 977-8555	7514 East Parkway Drive Lone Tree, 80124 (303) 649-9933

What to expect. . .

Krispy Kreme is open all day but plan to visit 6:00 AM - 11:00 AM or 5:00 PM - 10:00 PM, because that's when they are making the original glazed donuts that made them famous. A "Hot Now" neon sign will be lit up in the window. Come in and step onto the raised platform where you and your child can watch through the theater window as the dough travels through the conveyor and transforms into a fresh donut. A description of what is happening at each stage is on the glass. Every customer who comes in during this time receives a complimentary fresh donut. If you want to take one home,

purchase a Kid's Pack for $2.99 which includes a donut, your choice of milk or juice, and other surprises like tattoos, a curly straw, a paper hat like the employees wear, and a coloring sheet. You can get a free donut anytime by having your child color the sheet and returning it to the store.

The staff is very friendly, and if they have someone available, they will walk with you along the conveyor belt and tell you more information than is posted on the window. You can also make reservations for a group tour for a personalized experience. Men's and women's bathrooms are located inside the store, but they do not have diaper-changing tables.

Other destinations within 5 miles . . .

D.L. Parsons Theatre (Site 29) - 1 mile
E.B. Rains Jr. Memorial Park (Site 104) - 1 mile
The Hop - Thornton (Site 46) - 1 mile
Boondocks Fun Center (Site 151) - 1½ miles
Skate City - Westminster (Site 175) - 1½ miles
Jungle Quest (Site 49) - 3½ miles

Scales 'n' Tails - Northglenn (Site 139) - 4 miles
Thornton City Pool (Site 91) - 4½ miles
Little Monkey Bizness - Westminster (Site 53) - 5 miles
Paul Derda Indoor Pool (Site 74) - 5 miles
Kids Zone (Site 52) - 5 miles

NCAR ☆☆☆☆☆

Copyright UCAR Photo by Carlye Calvin

Hours:	8:00 AM - 5:00 PM, Monday - Friday 9:00 AM - 4:00 PM, Saturday, Sunday, and holidays
Admission:	FREE!
Parking:	Free parking lot.
Food:	The cash-only cafeteria offers a variety of healthful food and is open to the public weekdays only from 8:00 AM - 9:30 AM and from 11:30 AM - 1:30 PM. Tables and benches are located on site if you prefer to bring your own food and have a picnic lunch. The view from the picnic tables on the cafeteria patio is fabulous.

1850 Table Mesa Drive
Boulder, 80305
(303) 497-1000
www.eo.ucar.edu/visit

What to expect. . .

The National Center for Atmospheric Research (NCAR) may not sound like a facility for children, but we found quite a few things to get excited about. A variety of interactive weather exhibits are located on the first floor. Disrupt a mini-tornado and then watch it re-form, create fog, or view lightning in a tube. A theater at the end of this hallway shows two short videos on weather and climate change. The second floor has a Climate Discovery exhibit that covers the topic of past, present, and future climate, as well as a library that is open to the public. From this floor, you can access the Walter Orr Roberts Weather Trail in the northwest corner of the building.

The Walter Orr Roberts Weather Trail was inspired by a similar trail at the Swiss Meteorological Institute in Gstaad and is believed to be the only interpretive trail in North America devoted to weather and climate. The half-mile walking loop has 11 viewpoints; each point has a sign referring to a different weather phenomenon that may be visible from that spot, depending on the time of year you visit. Don't be surprised if you encounter deer on or near this path (they also tend to hang out in the grassy areas as you enter the parking lot). The view from this path is outstanding. Follow the loop back to where you started. A button near the door will call security, who can buzz you back into the building. You can also follow the path north and it will drop you on the side of the building, near the entrance. The path is dirt, firm enough for a stroller unless there has been a lot of rain or snow.

The parking lot and building are both enormous. Face the building from the parking lot and the entrance is located on the right (north) side near the flagpole. Guided tours are offered daily at noon and last about one hour. Two self-guided cell-phone audio tours are available, one created for adults and one geared toward children. Bathrooms are located throughout the facility. Diaper-changing tables are in the men's restroom on the first floor and the women's restroom on the second floor. Before or after your visit, check out **www.eo.ucar.edu/kids** for games, activities, experiments, and cool weather facts.

Annual Events . . .

Wild Earth Day is held the Saturday before Earth Day (April 22) each year.

Super Science Saturday is a large public event held on one Saturday each October (see the website).

Other destinations within 5 miles . . .

Boulder History Museum (Site 3) - 4 miles
Colorado Music Festival Children's Concerts (Site 25) - 4 miles
CU Museum of Natural History (Site 7) - 4 miles
Fiske Planetarium (Site 169) - 4 miles

Boulder Museum of Contemporary Art (Site 4) - 5 miles
Scott Carpenter Park (Site 121) - 5 miles
Storybook Ballet (Site 36) - 5 miles
Tebo Train (Site 160) - 5 miles

Pearl Street Mall ☆☆☆☆☆

Hodgepodge

Courtesy Boulder Parks & Recreation

Pearl Street between 11th and 15th St
Boulder, 80302
www.boulderdowntown.com

Admission:	FREE!
Parking:	Metered street parking and paid lots are available. Parking is free in the city-owned parking structures on Saturday and Sunday.
Food:	Choose from more than 100 different restaurants, cafés, or street vendors. Tables and benches are plentiful so you can bring your own lunch as well.

What to expect. . .

The Pearl Street Mall is a pedestrian mall that stretches for four blocks through the heart of downtown Boulder. What sets this mall apart from most other pedestrian malls is that approximately 85% of the businesses are locally-owned. Window-shop or people-watch as you walk along. A variety of street performers entertain here during the warmer months. The area is a historic district so you will see some of Boulder's oldest buildings here. You will also see a variety of public art, from fountains to sculptures. A play area with pop up water jets is located near 14th Street. Bring a change of clothes for your

Courtesy City of Boulder's Parks & Recreation Department

child, and maybe yourself, if you're visiting in the summertime. Many events are held here through the course of the year; you'll find them listed on the website under *Events*.

The Pearl Street Mall is also just two blocks from the Boulder Farmer's Market (**www.boulderfarmers. org**), located at 13th and Canyon Streets, which is open during the summer on Saturday mornings and early afternoons and Wednesday evenings. There is a public playground located at 15th and Spruce Street just off the east end of the Mall area, and there are more stores and restaurants on the East and West ends of Pearl Street.

Pearl Street Mall is stroller-friendly. It can get crowded, especially during rush hour and on the weekends. Public restrooms can be found at right in the middle at 13th and Pearl. Most businesses reserve their restrooms for customers only, but some will accommodate you if you have a toddler doing the potty dance.

Other destinations within 5 miles . . .

Skate City Pixie Class ☆☆☆☆☆

Hours:	10:00 AM - 11:30 AM, Thursday
Admission:	$4 (includes skate rentals)
Parking:	Free parking at all locations.
Food:	Price includes a drink and a snack.

www.skatecitycolorado.com

Multiple Locations. . .

15100 East Girard Avenue
Aurora, 80014
(303) 690-1444

200 West 121st Avenue
Westminster, 80234
(303) 457-0220

5801 South Lowell Way
Littleton, 80123
(303) 795-6109

What to expect. . .

Designed for children age 2 to 6, Pixie Class is an opportunity for your child to have fun while learning to skate to a mix of kid songs (think Barney) and kid-friendly songs (think "YMCA"). The class is led by dedicated Skate City staff members. Parents may watch but do not participate in skating. Skates can be "locked" for beginners, which simply means the wheels give more resistance and don't roll quite as easily. Helmets are available, but you may want to bring your own to ensure a good fit. While your child is having fun, you can check your email (all facilities have free WiFi), read a book, or visit with a friend.

The snack bar is closed during Pixie Class. Children are given a drink and a snack halfway through the class. Parents may bring a drink or snack for themselves. Bathrooms are available but do not have diaper-changing tables. If you plan to attend frequently, get a punch card. Your child gets a free Pixie Super Skater t-shirt after 10 visits.

Once your child is steady on her feet, make this physical activity a family affair. Parents with paying children skate free on Saturday morning from 10:00 AM - 12:00 PM ($4.50 admission for children, $1.50 skate rental for everyone or you can bring your own). Or try Family Night every Sunday from 6:00 - 8:00 PM and get a free slice of pizza for each paid skater ($4 admission, $1 skate rental or you can bring your own).

Other destinations within 5 miles . . .

See Cherry Creek State Park Swim Beach (Site 82) for destinations near Aurora location.
See The Town Hall Arts Center (Site 38) for destinations near Littleton location.
See EB Rains Jr Memorial Park (Site 104) for destinations near Westminster location.

The State Capitol Building ☆☆☆☆☆

200 East Colfax Avenue
Denver, 80203
(303) 866-2604
www.colorado.gov/capitoltour

Hours:	7:30 AM - 5:00 PM, Monday - Friday Three different types of guided tours are offered. Closed state and federal holidays.
Admission:	FREE!
Parking:	Metered street parking and paid lots are available.
Food:	Vending machines and a small coffee shop with a few lunch items are located in the basement. You may also bring in your own food and drink and eat at the tables in front of the cafeteria.

What to expect...

Built in the 1890s and designed to resemble the United States Capitol building, the Colorado State Capitol is exquisite. Gold plating was added to the dome in 1908 to commemorate the Colorado Gold Rush. The steps at the Western entrance do not lead to a public entrance, but you will find the words "One Mile Above Sea Level" engraved on the 15th step. A second mile-high marker was added to the 18th step in 1969 when CSU students resurveyed the elevation. In 2003, modern means determined that the 13th step is actually the mile-high step, and a third marker on this step was installed. The public entrances are through the first floor level on the north and south sides of the building, with the south side being stroller- and wheelchair-accessible. The inside of the building is as extraordinary as the out-side, with murals, stained glass, art work, and intricate details in every inch of design.

Three different guided tours are available: historical tours given year-round; legislative tours designed for students and only available during the legislative session; and dome tours for which reservations are required. The tours generally last about 45 minutes, but you can step out of the tour at any time if your child becomes fussy or bored. You can also do a self-guided tour at your leisure. Mr. Brown's Attic, an exhibit area between the third floor and the dome, is a small children's space with more information on Colorado's history and the Capitol building. From here, you can climb another 61steps to get to the top of the dome, where you will have a 360-degree panoramic view of Denver.

If your child enjoys riding in a stroller, this is a great place for a long walk, especially if it's cold outside. Toddlers and preschoolers will enjoy the wide, open spaces and the unusual architecture, but may not be interested in lingering as long. Bathrooms are located in several areas of the building; the men's and women's bathrooms in the basement have diaper-changing tables. A gift shop is also located in the basement. The building is very stroller-friendly up to the third floor, but Mr. Brown's Attic and the Dome are only accessible via stairs. A video tour near the third-floor elevators is available for those who are unable to make the climb.

Other destinations within 5 miles . . .

See Appendix I - Downtown Destinations
Kids Kourt (Site 51) - 3 miles
Sloan's Lake Park (Site 122) - 4 miles

The Bookery Nook (Site 59) - 5 miles
The Bookies (Site 60) - 5 miles
Four Mile Historic Park (Site 106) - 5 miles

DID YOU KNOW? It is against state law to build any building that would block the 120-mile long view of the mountains from the Colorado State Capitol.

Little Man
ICE CREAM

• (303) 455-3811 • 2620 16th St. Denver, CO 80211 •
• www.littlemanicecream.com •

The United States Mint ☆☆☆☆☆

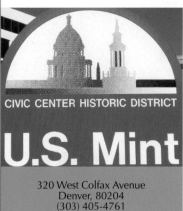

CIVIC CENTER HISTORIC DISTRICT

U.S. Mint

320 West Colfax Avenue
Denver, 80204
(303) 405-4761
www.usmint.gov

Hours:	8:00 AM - 2:00 PM, Monday - Friday Closed weekends and all federal holidays.
Admission:	FREE! (Reservations strongly recommended.)
Parking:	Metered street parking and paid lots are available.
Food:	No food or drink are allowed inside the Mint. Restaurants and parks are within walking distance.

What to expect. . .

The United States Mint can manufacture up to 40 million coins in one day. It does not print paper currency. During a tour, you will have the opportunity to learn about the history of the Mint and the current state of coin manufacturing, see antique coin presses and old coins, and possibly even watch coins being made. If coins are not being manufactured during your visit, a video demonstrates the process. My 5-year-old, who had recently started receiving an allowance and was beginning to gain an understanding of money, was fascinated. My 3-year-old, who would rather have a roll of stickers than any amount of money, was not nearly as intrigued. Fortunately, the tours only last about 30 minutes so he was able to make it through.

Guided tours begin on the hour, with the last tour departing at 2:00 PM. Although the tour is free, it is strongly recommended that you make reservations through the website, as only a limited number of stand-by tickets are available each day. You may need to make your reservations six to eight weeks in advance during spring and summer months, as this is the busiest time for tours. The United States Mint is a federal facility and has a number of restrictions. You may bring in a wallet or change purse to hold your identification and keys if it is small enough to fit in your pocket. Virtually everything else, including cell phones with built-in cameras, is prohibited. You may carry your child in a baby carrier or backpack, provided nothing else is in the backpack. Carefully read the information on the website prior to your visit.

As a souvenir, we received pennies that had not yet been pressed, although I'm not sure if this is done for every tour. If you're interested in coins, visit the gift shop at the end of the tour. Bathrooms are available before the tour starts, but I can't remember if they had diaper-changing tables (I did not have my digital voice recorder or pen and paper — see above paragraph). Before or after your visit, go to www. usmint.gov/kids for games and cartoons about coins and Mint history.

Note: Click on Tours, then choose Denver.

Other destinations within 5 miles . . .

See Appendix I - Downtown Destinations
Kids Kourt (Site 51) - 3½ miles
Sloan's Lake Park (Site 122) - 3½ miles

The Bookery Nook (Site 59) - 4½ miles
Fish Den (Site 138) - 5 miles

White Fence Farm ☆☆☆☆☆

6263 West Jewell Avenue
Lakewood, 80232
(303) 935-5945
www.whitefencefarm-co.com

Hours:	4:30 PM - 8:30 PM, Tuesday - Saturday 11:30 AM - 8:00 PM, Sunday Closed Thanksgiving, Christmas, and the entire month of January.
Admission:	FREE! American Express, Discover, MasterCard, Visa, checks and cash are accepted in the restaurant and gift shops.
Parking:	Free parking lot.
Food:	Outside food and drink are prohibited.
Discounts:	Purchase a Cheep Eats card for $7. Your beverages are complimentary on the day you purchase the card, and you will get $2 off adult meals and $1 off kid meals for three months, excluding Saturday. The card is valid for up to four meals. With the Cheep Eats card, you also get $1 off desserts and 20% off gift shop purchases.

What to expect. . .

White Fence Farm is primarily a restaurant with a variety of family entertainment and farm activities on the eight-acre property. Upon arrival, add your name to the restaurant's waiting list as seating is done on a walk-in basis. A very comfortable waiting area is located just outside the dining room if you need some time to relax. If you prefer, feel free to shop, play, or stroll the beautifully landscaped grounds while you wait. You can watch for your table number on the monitors located in the buildings or listen for the loudspeaker pages throughout the grounds and buildings. Entertainment and amusements include:

OK Corral, located just past the Country Cottage gift shop behind the main building's entrance, is a petting zoo with goats, sheep, and a pig. Tank, a huge steer, lives in the pen too, so you can only pet the animals through the fence.

The Treehouse and Playground in front of the restaurant is for children 10 and under. The climbing structure has monkey bars, a slide, a bridge, and a tire swing. The gazebo, an aviary, and several photo spots are also located in this area.

Waterside Walk, complete with bridge and waterfall, received a national landscape award. Bring a few quarters to purchase food for the ducks and fish.

Americana Barn is a separate building connected to the restaurant by a carriage museum. On the first floor of the building is a Christmas-themed gift shop, a fudge and pie shop, and a stage with live country and blue grass entertainment most evenings. Upstairs, you'll find a small arcade, tables with checkerboards, and a miniature barn play area for the younger children. Perhaps the most popular feature in this building is the Pig Chute, a two-story slide for those who are at least four feet tall. The Pig Chute is only open for the first 15 minutes of each hour.

Carriage Rides run during restaurant hours. Rides are $4 for adults and $3 for children, cash only.

White Fence Farm specializes in family-style farm chicken: half a fried chicken and mashed or baked potato or french fries (I recommend the mashed potatoes with gravy). Accompanying this meal are unlimited amounts of beets, coleslaw, bean salad (yum), and fritters (double-yum). Don't visit if you're dieting. The food is not low-calorie, and it is so delicious you will not want to deprive yourself. A manager will give you a tour of the kitchen upon request and you can see the fritters being made.

White Fence Farm is charming, family-oriented, and offers the "best fried chicken in Denver," according to *Westword*. Antique farm equipment located throughout the property provide great photo spots, as do the rocking chairs on the front porch of the Americana Barn and Country Cottage. The entire facility is stroller-friendly. Restrooms are located in the waiting area outside the dining room and on the second floor of the Americana Barn. Diaper-changing tables are in both the men's and women's, and family restrooms with lower toilets, diaper-changing tables, and stools for the sink are also available in these locations.

Other destinations within 5 miles . . .

Lakewood Link Recreation Center Pool (Site 71) - 1½ miles

Scales 'n' Tails - Lakewood (Site 139) - 5 miles

Sloan's Lake Park (Site 122) - 5 miles

Younger Generation Players (Site 40) - 5 miles

See Also

Cave of the Winds (Site 180)

Manitou Springs (Site 187)

White Fence Farm

Colorado Springs

Situated at the base of one of America's most famous mountains (Pikes Peak), the city of Colorado Springs is about 60 miles south of Denver. It is close enough for a day trip, or a great place for a weekend getaway. Colorado Springs offers a wide variety of activities for young children. This chapter is by no means all-inclusive, but focuses on the destinations that are a little different from what you might find in Denver.

America the Beautiful Park Courtesy City of Colorado Springs

Colorado Springs

America the Beautiful Park ☆☆☆☆☆

Courtesy City of Colorado Springs

Hours:	5:00 AM - 9:00 PM, November 1 through April 30 5:00 AM - 11:00 PM, May 1 through October 31
Admission:	FREE!
Parking:	Free street parking around the park and a parking lot across the street.
Food:	You may bring in your own food and drinks.

126 Cimino Drive
Colorado Springs, 80903
(719) 785-3323
www.springsgov.com

What to expect...

Located between downtown Colorado Springs and I-25, America the Beautiful Park features the Julie Penrose fountain, a rotating water sculpture that represents the life-giving movement of water between the sky and the earth. Atop the fountain is the Stargate Portal, and water flows from the top and the bottom. You are allowed to splash and play in the base of the fountain, which runs daily from 10:00 AM - 6:00 PM (till 8:00 PM on Wednesday). The fountain may periodically be turned off due to weather, limited staff, or budget constraints. Picnicking is allowed next

Courtesy City of Colorado Springs

to the fountain, but there are no tables and no shade. Summer events may include concerts in the park or farmer's markets. Check the website for the current year's calendar.

The large playground is quite unusual and creates a new opportunity for kids to use their imagination, explore, and try to figure out how to use the playground equipment. Children are invited to draw chalk designs on the Quirks, ride bikes or skateboard down the small ramp, or play Pirates on the sailboats. A few small awnings provide some areas of shade over the playground. The park also has baby swings, a pavilion with picnic tables that can be reserved, and benches all around. The bathrooms are next to the playground but do not include changing tables.

Note: On the website click on Play at the top, scroll down to the last paragraph and click on Community Parks.

Other destinations within 5 miles . . .
Uncle Wilber Fountain (Site 193) - 1 mile
Ghost Town and Wild West Museum (Site 186) - 3 miles

DID YOU KNOW? The first stanza of the song "America the Beautiful" was inspired by Pikes Peak ("purple mountain majesties") and the view from atop the mountain ("above the fruited plain").

Cave of the Winds ☆☆☆☆☆

Hours:	9:00 AM - 9:00 PM daily during summer months 10:00 AM - 5:00 PM daily during winter months Some days may have shorter hours; check the website. Closed Christmas Day.
Admission:	**Discovery Tour** - Under 6: Free; Age 6-11: $9; Age 12+: $18 **Lantern Tour** - Under 6 not permitted; Age 6-11: $12; Age 12+: $22 Discover, MasterCard, Visa, and cash accepted.
Parking:	Free parking lot.
Food:	No food or drink are allowed inside the cave. A concession stand and vending machines are located inside. You may bring in your own food and drink; tables are provided both indoors and outside.
Discounts:	Military discounts are available.

100 Cave of the Winds Road
Manitou Springs, 80829
(719) 685-5444
www.caveofthewinds.com

What to expect. . .

Cave of the Winds offers guided tours through 20 beautiful cavern rooms. The Discovery Tour lasts approximately 45 minutes. The path is about half a mile long with 200 steps and occasional ducking or turning sideways is required. For these reasons, strollers and children in carriers are not allowed. Along the way, we learned about how and why caves are formed. The Lantern Tour is twice as long and guided only by candle-lit lanterns; children 5 and younger are not permitted on the Lantern Tour.

Tours depart approximately every half hour in the winter months, and every 15 minutes or so in the summer. Expect a wait of at least half an hour from the time you purchase your tickets to the start of an available tour. Buying your tickets online may reduce your wait time, but it probably won't eliminate it entirely. While you wait, enjoy the incredible views, buy a bag of paleo mix from the Claim Jumper Mining Company and pan for goodies, visit the enormous gift shop, or have a bite to eat.

My 5-year-old loved this adventure. It was unlike anything we had ever done before. Personally, I think one of the main reasons to visit Cave of the Winds is just so you can use one of the funnest words in the English language: spelunking. My 3-year-old got very spooked as we entered the cave. We made it as far as the photo spot, and then he and my husband had to leave the tour. We were able to receive a refund for them without any problems, as they prefer not to have screaming children on the tour. There was another 3-year-old on our tour who seemed to enjoy it very much, so it really depends on the nature of your child. Before you visit Cave of the Winds, visit the *Kids Fun Center* section on the website for some cool cave-related games, quizzes, and activities.

The caverns are less than 60 degrees Fahrenheit regardless of the temperature outside, so dress appropriately. Both the men's and women's bathrooms provide diaper-changing tables. Lockers are available for 50 cents. An ATM is onsite.

Other destinations within 5 miles . . .

Manitou Springs (Site 187) - 1 mile
Ghost Town and Wild West Museum (Site 186) - 3 miles
Garden of the Gods (Site 185) - 4 miles
Rock Ledge Ranch (Site 190) - 4 miles

Cheyenne Mountain Zoo

Hours:	9:00 AM - 6:00 PM daily from Memorial Day weekend to Labor Day 9:00 AM - 5:00 PM daily from September to May Last admission is at 4:00 PM. Hours are shorter on some holidays.
Admission:	Under 3: Free; Age 3-11: $7.25; Age 12-64: $14.25; Age 65+: $12.25 American Express, Discover, MasterCard, Visa, in-state checks, and cash accepted.
Annual Pass:	$91.50 for 2 adults and their children under 18.
Parking:	Free parking lot.
Food:	You may bring in your own food and drink. Picnic areas are located throughout the zoo. Several restaurants and snack bars are available.
Discounts:	Military and AAA discounts are available. Visit the *Discounts & Promotions* section of the website for other ways to save.

4250 Cheyenne Mountain Zoo Road
Colorado Springs, 80906
(719) 633-9925
www.cmzoo.org

What to expect. . .

America's only mountain zoo, Cheyenne Mountain Zoo is home to more than 800 animals of every type. What makes the Cheyenne Mountain Zoo so unique, however, is that it provides many opportunities for children (and adults) to get up close and personal with the animals. The first exhibit is the giraffes. It is designed with the walkway higher than the exhibit so you can get face to face with these gentle giants. Buy a few crackers to feed them; you'll be fascinated by their long tongues. Surround yourself with budgies, finches, and cockatiels in the Budgies Buddies exhibit. In the warmer months, you may find a zookeeper holding a wallaby for you to pet. And the grizzly exhibit gets you so close (safely) you can "smell the fish on their breath."

Cheyenne Mountain Zoo offers much more than animals. It is said that you can see all the way to Kansas from the zoo. Ride the carousel that was an attraction at the 1932 World's Fair. Visit My Big Backyard and climb on giant mushrooms, sit in an oversized chair, or pet a goat. For the truly adventurous, hop on the Mountaineer Sky Ride, a chairlift-style ride that carries you above many of the zoo exhibits. More spectacular views and a playground are available at the top. Your admission to the zoo also includes a trip to the Will Rogers Shrine of the Sun, a historic monument 1.4 miles up the highway from the zoo entrance (you may drive). The elevation of the Shrine is over 8,000 feet on the top deck.

Many of the "extras" require an additional fee; bring extra dollar bills with you. The entire zoo is stroller-friendly, but it is also very hilly so prepare yourself for a great workout. Bathrooms are located throughout the zoo and most of them have diaper-changing tables in both the men's and women's. When we don't bring our own lunch, The Grizzly Grill, near the carousel, is our favorite place to eat because it has a variety of healthful options (although more expensive than the others). Visit the website with your child before your trip to the zoo. Click on the *Kids' Fun* tab and follow the links. You can watch YouTube videos of different areas of the zoo, listen to some of the animals, and play games. Visit the website again after your trip and talk about your favorite parts. The Zoo's blog gives you up to date information at www.cheyennemountainzooblog.blogspot.com. You can also become their fan on Facebook.

Annual Events . . .

Run to the Shrine is a 5K/10K event that takes place every May.

Teddy Bear Days, usually held in July, has special activities such as face painting, a teddy bear clinic for check-ups, and special bear demonstrations. Kids 12 and under accompanied by a teddy bear (or other stuffed animal) receive an admission discount.

Boo at the Zoo is after hours on select weekends in October.

Electric Safari is after hours on many evenings in December.

Other destinations within 5 miles . . .
Ghost Town and Wild West Museum (Site 186) - 5 miles

GO ONE STEP FURTHER - Serenity Springs Wildlife Center, home to more than 120 big cats, is the largest federal and state licensed placement facility in Colorado. Located about 22 miles east of Colorado Springs near Calhan, Serenity Springs provides a permanent sanctuary to displaced lions, tigers, cougars, caracals, leopards, and other exotic animals. For more information about how you can support this important facility or to schedule a tour, please go to

www.serenityspringswildlife.org.

Photo by Tracey Gazibara Courtesy Cheyenne Mountain Zoo

Colorado Springs Sky Sox Baseball ☆☆☆☆☆

Colorado Springs Sky Sox Baseball
Courtesy Security Service Field

4385 Tutt Boulevard
Colorado Springs, 80922
(719) 591-7699 (Tickets)
www.skysox.com

Hours:	Season runs from early April to September. Games are typically in the evening, with 1:00 PM Sunday starts and some weekday matinees. There are additional day games in April and May.
Admission:	Ticket prices range from $7 - $12. Children under 2 are free. Tickets can be purchased online using American Express, Discover, MasterCard, or Visa. The box office also accepts checks and cash.
Parking:	General parking is available west of the stadium for $5 per vehicle.
Food:	Only soft plastic water bottles may be brought into the stadium. Several concession stands are located throughout the stadium.
Discounts:	Youth, seniors 60 plus, and military discounts are available. "$2 Tuesdays" offers $2 tickets and parking. A variety of discounted ticket packages are offered. Specials occur throughout the season so visit the website often.

What to expect. . .

The Sky Sox are the top minor league baseball team affiliated with the Colorado Rockies (Site 146); dozens of players each year will split their time between each team. Many people consider minor league baseball to be more "pure" than major league baseball and feel that the players have "more heart." As a parent, taking my children to a Sky Sox game is an affordable way to teach my children about the sport that is as American as apple pie. Security Service Field has 6,200 fixed seats, plus the grass slope on the third base side and Skybox suite level. Because it is a smaller field, we can get closer to the action. A Fun Zone with inflatables and a pitching area is available to children 12 and under. You can purchase an unlimited wristband for $6, or pay $1 per child per ride or activity. Every day of the week during the season offers something special: Kids Eat Free Monday, $2 Tuesday, etc. Starting in May, all Friday night home games feature spectacular post-game firework displays. The Sky Sox full-color team magazine, "Inside Pitch," is issued free to all fans at the entrance gates.

Games generally last about three hours, but can go into extra innings. The seats at Security Service Field are comfortable, but it doesn't hurt to bring a cushion to sit on, especially for smaller children who might need a boost. The box seats (first 14 rows) are individual seats with cup holders. The reserved seats (next 14 rows) have fixed-back aluminum seating. Don't forget to pack a jacket for the night games.

DID YOU KNOW? Every minor league ballpark in the country is unique. The signature feature of the Sky Sox is that they have an original ballpark hot tub, which launched a whole industry of aquatics features in sports. Also, at 6,531 feet above sea level, it is the nation's highest altitude professional ball park, major leagues included.

rrara's Happy Apple Farm ☆☆☆☆☆

Courtesy Ferrara's Happy Apple Farm

1190 First Street
Penrose, 81240
(719) 372-6300
www.happyapplefarm.com

Site 182 Colorado Springs

Hours:	9:00 AM - 4:30 PM, Wednesday - Sunday from July to October Closed Monday and Tuesday.
Admission:	FREE! MasterCard, Visa, checks, and cash accepted for store purchases.
Parking:	Free parking, mostly on the sides of the dirt road leading to the farm.
Food:	You may bring your own lunch to enjoy at one of their picnic tables. A reasonably-priced deli is located in the lower area of the store. On weekends, Sunflowers Grill sells applewood-smoked brisket, turkey legs, and grilled corn.

What to expect. . .

Ferrara's Happy Apple Farm is a pick-your-own produce farm with 14 varieties of apples, pears, blackberries, raspberries, gooseberries, and pumpkins. Pick up your baskets and boxes in the building, then take a free tractor-trailer ride down to the berry and pumpkin patches, where the staff will point out what is growing where. Even very little children can tell the difference between a berry and a leaf (although they can't always tell the difference between a ripe berry and one that isn't quite ready to be picked). My children seemed to have a greater appreciation for "where food comes from" after our visit. Our entire family had a wonderful time picking our fruit and later making apple crumb together. Most of the berries were eaten before we arrived home!

The fruit is less expensive than the grocery store, and it is fresher and tastes better too. The store sells apples and a variety of foods made from their own produce, such as jams, jellies, and pumpkin butter. You can also purchase fresh-pressed apple cider and local honey. The only bathrooms available are port-a-potties, but they are much cleaner than many I've experienced. The fruits reach their peak at different times; making three or four trips each season affords a different experience each time. Check the website before your visit to see the current status of the produce.

Annual Events . . .

The **Apple Blossom Festival**, held over two weekends in April, gives you the chance to see the orchard in full bloom.

Happy Apple's Pumpkin Festival is one weekend in mid-to-late September.

APPLE POCKETS

2-3 apples
2 tablespoons sugar
1 tablespoon butter, melted

1 teaspoon cinnamon
1 package refrigerated biscuits
Dash vanilla

Heat oven to 350°. Peel and core apples; grate them into a medium bowl. In a small bowl, combine sugar and cinnamon. Stir half of cinnamon-sugar into grated apples. Roll each biscuit to about a 5" circle. Spoon apple mixture onto circles. Fold circles over and pinch edges to make half-moons. Place on a baking sheet. Combine the rest of the cinnamon-sugar with melted butter and vanilla; brush onto pockets. Bake 18-20 minutes.

Flying W Ranch ☆☆☆☆☆

Courtesy Flying W Ranch

3330 Chuckwagon Road
Colorado Springs, 80919
(719) 598-4000
www.flyingw.com

Hours:	4:30 PM - 10:00-ish PM, Monday - Sa[...] Memorial Day weekend through August 4:30 PM - 10:00-ish PM, Thursday - Saturday in September Closed Sunday.
Admission:	Under 2: Free; Age 3-5: $5; Age 6-12: $12; Age13-59: $22; Age 60+: $20 Price includes admission, supper, show, tax, and tip. Visa, MasterCard, traveler's checks, and cash accepted.
Parking:	Free parking lot. However, the cars are really packed in so you may have difficulty if you want to leave early.
Food:	No outside food or drink allowed.
Discounts:	Coupons may be available on Pikes-Peak.com. Military discounts are available.

What to expect. . .

The Flying W Ranch is a working, mountain cattle ranch that has specialized in Western food and entertainment since 1953. Come early, as seating is on a first-come, first-served basis and in the high season they may have as many as 1,000 guests each night. Until suppertime, you and your child can explore the Western town. Some of the buildings are reproductions, but others are originals that were brought over piece by piece and assembled on the ranch. Stop at the Blacksmith Shop to see them shoe a horse. Definitely visit the Biscuit Hut, watch how biscuits were made out on the ranch, and enjoy the free sample with honey. Hike the easy trail up to Christmas Walk Overlook. Have a pre-dinner treat at an old-fashioned soda fountain. Ten different shops offer a large variety of gifts and souvenirs. The dinner bell rings at 6:45, and you can hear it everywhere in the town.

The Flying W has perfected a serving system where they can get food to everyone in about half an hour. They serve trail beans, barbecue beef or chicken, foil-wrapped baked potatoes, homemade applesauce, spice cake, lemonade, ice tea, and coffee. One of the cowboys saw me standing in line with my 3-year-old trying to balance both of our plates. He offered to help and walked with us through the line and back to our seats, carrying one of the plates. An emcee entertains the guests who are waiting to get in line. He is pretty funny, but his jokes are geared more toward adults than to children. The evening is topped with a performance by the Flying W Wranglers, the world's second oldest western singing group. They were inducted into the Western Music Association's Hall of Fame in 2009. The Wranglers are great singers and musicians, and they provide a bit of comic relief in between songs. Again, the jokes are geared more toward the adults than the children but nothing inappropriate is ever said.

The only bathrooms are located at the entrance, next to the dining hall. They are large but do not have diaper-changing tables. The path throughout the town is paved brick but is quite uneven in some places so watch your step, and your child's too. If you love the Flying W Ranch, you can visit the steakhouse in the winter months (except January and February) and enjoy the food and the performance of the Flying W Wranglers.

Other destinations within 5 miles . . .

Garden of the Gods (Site 185) - 3 miles
Rock Ledge Ranch (Site 190) - 3 miles
Pro Rodeo Hall of Fame (Site 189) - 4½ miles

Garden of the Gods ☆☆☆☆☆

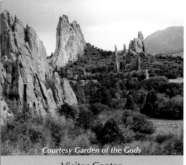

Courtesy Garden of the Gods

Visitor Center
www.gardenofgods.com

Trading Post
www.gardenofthegodstradingpost.com

Hours:	**Visitor Center and Trading Post** 8:00 AM - 8:00 PM daily Memorial Day to Labor Day 9:00 AM - 5:00 PM daily in the winter months Closed Thanksgiving, Christmas, and New Year's Day. **Park** 5:00 AM - 11:00 PM, May1 through October 31 5:00 AM - 9:00 PM, November 1 through April 30
Admission:	FREE!
Parking:	Free parking at the Visitor Center and the Trading Post. Limited parking throughout the park.
Food:	You may bring your own food and drink into the park. Picnic tables are scattered throughout the park. No outside food or drink allowed in the Visitor Center or the Trading Post. Both buildings have restaurants.
Discounts:	Coupons for the Trading Post gift shop and restaurant may be available on Pikes-Peak.com.

Multiple Locations. . .

Visitor Center 1805 30th Street Colorado Springs, 80904 (719) 634-6666	Trading Post 324 Beckers Lane Manitou Springs, 80829 (719) 685-9045

What to expect. . .

One visit to Garden of the Gods and you will understand why legend has it that this was an area where Native Americans gathered to worship. Few natural landmarks are as spectacular as these red sandstone plates, some as high as 300 feet, with the blue Colorado sky behind them. I honestly don't know what to say about the park except, if you have never been, go. The Ridge Trail is only ½ mile roundtrip, with less than a 150-foot climb. The Siamese Twins Trail is one mile roundtrip, with less than a 150-foot climb. Both trails are easy enough for most younger children, or for most adults carrying a child in a backpack.

Stop at the Visitor Center before you enter the park to get a map of the trails and roads. You can also listen to free nature talks, explore 30 interactive nature exhibits, watch a video about the formation of the park (fee applies), or buy tickets for a guided bus tour through the park (available in the summer only). Purchase Colorado-made gifts and souvenirs in the gift shop, or enjoy the view while dining at the Balcony Café. Bathrooms with diaper-changing tables are also available.

Inside the park, you may want to visit the Garden of the Gods Trading Post, Colorado's "oldest and largest art gallery and gift shop." Enjoy a buffalo burger at the Balanced Rock Café or simply admire the Native American pottery and jewelry, Navajo rugs, Pueblo pottery, and sand paintings.

Don't forget your camera! As you walk, bike, or drive through the park, you'll find scores of photo op-portunities. Some of the most popular spots are near the Scotsman and under Balanced Rock.

Annual Events . . .

Bighorn Sheep Day celebrates our state mammal every February.

Earth Day is celebrated in April in sync with Rock Ledge Ranch (Site 190).

Other destinations within 5 miles . . .

Rock Ledge Ranch (Site 190) - less than 1 mile
Flying W Ranch (Site 184) - 3 miles
Ghost Town and Wild West Museum (Site 186) - 3 miles

Cave of the Winds (Site 180) - 4 miles
Manitou Springs (Site 187) - 5 miles

Ghost Town and Wild West Museum ☆☆

Hours:	9:00 AM - 6:00 PM, Monday - Saturday through August 10:00 AM - 6:00 PM, Sunday, June through August 10:00 AM - 5:00 PM daily from Sept. through May Closed Christmas and New Year's Day.
Admission:	Under 6: Free; Age 6-16: $5; Age 17+: $6.50 American Express, MasterCard, Visa, checks, and cash accepted.
Parking:	Free parking lot.
Food:	You may bring in your own food and eat at the picnic tables out front or in the gold panning area.
Discounts:	Coupons may be available on their own website and at Pikes-Peak.com.

400 South 21st Street
Colorado Springs, 80904
(303) 449-3464
www.ghosttownmuseum.com

What to expect. . .

Selected by *Family Circle Magazine* as one of America's 55 special attractions, Ghost Town offers a chance to step back in time to visit an 1800s western town. Actual buildings brought in from abandoned towns display hundreds of artifacts from the 1890s to the 1920s. Look into a saloon, hotel, apothecary, print shop, blacksmith, barbershop, jail, and a general store. Visit a replica of a Victorian home, decorated with furniture and artifacts from that era, including a bed that belonged to President Chester A. Arthur. Bring quarters for the organ, shooting gallery, and old-time crank movies. Stagecoaches and carriages are placed throughout the museum, and one can be climbed into. Most of the artifacts are for looking only (which my children didn't seem to mind at all), but there are some hands-on activities for children including panning for gold in the summer months.

The museum gift shop offers a huge selection of Western gifts and collectibles. The town and Victorian home are set up indoors, so you don't have to worry about the weather. Bathrooms are available inside the town section of the museum, but do not have diaper-changing tables.

Other destinations within 5 miles . . .

America the Beautiful Park (Site 179) - 3 miles
Cave of the Winds (Site 180) - 3 miles
Garden of the Gods (Site 185) - 3 miles
Rock Ledge Ranch (Site 190) - 3 miles

Manitou Springs (Site 187) - 4 miles
Uncle Wilber Fountain (Site 193) - 4 miles
Cheyenne Mountain Zoo (Site 181) - 5 miles

Manitou Springs ☆☆☆☆☆

Getting there...

From Denver, take I-25 South to Highway 24 West (Exit 141), then follow the signs to Manitou Springs.

Visitor Center (719) 685-5089
www.manitousprings.org

What to expect...

It might seem odd to make a town a destination of its own, but Manitou Springs is a wonderfully odd town. (Full disclosure: I spent my middle school and high school years in this town.) The history of Manitou Springs is linked with the natural springs found within it. The Utes, Cheyenne, Arapahoe, and other Native American tribes came to these waters for healing (the bubbles were considered to be the breath of the Great Spirit) and this area was considered sacred and neutral territory.

Situated at the foot of Pikes Peak, Manitou Springs continues to be a town of mystery and spirituality. The mineral springs continue to flow. Bring your own containers, and you can fill them up and take the water home with you. Personally, I'm not too keen on the flavor of the water but it makes fantastic lemonade.

The heart of the town is the Downtown District, located on Manitou Avenue in the blocks between Pawnee Avenue and Park Avenue. In these few blocks, you'll discover more than 80 restaurants, bars, antiques, art galleries, bookstores, clothing and jewelry stores, and specialty gift shops. Visit the Penny Arcade, have an Old West picture taken at Old Tyme Photography, and pick up a treat at Pikes Peak Chocolate Company. For a fun break from window-shopping, visit the playground at the elementary school. It was designed by the children and built by the parents of Manitou. The summer is tourist season and it can get quite crowded, but this is also the time with the most activity and events.

Annual Events...

The Great Fruitcake Toss takes place in early January.

Mumbo Jumbo Gumbo Cookoff and Carnivale Parade marks the occasion of Mardi Gras in February.

Huck Finn Days is celebrated in mid-June.

Summer Concerts and Farmer's Market take place on Wednesday from mid-June through Labor Day at Soda Springs Park.

Colorado Springs

Fireworks on Red Mountain are shot off every Independence Day, if there has been enough rain.

Pikes Peak Ascent and Marathon are in mid-August.

Mountain Music Festival is usually the weekend after the Ascent and Marathon.

Emma Crawford Festival and Coffin Race and Parade is a must-do in late October.

Victorian Christmas at Miramont Castle is celebrated for three days after Thanksgiving.

Snowflakes and Smiles Parade is in mid-December. Breakfast with Santa may take place beforehand.

Other destinations within 5 miles (from downtown Manitou) . . .

Cave of the Winds (Site 180) - 2 miles
Ghost Town and Wild West Museum (Site 186) - 4 miles

Garden of the Gods (Site 185) - 5 miles
Rock Ledge Ranch (Site 190) - 5 miles

GO ONE STEP FURTHER - Interested in checking out the view from atop Pikes Peak? From Manitou Springs, you can get on the Pikes Peak Highway and drive up (www.pikespeakcolorado.com), take the Cog Railway (www.cograilway.com), or hike the trail that starts at the top of Ruxton Avenue.

May Natural History Museum of the Tropics ☆☆☆☆☆

Colorado Springs

710 Rock Creek Canyon Road
Colorado Springs, 80926
(719) 576-0450
www.maymuseum-camp-rvpark.com

Hours:	9:00 AM - 6:00 PM daily from May 1 through Sept. 30. By appointment in the winter months.
Admission:	Under 6: Free; Age 6-12: $3; Age 13-59: $6; Age 60+: $5. Discover, MasterCard, Visa, checks, and cash accepted.
Parking:	Free parking.
Food:	No food or drink are allowed inside the museum. A small convenience store is located on site. You may bring in your own food and drink; picnic tables are located near the Museum of Space Exploration.
Discounts:	Coupons may be available on Pikes-Peak.com.

What to expect. . .

John May began his vast collection in 1903. For over 80 years, he traveled extensively and accumulated specimens for what is considered one of the world's most outstanding collections of giant tropical insects and other interesting creatures. The museum has a small theater showing a short National Geographic movie about butterflies and bees. After viewing the movie, enter the May Natural History Museum where some of his collection, about 7,000 different invertebrates, are on display, including some of the world's largest specimens. From beetles and grasshoppers to butterflies and spiders, you can see literally thousands of different species of the creepy-crawly variety.

This museum is located in the midst of one of Colorado's largest private RV Parks and Campgrounds, which means beautiful surroundings, but also dirt roads and dirt paths. If you must bring a stroller, make sure it's a sturdy one. Bathrooms are conveniently located at the entrance of the museum, but lack diaper-changing tables. The Museum of Space Exploration is also on site, with hundreds of space photos and models. It is geared more toward adults than to children, but is worth a walk-through.

Pro Rodeo Hall of Fame ☆☆☆☆☆

Courtesy Pro Rodeo Hall of Fame

101 Pro Rodeo Drive
Colorado Springs, 80919
(719) 528-4764
www.prorodeohalloffame.com

Hours:	9:00 AM - 5:00 PM daily during summer months 9:00 AM - 5:00 PM, Wednesday - Sunday, early September through March Closed New Year's Eve, New Year's, Easter, Thanksgiving, Christmas Eve, and Christmas.
Admission:	Under 6: Free; Age 6-12: $3; Age 13-54: $6; Age 55+: $5. Discover, MasterCard, Visa, checks, and cash accepted.
Parking:	Free parking lot.
Food:	The museum asks that you not bring food or drinks, other than water, into the museum. An outdoor area in the back of the museum provides tables if you would like to bring a picnic lunch.
Discounts:	Coupons may be available on Pikes-Peak.com and in the Entertainment Book (Colorado Springs edition). Military discount available with ID.

What to expect. . .

As we entered the Pro Rodeo Hall of Fame, I was thinking that this really isn't a good fit for children under 5, but then both my sons exclaimed, "This place is awesome!" Filled with busts of legends, statues (including a larger-than-life one of Casey "The Champ" Tibbs), and display cases, this is the only museum in the world dedicated solely to the sport of Professional Rodeo. The museum is made up of two very large galleries housing clothing, gear, artifacts, and information on the history of rodeo. The Hall of Champions features contestants from each rodeo event, as well as stock contractors, rodeo clown, announcers, and animals. A multimedia presentation shows highlights from various events.

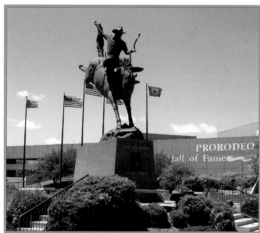

Courtesy Pro Rodeo Hall of Fame

As you drive up to the building, you'll see the Cowboy Association located at the front of the building. Drive around to the back where you can park and enter the museum. The Pro Rodeo Hall of Fame is not interactive and does not have any hands-on exhibits, but my children didn't mind, although we never stayed in front of a display case long enough for me to read much of the information. They asked to watch the highlights over and over again. Bathrooms are located in the front and the back of the museum; the bathrooms in the back have diaper-changing tables in both the men's and women's. The entire hall is stroller-friendly. The gift shop is very large and has any cowboy-related item you can think of, including Lincoln Logs, cowboy hats, gun and holster sets, shirts, buckles, books, and more.

Other destinations within 5 miles . . .

Flying W Ranch (Site 184) - 4½ miles

Rock Ledge Ranch ☆☆☆☆☆

Courtesy Rock Ledge Ranch

Gateway Road and North 30th Street
Colorado Springs, 80904
(719) 578-6777
www.rockledgeranch.com

Hours:	10:00 AM - 5:00 PM, Wednesday - Saturday, early June through mid-August Closed Sunday, Monday, and Tuesday.
Admission:	Under 5: Free; Age 6-12: $2; Age 13-18: $4; Age 18-54: $6, Age 55+: $4 MasterCard, Visa, checks, and cash accepted.
Membership:	$30 for two named adults and their children under 18.
Parking:	Free parking lot.
Food:	You may bring in your own food and drink. Picnic tables are located throughout the ranch. The gift shop sells old-fashioned soda (including Sarsaparilla) and candies

What to expect. . .

With gorgeous Garden of the Gods (Site 185) serving as its backdrop, Rock Ledge Ranch is a living history farm and museum depicting life in the Pikes Peak region from the late 1700s to the early 1900s. Travel through time as you explore four different eras, including:

A 1775 Native American Settlement, including a tipi made from genuine elk hide. It is one of only half a dozen left in the United States.

An 1860s Pioneer Log Cabin, which is just a one-room cabin, filled with artifacts from that time.

An 1880s Victorian Farm House demonstrates the challenges of farm life in the late 19th century.

A 19th Century Blacksmith Shop provides daily demonstrations as it repairs farm implements and tools and creates hand-forged items available for purchase in the Heritage Shop.

A 1907 Edwardian Estate shows the progress made in American life in less than three decades.

The Carriage House is a small museum building that may be used for meetings or certain exhibits.

These various periods of development all took place on this 220-acre property and several of the buildings are historic structures that have been restored. Each area looks just as it would have at the time with genuine supplies, tools, furniture, and decor. Knowledgeable docents in period clothing can tell you more about the particular time you are visiting. I was quite impressed by the amount of information they could share with us. More than simply hearing about the history, though, visitors may have the opportunity to participate in various activities, providing an educational experience through action. The day we visited, the homesteaders at the log cabin were building an outdoor bread oven and guests were invited to assist in the process if they desired.

Your walk through the ranch from era to era is self-guided and is approximately one mile. The walking paths are dirt, so wear closed-toe shoes and bring a rugged stroller if your child prefers to ride. Little shade is available along the path; plenty of sunscreen and hats are recommended. Once you arrive at each site, guided tours are available through the buildings. My children were horrified to learn that emptying the chamber pots was the responsibility of children, and instantly became more appreciative of the luxuries we have. Bathrooms are located at the Carriage House at the start of your tour and also near the Heritage Shop about halfway through the walk. In addition to sodas and candies, the Heritage Shop offers a variety of books, reproductions, and other related items. Because it is a working farm, animals are also on the property. Horses and cows are penned while the sheep and chicken may roam free. Don't be alarmed, though, as they really keep to themselves.

Annual Events . . .

Earth Day is celebrated in sync with the Garden of the Gods (Site 185) in April.

An Independence Day Celebration takes place on the Fourth of July.

An 1880s baseball game is played on Labor Day.

The Harvest Festival occurs in early October.

A Holiday Evening is celebrated each year in December.

Other destinations within 5 miles . . .

Garden of the Gods (Site 185) - less than 1 mile

Flying W Ranch (Site 184) - 3 miles

Ghost Town and Wild West Museum (Site 186) - 3 miles

Cave of the Winds (Site 180) - 4 miles

Manitou Springs (Site 187) - 5 miles

Courtesy Rock Ledge Ranch

y Mountain Dinosaur Resource Center ☆☆☆☆☆

Site 190 Colorado Springs

Courtesy Rocky Mountain DinosaurResource Center

201 South Fairview Street
Woodland Park, 80863
(719) 686-1820
www.rmdrc.com

Hours:	9:00 AM - 6:00 PM, Monday - Saturday 10:00 AM - 5:00 PM, Sunday Closed New Year's Day, Easter, Thanksgiving, and Christmas
Admission:	Under 5: Free; Age 5-12: $7.50; Age 13-64: $11.50; Age 65+: $10.50 American Express, Discover, MasterCard, Visa, checks, and cash accepted.
Membership:	$95 for two named adults and their children under 18.
Parking:	Free parking lot.
Food:	Food and drink are not allowed inside the museum. Picnic tables are available in the plaza and a soda vending machine is located just inside the front door.
Discounts:	Coupons can be found in the Entertainment Book - Colorado Springs edition, and usually on their own website. Half-price admission for military families on Independence Day and Veterans Day. The last Tuesday of the year is Kids' Free Day, when two children (age 5-12) are free with each paid adult admission.

What to expect. . .

The Rocky Mountain Dinosaur Resource Center is home to a
vast display of dinosaurs, prehistoric marine reptiles, pterosaurs,
and fish from the late Cretaceous period (which, sadly, means
more to my children than it does to me). With one of the largest paleo labs in North America, you and your child have the
opportunity to watch paleontologists uncovering fossils and
making commercial casts for other museums (weekdays only).
The center is for-profit, which means they collaborate with sci-
entists to properly place fossils and casts in institutions around
the world. The benefit to this is that their exhibits are changing
regularly while they showcase items before they are transferred
to another facility. They have a number of permanent exhibits as
well in this 20,000 square foot building.

Courtesy Rocky Mountain Dinosaur Resource Center

The center is divided into two main rooms: Dinosaur Hall
and Prehistoric Ocean. In Prehistoric Ocean, you can watch a short video highlighting some of the
specimens currently on display. Woody's Play Area, located in Dinosaur Hall, gives your child an opportunity to explore and discover. Uncovering genuine fossil replicas in a dig area, creating a dinosaur
using magnets, and touching real fossils — including dinosaur poop — are just a few of the hands-on
activities available. A child-friendly video about dinosaurs plays throughout the day in this area.

Story time generally takes place around 11:00 AM most mornings, although it may not always occur
during the summer since that is their busiest time. Guided tours are available all day, occurring more frequently in the summer months. The guided tours are adjusted and somewhat customized for the group,
and the docents are extremely knowledgeable. You can step out of the tour at any time if your child becomes disinterested. The aisles are wide and stroller-friendly, and all the displays provide a large amount
of information. Bathrooms are located near the Prehistoric Paradise gift shop, with diaper-changing
tables provided in both the men's and women's. Prehistoric Paradise has an extensive array of dinosaur
merchandise, from apparel to toys and paleontologist outfits to more unusual items, like chess sets.

Annual Events . . .

An Anniversary Party for the center is celebrated in June with a big party.

Critter Fest is an outdoor event with animal rescue groups held the first weekend in August.

Earth Science Week is observed in October, with different activities throughout the week.

Santa's Workshop at the North Pole ☆☆☆☆

NORTH POLE
HOME OF Santa's
WORKSHOP

5050 Pikes Peak Highway
Cascade, 80809
(719) 684-9432
www.santas-colo.com

Hours:	10:00 AM - 5:00 PM, most days from mid-May through Christmas Eve. Check the website or call for exact hours and dates.
Admission:	Under 2 and 60+: Free; Age 2-59: $17.95 American Express, Discover, MasterCard, Visa, and cash accepted.
Annual Pass:	$150 for four people living at the same address.
Parking:	Free parking lot.
Food:	Three restaurants are located inside the park. You may bring in your own food and drink and picnic at the tables below the Train Station.
Discounts:	Coupons are generally available on their website and on Pikes-Peak.com. Military discounts are given with valid ID.

What to expect...

The Christmas Spirit is alive and well even in the summer months at this family amusement park. The park offers dozens of child-friendly rides such as a carousel, ferris wheel, train, and mini coaster. Most of the rides have restrictions (e.g., must be accompanied by a parent, can not be over or under a certain height), and very few of them can be ridden by anyone under the age of one. In addition to the rides, the North Pole offers eight gift shops (mostly toy-themed), magic shows, llamas and goats that you can feed, an arcade, and of course a visit with the Big Guy himself in Santa's house. You can purchase a picture with Santa or use your own camera.

Other than for the arcade games and the animal food dispenser, no money is exchanged inside the park. Instead, you receive an admission card when you arrive. Any time you want to make a purchase at one of the gift shops or restaurants, a note is made on the card. Do not lose your card; you'll need it to leave the park. The benefit to this process is that you don't have to carry cash around. The down side is that you can easily spend much more than you intended. Bathrooms are located on both sides of the park and diaper-changing tables are provided in both the men's and women's. The entire path is paved and stroller-friendly, but some of it is steep. As an adult, the North Pole can feel a little too commercialized. But if your child is in those years between being afraid of Santa and no longer believing in him, a visit here can really be a magical experience.

Uncle Wilber Fountain ☆☆☆☆☆

East Bijou Street & North Tejon Street
Colorado Springs, 80903
(719) 385-6035
www.unclewilberfountain.org

Hours:	10:00 AM - 7:00 PM, Sunday - Thursday, mid-May through late August 10:00 AM - 9:00 PM, Friday and Saturday, mid-May through late August The park itself is open 5:00 AM - 11:00 PM in the summer months.
Admission:	FREE!
Parking:	A Parking garage is one block away at Cascade and Bijou. The prices for the garage are the same as metered parking. The garage is free on Saturday and Sunday.
Food:	You may bring in your own food and drinks. No alcohol and no eating or drinking while playing in the fountain. Several restaurants are within walking distance.

What to expect. . .

Located in Acacia Park, the whimsical Uncle Wilber Fountain has 52 vertical pop jets, over 200 unpredictable streams of water, and a cascading waterfall. Starting at 10:00 AM, the colorful sculpture opens up on the hour and half hour and that's when the real fun begins. Dozens of colorful lights and fun music create a wet dance floor and the kids (and sometimes adults) really go crazy! So entertaining and fun, the fountain has received a Partnership for Community Design award, was voted "Best Addition to Downtown" in 2001, and was featured in the national publication *Landscape Architect*. Dogs, smoking, bikes, and skateboards are prohibited. Swim diapers are required for children who are not yet potty-trained.

The City of Colorado Springs occasionally experiences staff shortages that affect their ability to keep the Fountain open, especially in the late weeks of summer. The fountain follows the same inclement weather policy as the outdoor pools. For these reasons, I recommend that you call before you go to make sure the fountain is open.

Acacia Park also has a small playground with slides and monkey bars, as well as a shuffleboard court. Plenty of benches and picnic tables, many of which are shaded by the large trees, provide a comfortable spot for lunch. The bathrooms are in a small building that is not well marked, facing Bijou Street. They are small and do not have changing tables.

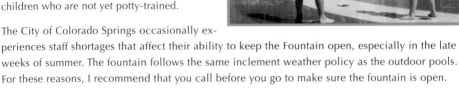

Other destinations within 5 miles . . .

Western Museum of Mining and Industry ☆☆☆☆☆

225 Old North Gate Road
Colorado Springs, 80921
(719) 488-0880
www.wmmi.org

Hours:	9:00 AM - 4:00 PM, Monday - Saturday from September through May 9:00 AM - 5:00 PM, Monday - Saturday from June through August Closed Sundays and major holidays.
Admission:	Under 3: Free; Age 3-12: $4; Age 18-59: $8; Students and Seniors 60+: $6 Discover, MasterCard, Visa, checks, and cash accepted.
Membership:	$50 for all immediate family members.
Parking:	Free parking lot.
Food:	Food, drink, and gum are not allowed inside the museum. Picnic tables are available outside.
Discounts:	AAA and military discounts are offered. Coupons may be available on Pikes-Peak.com, on their own website, and in the Entertainment Book (Colorado Springs edition).

What to expect...

The Western Museum of Mining and Industry preserves the history of mining for gems, gold, and minerals in Colorado and the American West. The museum sits on 27 acres of wetlands and prairie grounds, and has a variety of equipment and exhibits both indoors and out. Guided tours of the museum are available at 10:00 AM and 1:00 PM. You may explore the museum on your own, but only on the tour can you see the docent operate real steam engines and mining machines, including the 37-ton Corliss Steam Engine. Several hands-on activities are available for children, including panning for gold, donning a hard hat and walking through a mine replica, and operating models of steam engines and stamp mills with the push of a button. "What's Yours is Mined" is an exhibit with a number of minerals on display, as well as every day products like baking soda and M&M candies that contain these minerals. The minerals here can be touched, weighed on a scale, and viewed more closely with magnifying glasses.

The museum has two donkeys, Oro and Nugget, who represent all the hard-working donkeys that were used in mining. They have a pen near the picnic tables, but may roam freely around the property in the warmer months; bring a carrot or an apple to offer as a treat. From June through August, gem mining and gold panning are offered outside (purchase the bags containing the goods for $5). A small gift shop sells gold-panning kits, rocks, gems, books, and a few other items. The only bathrooms are located inside the museum; they do not have changing tables. While the museum is stroller-friendly, the property itself is not. Bring a wagon instead.

Annual Events...

Spring Break with the Burros takes place on the Saturday at the end of El Paso County's break.

Picnic and Planes occurs in May on the day of the Air Force Academy graduation. For a small donation for parking, you can watch the Thunderbirds fly overhead.

A Rock Fair is the weekend following Father's Day; the only time of year they run the stamp mill outside.

The Burro Birthday Bash is a huge party in August with bands and family-friendly activities.

A Farmer's Market is all day on Monday and Wednesday from June through October.

Family Exploration Days occur three or four times throughout the year, each with a different theme.

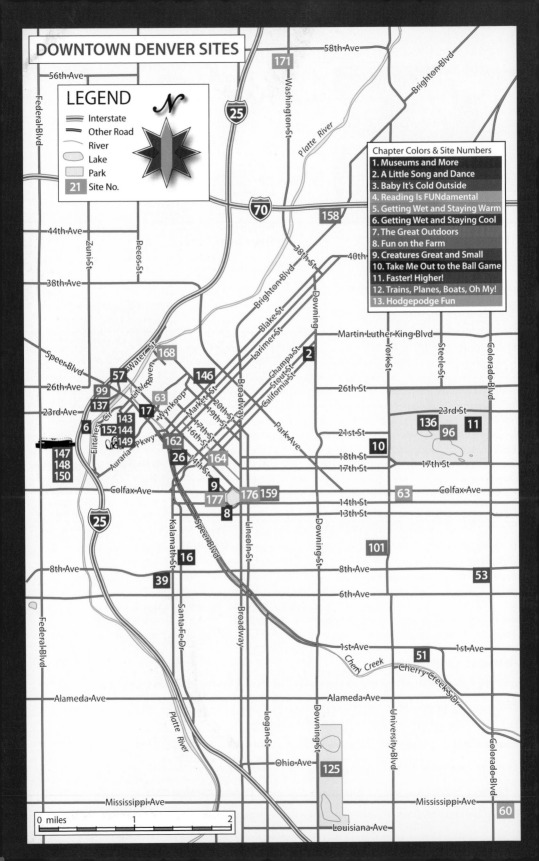

DOWNTOWN DENVER SITES

LEGEND

N

Interstate
Other Road
River
Lake
Park
21 Site No.

Chapter Colors & Site Numbers

1. Museums and More
2. A Little Song and Dance
3. Baby It's Cold Outside
4. Reading Is FUNdamental
5. Getting Wet and Staying Warm
6. Getting Wet and Staying Cool
7. The Great Outdoors
8. Fun on the Farm
9. Creatures Great and Small
10. Take Me Out to the Ball Game
11. Faster! Higher!
12. Trains, Planes, Boats, Oh My!
13. Hodgepodge Fun

0 miles   1   2

Downtown Destinations
Appendix I

Because there are so many places to visit in our downtown area, a separate section is needed to list them all. All of these destinations are within an eight-mile radius, and most are less than five miles from each other.

16th Street Mall - Site 164

Black American West Museum - Site 2

The Children's Museum of Denver - Site 6

City Park - Site 96

Colorado Avalanche - Site 143

Colorado Mammoth - Site 144

Colorado Rockies - Site 146

Colorado Sports Hall of Fame - Site 147

The Colorado Symphony Family Series - Site 26

Confluence Park - Site 99

Denver Art Museum - Site 8

Denver Broncos - Site 148

Denver Botanic Gardens - Site 101

Denver Firefighters Museum - Site 9

Denver Museum of Miniatures - Site 10

Denver Museum of Nature and Science - Site 11

Denver Nuggets - Site 149

Denver Outlaws - Site 150

Denver Skate Park - Site 168

Denver Zoo - Site 136

Downtown Aquarium - Site 137

Elitch Gardens - Site 152

Forney Museum of Transportation - Site 158

Hammond's Candies - Site 171

Little Monkey Bizness (Denver) - Site 53

Museo de las Americas - Site 16

Museum of Contemporary Art - Site 17

Platte Valley Trolley - Site 159

REI - Site 57

State Capitol Building - Site 176

Tattered Cover Bookstore (Denver) Site 63

Trunks - Site 39

The United States Mint - Site 177

Venice on the Creek - Site 162

Washington Park - Site 125

Kids Eat Free (or Cheap)
Appendix II

Denver has plenty of family-friendly restaurants that offer children's meals for free or at a reduced price. Most restaurants offer one child's meal per adult's meal purchased and most consider a child to be age 12 or under. When there are multiple locations, not all locations participate. Additional restrictions may apply and the deal may change without notice, so be sure to call ahead.

Daily

The Bent Noodle: Aurora
Dinner only.
www.bentnoodle.com.

Deli Tech: Denver
www.delitech.com.

IHOP: Various locations
Kids eat for 99 cents, 3:00 PM - 9:00 PM.
www.ihop.com.

McAlister's Deli: Aurora
After 5:00 PM.
www.mcalistersdeli.com.

Saj Mediterranean Grill: Centennial
Excluding Friday and Saturday.
www.sajgrill.com.

Texas de Brazil: Denver
www.texasdebrazil.com.

Sunday

Bombay Bowl: Centennial
www.bombaybowl.com.

Bono's BBQ: Aurora and Centenniall
www.bonosbarbq.com.

Casey's Bistro and Pub: Denver
www.caseysbistroandpub.com.

Darcy's Bistro and Pub: Denver
www.darcysbistroandpub.com.

Dickey's Barbecue Pit: Various locations
www.dickeys.com.

Garcia's Mexican Restaurant: Denver
www.garciasmexicanrestaurants.net.

Jordan's Bistro and Pub: Denver
www.jordansbistroandpub.com.

Lansdowne Arms: Highlands Ranch
After 4:00 PM.
www.lansdownearmsbistroandpub.com.

Lil Ricci's NY Pizzeria: Various locations
www.lilriccispizza.com.

Lodo's Bar and Grill: Various locations
Kids eat for $2.99.
www.lodosbarandgrill.com.

McCabe's Bistro and Pub: Aurora
www.mccabesbistroandpub.com.

The Melting Pot: Littleton
3:00 - 5:00 PM.
www.meltingpot.com.

Randolph's: Denver
www.randolphsdenver.com.

Rox Bar and Grill: Littleton
Kids 10 and under.
www.roxbargrill.com.

Souper Salad: Various locations
www.soupersalad.com.

Via Baci: Lone Tree
Two children per adult purchase.
www.viabaci.com.

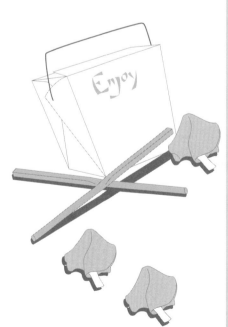

Monday

3 Margaritas: Various locations
Kids eat for 99 cents.
Each location has its own website.

Bono's BBQ: Aurora and Centennial
www.bonosbarbq.com.

Boston's - The Gourmet Pizza:
Highlands Ranch and Parker
www.bostons.com.

Brothers BBQ: Various locations
www.brothers-bbq.com.

Buffalo Wild Wings: Various locations
Kids eat for 99 cents.
www.buffalowildwings.com.

C.B. & Potts: Various locations
www.cbpotts.com.

Carino's Italian: Various locations
www.carinos.com.

Chick Fil-A: Various locations
www.chickfila.com.

Cinzzetti's Italian Market: Northglenn
5:00 PM - 9:00 PM.
www.cinzzettis.com.

Costa Vida: Lone Tree
www.costavida.net.

Fuddruckers: Various locations
Kids eat for 99 cents.
www.fuddruckers.com.

Gunther Toody's: Various locations
After 11:00 AM.
www.gunthertoodys.com.

Heidi's Brooklyn Deli: Various locations
www.heidisbrooklyndeli.com.

Islands: Boulder
www.islandsrestaurants.com.

La Estrellita: Brighton and Westminster
After 4:00 PM.
www.salsalaest.com.

Luigi's Italian Restaurant: Centennial
Dinner only.
www.luigisitalian.net.

Miyama of Colorado: Lone Tree
www.miyamaofcolorado.com.

Rio Grande: Denver and Lone Tree
www.riograndemexican.com.

Rox Bar and Grill: Littleton
Kids 10 and under.
www.roxbargrill.com.

Texas Roadhouse: Various locations
www.texasroadhouse.com.

TGI Friday's: Various locations
 www.tgifridays.com.

Woody's Wood Fired Pizza: Golden
www.woodysgolden.com.

The Yard House: Lakewood
www.yardhouse.com.

Deals on Meals!

Kids Eat Free (or Cheap)
Appendix II

Tuesday

3 Margaritas: Various locations
Each location has its own website.

Atlanta Bread Company:
Various locations
After 4:00 PM.
www.atlantabread.com.

The Bagel Deli and Restaurant: Denver
After 4:00 PM.
www.thebageldeli.com.

Black-Eyed Pea: Various locations
After 5:00 PM.
www.blackeyedpeacolorado.com.

Brothers BBQ: Various locations
www.brothers-bbq.com.

Carino's Italian: Various locations
www.carinos.com.

Champps: Littleton
www.champps.com.

Chick Fil-A: Various locations
www.chickfila.com.

Cinzzetti's Italian Market: Northglenn
www.cinzzettis.com.

Denny's: Various locations
Kids 10 and under from 4:00 - 10:00 PM.
www.dennys.com.

Famous Dave's: Broomfield and Denver
Kids 10 and under.
www.famousdaves.com.

Fazoli's: Various locations
Kids eat for 99 cents, 5:00 - 8:00 PM.
www.fazolis.com.

Fuddruckers: Various locations
Kids eat for 99 cents.
www.fuddruckers.com.

Heidi's Brooklyn Deli: Various locations
www.heidisbrooklyndeli.com.

Joe's Crab Shack: Various locations
Kids eat for $2.99.
www.joescrabshack.com.

La Estrellita: Brighton and Westminster
After 4:00 PM.
www.salsalaest.com.

Le Peep: Various locations
www.lepeep.com.

Lone Star Steakhouse: Various locations
Two kids per adult.
www.lonestarsteakhouse.com.

Luigi's Italian Restaurant: Centennial
Dinner only.
www.luigisitalian.net.

The Melting Pot: Littleton
5:00 - 7:00 PM.
www.meltingpot.com.

Miyama of Colorado: Lone Tree
www.miyamaofcolorado.com.

Pasquini's Pizzeria: Various locations
www.pasquinis.com.

Perkins: Various locations
4:00 PM - 10:00 PM.
www.perkinsrestaurants.com.

The Rockyard: Castle Rock
www.rockyard.com.

Silver Mine Subs: Boulder and Denver
www.silverminesubs.com.

Wednesday

Applebees: Various locations
Kids eat for 99 cents after 3:00 PM.
www.applebees.com.

The Bagel Deli and Restaurant: Denver
After 4:00 PM.
www.thebageldeli.com.

C-Level Waterfront Hideaway: Arvada
5:00 PM - 7:00 PM
www.hiddenlakerestaurants.com.

Fish City Grill: Lone Tree
www.fishcitygrill.com.

Great Scott's Eatery: Broomfield and Denver
www.greatscottseatery.com.

Gunther Toody's: Various locations
www.gunthertoodys.com.

Heidi's Brooklyn Deli: Various locations
www.heidisbrooklyndeli.com.

Jason's Deli: Various locations
Up to three children with each adult.
www.jasonsdeli.com.

Luigi's Italian Restaurant: Centennial
Dinner only.
www.luigisitalian.net.

Miyama of Colorado: Lone Tree
www.miyamaofcolorado.com.

Woody's Wood Fired Pizza: Golden
www.woodysgolden.com.

Thursday

Buffalo Wild Wings: Various locations
Kids eat for 99 cents.
www.buffalowildwings.com

C.B. & Potts: Various locations
www.cbpotts.com.

Captain D's: Aurora
Two kids eat free with each adult meal
purchase.
www.captainds.com.

Heidi's Brooklyn Deli: Various locations
www.heidisbrooklyndeli.com.

Luigi's Italian Restaurant: Centennial
Dinner only.
www.luigisitalian.net.

Miyama of Colorado: Lone Tree
www.miyamaofcolorado.com.

Friday

See Daily deals.

Saturday

Bombay Bowl: Centennial
www.bombaybowl.com.

Bono's BBQ: Aurora and Centennial
www.bonosbarbq.com.

Denny's: Various locations
Kids 10 and under from 4:00 - 10:00 PM.
www.dennys.com.

Lodo's Bar and Grill: Various locations
Kids eat for $2.99.
www.lodosbarandgrill.com.

Lone Star Steakhouse: Various locations
Two kids per adult.
www.lonestarsteakhouse.com.

Perkins: Various locations
4:00 PM - 10:00 PM.
www.perkinsrestaurants.com.

Texas Roadhouse: Various locations
www.texasroadhouse.com.

Free Summer Fun
Appendix III

Outdoor Concerts

Arvada: McIlvoy Park
www.apexprd.org

Aurora: various parks
www.auroragov.org

Boulder: Pearl Street Mall
www.boulderdowntown.com

Brighton: Brighton Pavilions
www.brightonco.gov

Broomfield: FlatIron Crossing Mall
www.flatironcrossing.com

Broomfield: Community Park
www.ci.broomfield.co.us

Castle Rock: Butterfield Crossing Park
www.meadowslink.com

Denver: City Park
www.cityparkjazz.org

Denver: Confluence Park
www.greenwayfoundation.org

Evergreen: Evergreen Lakehouse
www.evergreenrecreation.com

Golden: Parfet Park
www.goldengov.org

Highlands Ranch: Civic Green Park
www.highlandsranch.org/civicgreen

Highlands Ranch: Highlands Heritage Park
www.hrcaonline.org

Lafayette: Waneka Lake Park
www.cityoflafayette.com

Littleton: Robert F Clement Park
www.ifoothills.org

Lone Tree: Sweetwater Park
www.cityoflonetree.com

Longmont: Roosevelt Park Pavilion
www.ci.longmont.co.us

Louisville: Louisville Community Park
www.ci.louisville.co.us

Louisville: Steinbaugh Pavilion
www.downtownlouisvilleco.com

Niwot: Whistle Stop Park
www.niwot.com/events/rhythm_on_the_rails

Northglenn: E.B. Rains Park
www.northglenn.org

Parker: O'Brien Park
www.parkeronline.org

Westminster: Westminster Promenade
www.thewestminsterpromenade.com

Westminster: Westminster City Park
www.ci.westminster.co.us

Singer/Songwriter Katelyn Benton Photo by Brig Van Osten

more **Free Summer Fun**

Outdoor Movies

Arvada: Old Towne Square
www.historicarvada.org

Aurora: Fletcher Plaza
www.auroragov.org

Boulder: Downtown Boulder
www.boulderoutdoorcinema.com

Broomfield: Broomfield Commons Park
www.yourlocalcreditunion.com

Castle Rock: Festival Park
www.downtowncastlerock.com

Denver: Confluence Park
www.greenwayfoundation.org

Denver: Fillmore Plaza
www.cherrycreeknorth.com

Denver: Founder Green Town Center
www.stapletondenver.com

Golden: Parfet Park
www.goldengov.org

Highlands Ranch: Civic Green Park
www.highlandsranch.org/civicgreen

Highlands Ranch: Southridge Recreation Center
www.hrcaonline.org

Littleton: Aspen Grove Shopping Center
www.shopaspengrove.com

Longmont: Thompson Park
www.ci.longmont.co.us/rec

Parker: O'Brien Park
www.parkerchamber.com

Thornton: Multipurpose Fields
www.yourlocalcreditunion.com

Westminster: City Park
www.ci.westminster.co.us

Calendar of Events & Festivals
Appendix IV

In addition to the annual events offered in each destination, a number of other festivals, fairs, and seasonal events occur each year. Following is a monthly list of the ones that seem to be the most child-friendly and the most popular. Some of the more unique events in Colorado, such as the International Snow Sculpture in Breckenridge and the Mike the Headless Chicken Festival in Fruita, are well outside Denver but are worth mentioning. Events that occur in the Denver metropolitan area are in **BOLD**.

January

Denver Kids Expo (Denver)
www.denverkidsexpo.com

Family Snow Festival (Steamboat Springs)
www.steamboat.com

International Snow Sculpture Championship (Breckenridge)
www.gobreckevents.com

Lafayette Oatmeal Festival (Lafayette)
www.lafayettecolorado.com

Martin Luther King Marade (Denver)
www.denver.org/events

National Western Stock Show, Rodeo, and Horse Show (Denver)
www.nationalwestern.com

Ullr Fest (Breckenridge)
www.gobreckevents.com

February

Chinese New Year Celebration (Highlands Ranch)
www.denverchineseschool.org

Chocolate Affair in Arvada (Arvada)
www.oldetownarvada.org

Snowdown Winter Festival (Durango)
www.snowdown.org.

Snowscape Festival (Silverton)
www.silvertoncolorado.com

Winter Carnival (Steamboat Springs)
www.steamboatchamber.com

March

All About Kids Expo (Denver)
www.all-about-kids.org

March PowWow (Denver)
www.denvermarchpowwow.org

Frozen Dead Guy Days (Nederland)
www.nederlandchamber.org

St. Patrick's Day Parade (Colorado Springs)
www.csstpats.com

St. Patrick's Day Parade (Denver)
www.denverstpatricksdayparade.com

April

Arvada Kite Festival (Arvada)
www.arvadafestivals.com

Fairplay's Early Childhood Fun Fair (Fairplay)
http://tpecc.blogspot.com.

Kidsfest (Woodland Park)
http://tpecc.blogspot.com.

Spring Blast Family Weekend (Winter Park)
www.winterpark-info.com/events

May

Balloons-n-Varoooms (Ridgway)
www.ridgwaycolorado.com

Boulder Creek Festival (Boulder)
www.bceproductions.com

Cinco de Mayo (Denver)
www.cincodemayodenver.com

Highlands Ranch Music Arts Festival (Highlands Ranch)
www.hrmafestival.org

Mike the Headless Chicken Days (Fruita)
www.miketheheadlesschicken.org

Music and Blossom Festival (Canon City)
www.ccblossomfestival.com

Old South Gaylord Memorial Day Weekend Festival (Denver)
www.southgaylordstreet.com

Spring Fling (Lone Tree)
www.ssprd.org/southsubNew/springFling.asp

Thornton Fest (Thornton)
www.cityofthornton.net

Tulip Fairy and Elf Parade (Boulder)
www.boulderdowntown.com

June

Boulder Jewish Festival (Boulder)
www.boulderjewishfestival.com

Capitol Hill People's Fair (Denver)
www.peoplesfair.com

Cherry Blossom Festival (Denver)
www.tsdbt.org

Colorado Music Festival (Boulder)
www.coloradomusicfest.org

Colorado Renaissance Festival (Larkspur)
www.coloradorenaissance.com

Denver Chalk Art Festival (Denver)
www.larimerarts.org

Denver International Buskerfest (Denver)
www.denver.com/festivals

Donkey Derby Days (Cripple Creek)
www.visitcripplecreek.com

Evergreen Rodeo (Evergreen)
www.evergreenrodeo.com

Family Fire Muster (Lakewood)
www.westmetrofire.org.

Fiesta Aurora! (Aurora)
www.auroragov.org

Gold Strike Festival (Arvada)
www.historicarvada.org

The Greek Festival (Denver)
www.thegreekfestival.com

Greeley Independence Stampede (Greeley)
www.greeleystampede.org

Highlands Square Street Fair (Denver)
www.highlands-square.com

Juneteenth (Denver)
www.denverjuneteenth.org

Parker Country Festival (Parker)
www.parkerchamber.com

Scandinavian Midsummer Festival (Estes Park)
www.estesmidsummer.com

Strawberry Days (Glenwood Springs)
www.strawberrydaysfestival.com

A Taste of Puerto Rico (Denver)
www.atasteofpuertoricofestival.com

Teddy Bear Picnic (Estes Park)
www.estesparkcvb.com

Wild West Auto Roundup (Golden)
www.2hourvacation.com

July

Arapahoe County Fair (Aurora)
www.arapahoecountyfair.com

Boulder County Fair (Boulder)
www.bouldercountyfair.org

Buffalo Bill Days (Golden)
www.buffalobilldays.com

Colorado Black Arts Festival (Denver)
www.denbaf.org

Colorado Dragon Boat Festival (Denver)
www.cdbf.org

Colorado Irish Festival (Littleton)
www.coloradoirishfestival.org

**Colorado Renaissance Festival
(Larkspur)**
www.coloradorenaissance.com

Cowboys Roundup Days
(Steamboat Springs)
www.steamboatprorodeo.com

Elbert County Fair (Kiowa)
www.elbertcountyfair.com

Hot Air Balloon Rodeo
(Steamboat Springs)
www.steamboat-chamber.com

KidSpree (Aurora)
www.auroragov.org/kidspree

National Little Britches Rodeo Finals
(Pueblo)
www.nlbra.com

Paonia Cherry Days (Paonia)
www.paoniachamber.com

Pikes Peak or Bust Rodeo
(Colorado Springs)
www.coloradospringsrodeo.com

Rooftop Rodeo (Estes Park)
www.rooftoprodeo.com

Russian Festival (Denver)
www.russianfestivaldenver.com

Weld County Fair (Greeley)
www.weldcountyfair.com

August

Adams County Fair and Rodeo (Brighton)
www.adamscountyfair.com

Boom Days (Leadville)
www.leadvilleboomdays.com

Boulder Asian Festival (Boulder)
www.bapaweb.org

**The Colorado Scottish Festival
(Highlands Ranch)**
www.scottishgames.org

Colorado State Fair (Pueblo)
www.coloradostatefair.com

Corn Roast Festival (Loveland)
www.engaginglovelandinc.org

**Douglas County Fair and Rodeo
(Castle Rock)**
www.douglascountyfairandrodeo.com

Gilpin County Fair (Blackhawk)
www.co.gilpin.co.us

Lafayette Peach Festival (Lafayette)
www.lafayettecolorado.com

Olathe Sweet Corn Festival (Olathe)
www.olathesweetcornfest.com

Palisade Peach Fest (Palisade)
www.palisadepeachfest.com

Western Welcome Week (Littleton)
www.westernwelcomeweek.org

Westminster Faire (Westminster)
www.westminsterfaire.com

**Wheat Ridge Carnation Festival
(Wheat Ridge)**
www.wheatridgecarnationfestival.org

September

Arvada Harvest Festival (Arvada)
www.arvadaharvestfestivalparade.com

Boulder Creek Hometown Fair (Boulder)
www.bceproductions.com

Colorado Balloon Classic (Colorado Springs)
www.balloonclassic.com

Colorado Baby & Kidz Expo
(Colorado Springs)
www.theexpopros.com/colosprings.html

Festival International (Aurora)
www.aurorachamber.org

Festival Italiano (Lakewood)
www.belmarcolorado.com

Highlands Ranch Days (Highlands Ranch)
www.hrcaonline.org

Longmont Oktoberfest (Longmont)
www.bceproductions.com

Oktoberfest (Denver)
www.oktoberfestdenver.com

Potato Day Festival (Greeley)
www.greeleygov.com

Scottish/Irish Highland Festival (Estes Park)
www.scotfest.com

Snowmass Balloon Festival (Snowmass)
www.snowmassballoon.com

Summerset Festival (Littleton)
www.summersetfest.com

A Taste of Colorado (Denver)
www.atasteofcolorado.com

October

See **Fun on the Farm** chapter for a
variety of fall events.

November

Georgetown Bighorn Sheep Festival
(Georgetown)
www.wildlife.state.co.us

December

Lights of December Parade (Boulder)
www.boulderdowntown.com

**Olde Golden Christmas on Parade
(Golden)**
www.2hourvacation.com

Parade of Lights (Denver)
www.denverparadeoflights.com

**World's Largest Christmas Lighting Display
(Denver)**
www.downtowndenver.com

Online Resources
Appendix V

Breastfeeding Support

Bosom Buddies
www.bosombuddies.com

Breastfeeding for Working
Mothers/Better Breastfeeding
www.injoyvideos.com

Colorado Breastfeeding Coalition
www.cobfc.org

Colorado Department of Public Health and
Environment
www.cdphe.state.co.us

La Leche League
www.lalecheleague.org

Childcare Resources

Adams County Association of Family
Child Care
www.childcareinadamsco.org

Arapahoe County Family
Child Care Association
www.acfcca.org

Boulder County Family
Child Care Association
www.bouldercounty.gov

Douglas County Child Care Association
www.douglascountychildcare.com

Jefferson County Child Care Association
www.jeffcochildcare.org

Metro Denver Child Care
Resource and Referral
www.frcce.org

Dads Groups

Denver Dads
www.groups.yahoo.com/group/Denver_Dad

Meet Up Groups
www.dadsmeetup.com

Denver at a Discount

www.bocodeals.com (Boulder area only)

www.coloradokids.com

www.crowdsavings.com

www.dailydealsformoms.com

http://deals.mamapedia.com/denver
{Mamapedia gives 5% to your child's school)

www.deals.voiceplaces.com/denver

www.denverdailydeals.com

www.doubletakedeals.com

www.eversave.com/denver

www.getmyperks.com/denver

www.groupon.com/denver

www.kgbdeals.com/denver

www.livingsocial.com

www.sobiz10.com

www.spreesy.com

www.thedealmap.com

www.weeklyplus.com/denver/

www.woodeal.com

www.yolodeals.com

www.zowzee.com

Gay and Lesbian Family Support

The Center
www.glbtcolorado.org/families.aspx

Gay Parent Magazine
www.gayparentmag.com

Parents, Families, and Friends of
Lesbians and Gays
www.pflag.org

Grandparent Resources and Support

Colorado Grandparent Support Center
www.grandsplace.org

Grandparents Raising Grandchildren
www.raisingyourgrandchildren.com

Grandparents Resource Center
www.grc4usa.org

Living Frugally

America's Cheapest Family
www.americascheapestfamily.com

The Coupon Mom
www.couponmom.com

The Dollar Stretcher
www.stretcher.com

Home Energy Saver
www.hes.lbl.gov

Miserly Moms
www.miserlymoms.com

Mom Advice
www.momadvice.com

Mommy Savers
www.mommysavers.com

Moms Groups

Colorado Moms
www.coloradomoms.com

International MOMS Club
www.momsclub.org

Meetup Groups
www.momsmeetup.com

MOMS Club
www.modmoms.org

Moms Like Me
www.denver.momslikeme.com

MOPS International
www.mops.org

Mothers and More
www.mothersandmore.org

Moxie Moms
www.moxie-moms.com/boulder/index.php

Multiples Groups

Boulder County Parents of Twins and More
www.bouldertwins.org

Darling Doubles
www.darlingdoubles.org

Double Delights of Denver
www.orgsites.com/co/doubledelights

Mothers of Multiples Society
www.mothersofmultiples.com

Super Twins of the Rocky Mountains
www.stormcolorado.com

Parent Magazines

American Baby
www.parents.com/american-baby-magazine

Brain, Child
www.brainchildmag.com

Colorado Parent
www.coloradoparent.com

Exceptional Parent
www.eparent.com

Fathering Magazine
www.fathermag.com

Gay Parent Magazine
www.gayparentmag.com

Kids Pages
www.kidspages.org

Parenting
www.parenting.com

Parents
www.parents.com

Working Mother Magazine
www.workingmother.com

Parenting Education

Bagels and Blocks
Discussion and Playgroup
www.jccdenver.org

Boot Camp for New Dads
www.bootcampfornewdads.org

Colorado Foundation for
Families and Children
www.coloradofoundation.org

Families First
www.familiesfirstcolorado.org

Incredible Internet
www.incredibleinternet.com

Love and Logic
www.loveandlogic.com

A Parent Connection
www.aparentconnection.com

Postpartum Depression Support

A Mother's Wings
www.mhacolorado.org

Postpartum Depression Intervention
www.kempecenter.org

Postpartum Support International
www.postpartum.net

Saving and Investing for College and Retirement

FINRA
www.finra.org

The Investor's Clearinghouse
www.investoreducation.org

My Money
www.mymoney.gov

Upromise
www.upromise.com

US Securities and Exchange Commission
www.sec.gov/investor.shtml

Single Parents

Parents without Partners
www.parentswithoutpartners.org

Special Needs Resources and Support

Autism Society of America
www.autismcolorado.org

Cerebral Palsy of Colorado, Inc.
www.cpco.org

Children and Adults with
Attention Deficit Disorder
www.chadd.org

Colorado Department of
Public Health and Environment
www.cdphe.state.co.us

Mile High Down Syndrome Association
www.mhdsa.org

Parent to Parent of Colorado
www.p2p-co.org

PEAK Parent Center
www.peakparent.org

Special Kids/Special Families
www.sksfcolorado.org

Colorado Horse Park Photo by Angel McCall

Redstone Park Courtesy Highlands Ranch Metro District

Visitor Centers

Arvada Chamber of Commerce
www.arvadachamber.org

Boulder Convention and Visitors Bureau
www.bouldercoloradousa.com

City of Aurora Visitors Promotion Advisory Board
www.visitaurora.com

Colorado Springs Convention and Visitors Bureau
www.visitCOS.com

Experience Jefferson County
www.experiencejeffersoncounty.org

Golden Visitors Center
www.goldenvisitorscenter.com

Manitou Springs Chamber of Commerce
www.manitousprings.org

Parker Chamber of Commerce
www.parkerchamber.com

Pikes Peak Country Attractions
www.pikes-peak.com

Visit Brighton
www.visitbrighton.com

Visit Denver: The Convention and Visitors Bureau
www.denver.org

Working Mothers

Blue Suit Mom
www.bluesuitmom.com

Working Moms Against Guilt
www.workingmomsagainstguilt.com

Working Moms Refuge
www.momsrefuge.com

Working Mother Magazine
www.workingmother.com

Washington Park

INDEX

Alphabetical Site Index

Notes

Are We Missing Anything?

If you have discovered a great place to take your child that isn't mentioned in this book, or if you have found an error, please bring it to my attention. Just fill out this form and return it to the address at the bottom of this page. You may also contact me through the website at **www.PlaydateWithDenver.com.**

Include the following:
Name of Destination
Phone Number
Website
Other Information

Return to:
Sharp End Publishing
PO Box 1613
Boulder, CO 80306

Kyrie Collins

Kyrie Collins and her awesome husband have two beautiful, very energetic boys. Prior to mommyhood, Kyrie enjoyed reading novels, going to the theater, and sleeping. She makes a mean pumpkin spice bread and is a "spectacular fun planner." Read her blog, I Wanna Be a Giraffe, at **http://iwannabeagiraffe.blogspot.com/** or follow her on Twitter @playdatewithden.

Playdate Publishing
An imprint of Sharp End Publishing

www.PlaydatePublishing.com

Playdate with Denver
& Colorado's Front Range

nearly 200 Local Adventures

A child's first years seem to pass in a moment, but how they are spent will last a lifetime. Opportunities to explore and try new things will enhance your child's ability to learn and stimulate his or her imagination. *Playdate with Denver & Colorado's Front Range* is a dreamer book—a book to browse and plan adventures. Local writer and mother Kyrie Collins presents insightful reviews from the parenting trenches, offering insight and relevant information to help make your day filled with smiles, not epics!

- Designed for parents, grandparents and caregivers
- Nearly **200** local adventures
- 15 activity categories
- What to expect at each site

- Authentic, first-hand reviews
- Hours, prices, discount tips
- Special attraction events
- Nearby sites included with each description

Printed in the USA
$22.00

ISBN 978-1-892540-73-7
52200 >
9 781892 540737